Design as Democratic Inquiry

Design as Democratic Inquiry

Putting Experimental Civics into Practice

Carl DiSalvo

The MIT Press
Cambridge, Massachusetts
London, England

The MIT Press would like to thank the anonymous peer reviewers who provided comments on drafts of this book. The generous work of academic experts is essential for establishing the authority and quality of our publications. We acknowledge with gratitude the contributions of these otherwise uncredited readers.

This book was set in Stone by Westchester Publishing Services, Danbury, CT.

Library of Congress Cataloging-in-Publication Data

Names: DiSalvo, Carl, 1971– author.
Title: Design as democratic inquiry : putting experimental civics into practice / Carl DiSalvo.
Description: Cambridge, Massachusetts : The MIT Press, [2022] | Includes bibliographical references and index.
Identifiers: LCCN 2021016745 | ISBN 9780262543460 (paperback)
Subjects: LCSH: Design—Social aspects.
Classification: LCC NK1520 .D574 2022 | DDC 745.4—dc23
LC record available at https://lccn.loc.gov/2021016745

152941459

In memory of Victor Margolin

Contents

Acknowledgments

My work in community-based participatory design began with a series of workshops I held in Pittsburgh, Pennsylvania, in 2007, but it would have never progressed to this without the support of a community of designers and scholars. Most notably, I am indebted to Pelle Ehn for all the conversations over the years, and throughout those conversations the constant encouragement. The underlying concept for this book was inspired by the work of Thomas Binder, Eva Brandt, Pelle Ehn, and Jochaim Halse. Thomas, Eva, Pelle, and Jochaim, this book would not be what it is without your ideas and the examples you set through your practice and scholarship. Thank you. Time and again, colleagues from Denmark and Sweden generously invited me to participate in discussions with them. Those discussions inform this book, and their bold work continues to move me. In particular, I am so appreciative of the opportunities to learn from Brandon Clark, Per-Anders Hillgren, Li Jönsson, Tau Ulv Lenskjold, Ann Light, Per Linde, Kristina Lindström, Ramia Mazé, Sissel Olander, Maria Hellström Reimer, Anna Seravalli, and Åså Ståhl. Many of these ideas also emerged in ongoing conversations with colleagues at the Umeå Institute of Design. Jamer Hunt, Johan Redström, Aditya Pawar, Søren Rosenbak, Heather Wiltse, Anna Valtonen, and Maria Göransdotter, thank you for listening through early versions of the stories that make up this book, often over breakfast, or fika, or soup at the bookstore.

Over the past few years, several colleagues have heard versions of this work in talks and provided valuable feedback—in particular, ken anderson, Paul Dourish, Jodi Forlizzi, Sarah Fox, Eric Gordon, Mel Gregg, Steve Jackson, Stacey Kuznetsov, James Pierce, and John Zimmerman.

My colleagues at *Design Issues* provide invaluable opportunities for thinking about design, and I am grateful to the opportunities we have to explore ideas together. Thank you Richard Buchanan, Bruce Brown, Dennis Doordan, Kip Lee, Ramia Mazé, Teal Triggs, and of course Victor Margolin. We miss you, Victor.

Completing a book is a daunting endeavor. Special thanks go to Doug Sery, who believed and encouraged me every time I saw him and told him that I was, in fact, working on my book project. For the last several months of drafting the manuscript, Phoebe Sengers and I exchanged daily texts, checking in with each other on our writing, in the midst of a pandemic. Those daily texts motivated the writing and validated the struggle of all we were in the midst of.

I am also deeply grateful for the opportunity to work with Andrew Schrock as an editor. He helped me to find a voice as well as a structure, and to give form to these stories and ideas.

Support for this work came from a variety of sources. I am particularly thankful for the support of the Intel Science and Technology Center for Social Computing, made possible by Paul Dourish, Bill Mauer, Scott Mainwaring, and Melissa Greg. The freedom provided through this center made it possible to do work that otherwise would not have gotten done, and the vision of this center set an exemplar for how daring scholarship from the social sciences and humanities might contribute to diverse visions of computing. Support was also provided through a National Science Foundation grant authored with Daniela Rosner. Thank you for your collaboration on that grant, Daniela, and for all of the conversations it prompted. Support was also provided by the Serve-Learn-Sustain Center at the Georgia Institution of Technology, which is boldly attempting to change the culture of research at Georgia Tech.

This is very much a collaborative project. It would not have happened without partnerships with community members, organizations, students, colleagues, and friends. Thank you to Ms. Pamela for the trust you put in us and the challenges you put before us to live up to that trust. Thank you, Les, for your passion for your neighborhood and your willingness to invite us into sharing and serving that passion. Thank you to Concrete Jungle, in particular Craig Durkin and Katherine Kennedy. Your commitment to serving those in need with care moves me, and the opportunity to work with you is a privilege. Thank you to the numerous employees of the city of Atlanta, across city government and services, who listened and collaborated as we tried to make a difference. Thank you, Cicely Garret, for your belief in this work for over ten years and for setting the highest of standards for serving communities.

Thank you to all of the students and colleagues who contributed to these projects. Thank you to Karl Kim, Catherine Meeschia, Sean McKaye, and Natalie Larkins for your work with Concrete Jungle. Thank you to all of the participants in the Careful Coding project studio, in particular Qing Tian, Nick Tippens, and Morgan Orangi. Special thanks to Cookie Nguyen—you took a vague idea and made it into something meaningful and wonderful with *PARSE*—and Tom Jenkins, you persevered through all sorts of challenges and made the *Fruit Are Heavy* project happen. Thank you to Mariam Asad, Tom Jenkins, Thomas Lodato, Firaz Peer, and Sanjdar Kozubaev for the opportunity to think and write together about the ideas that permeate these projects. Thank you, Ellen Zegura, for your friendship, for believing in this work, for supporting it, and for the many conversations we had about care and data and what else computing might be. Thank you, Chris Le Dantec and Ian Bogost, for your friendship and support, personally and professionally. And thanks for reminding me that at some point, it's good enough.

Among all of my collaborators, I am most indebted to Amanda Meng. Amanda taught me how to accompany our partners in their activism and advocacy, to be more than an ally. The hours and hours she spent with our partners, and her belief in the value of this work made this book possible. Thank you, Amanda.

Betsy, Evy, and Elliott, thank you for your tolerance of my evenings and weekends spent elsewhere or writing. But more than that, thank you for your inspiration. Evy and Elliott, thank you for showing me how to be brave in the world. Betsy, in addition to everything you do every day, thank you for being a role model for a truly engaged and committed scholar, as well as the best possible partner.

Introduction

One of the reasons for the current popularity of design is that design methods are useful for structuring and amplifying creativity, and creativity is valued in contemporary society. In fact, design is so pervasive, it is fair to say that design has become an institution in the twenty-first century (Lee 2020). In some respects, we might take that to be a good thing. After all, a basic premise of design is that the products and services designers make should be of value to people. Orienting design around concepts such as empathy seems, at least on the surface, to be beneficial. But the relentless pursuit of innovation, the uncritical embrace of the new and novel, and the treatment of all problems as design problems can produce a kind of cultural imperialism. Claiming design as a universal method is appealing to many people and organizations precisely because it can be used to assert authority and dominion.

Design *does* offer ways of thinking and doing that can be oriented toward imagining and making worlds that are more just, sustainable, and democratic. But the profession of design tends to be oriented toward other contexts, with other commitments. Those are the contexts and commitments of free-market capitalism, which have come to infuse not only industry but also much of government and civil society. In this book I will offer a perspective on thinking and doing design otherwise. What I mean by this is thinking and doing design in different ways than are typical; it's still design, but it's not the prevailing ways of talking about and doing design. In particular, my interest is how design might work as a mode of democratic inquiry into diverse civics. In such a practice designing is, at one and the same time, a way of participating in anticipatory worlds through making and an endeavor through which to reflect on the conditions that might make those worlds possible, desirable, or not. Designing becomes a way to care, together, for our collective futures.

In this book I tell stories that help us theorize how practitioners and scholars might contribute to democracy through what I call design experiments in civics. Like other forms of democracy "in the small," (Binder et al. 2015; Ehn 2017) the projects in these pages are socially and culturally situated, both because of when and where they happened and because of who I am. They occurred in a particular place over a span of time: a city in the southern United States in the early part of the twenty-first century. They are set, in part, within academia. And they unfold in relation to existing practices and discourses of design. While my arguments about design and democracy gradually develop throughout this book, it is worthwhile to introduce some of these contexts before delving into the particulars in following chapters.

A Confluence of Design Otherwise

First and foremost, this work is situated in existing practices and discourses of design. Of particular interest is the potential that exists in the confluence of critical and speculative, social and participatory design. When these modes of designing swirl together, there is a possibility of emergent practices that blend imaginative making and politics toward engaged inquiry (Sanders and Stappers 2008, 2012).

Since the early 2000s, critical and speculative practices have become increasingly common in design. These practices were not new when they came to the fore, but they were novel, outside of familiar ways of doing design at the time. And that was part of the point: to offer another perspective on what the objects of design, designers, and the field of design might be doing. Much of what we today call critical and speculative design is often traced to the work of Tony Dunne and Fiona Raby (Dunne 2008; Dunne and Raby 2001, 2013). Over a series of books and projects they articulated a field of practice. Within those texts, Dunne and Raby make clear that critical and speculative design is not a break from design; rather, critical and speculative design draws together histories and practices of making that span art and design. As Dunne and Raby note, contemporary speculative design can be traced farther back to the radical design of the 1960s and 1970s and the work of collectives and studios such as Archigram, Superstudio, Global Tools, and

Archizoom (Coles and Rossi 2013). What is often overlooked is the political aspirations of those collectives and studios (Elfline 2016).

One distinctive quality of critical and speculative design is that it casts the designer as an author of sorts, capable of and responsible for producing content as well as form, or perhaps more accurately, producing content through form. When making in the mode of critical and speculative design, the designer is just as much engaged in storytelling as they are in rendering materials. Coupled with the notion of the designer as author, critical and speculative design is distinctive because it remains as a concept. Usually, concepts are steps in the design process toward a product or service that is ultimately realized through mass production and use. But in critical and speculative design, the concept is enough; the valuation of design is found in expressivity of that concept and its capacity to incite consideration.

Much of the work of critical and speculative design in the early 2000s shared a set of themes and aesthetics. This is unsurprising, given that it emerged from a small number of schools and studios. Critiques of those shared themes and aesthetics brought to light the need to develop pluralistic practices and discourses of critical and speculative design. In particular, critiques were brought to bear on critical and speculative design as being too Western, too northern, too white, and too enmeshed in and expressive of the privilege that often accompanies design (de Oliveira and de O. Martins 2014). This debate led to an exciting articulation of critical and speculative design with postcolonial theory, feminism, and queer theory (S. Bardzell 2018; de Oliveira and de O. Martins 2019; de O. Martins and de Oliveria 2016; Sengers, Williams, and Khovanskaya 2021) along with other speculative practices and discourses, such as Afrofuturism (Harrington and Dillahunt 2021; Winchester 2018).

Since the early 2000s there has also been a renewed attention on the social capacities and potentials of design. This manifests across a range of terms such as social design, social innovation, and design for social innovation. As with critical and speculative design, this is not new to design. One common origin point for much of this work is Victor Papanek and his canonical text *Design for the Real World: Human Ecology and Social Change* (1971). Papanek was critical of design and sought to reconstruct it as a practice for the good of people, beyond market imperatives. Contemporary social design continues this impulse, employing design techniques to address a range of pressing societal issues such as education, healthcare, justice reform, climate change, and food systems. In many ways, social design is fairly customary. Social design projects tend to use familiar techniques to address societal issues, and the outcomes of those techniques also tend to be familiar design things such as products and services, communications, and environments.

Similar to critical and speculative design, the histories and contemporary practices of social design are complicated. As design historian Allison Clarke (2021) describes, Papanek's practice was very much informed by agendas and strategies of international development. These agendas and strategies often purported to be emancipatory but in fact reproduced the hegemony of the West, grounded in the values and motives of Western nationalism and industry. Comparable histories that complicate utopian or progressive thinking have been drawn out by Fred Turner (2010) and his inquiries into the relationships between the counterculture of the 1960s and 1970s and contemporary Silicon Valley. During the early surge of social design, journalist Bruce Nussbaum questioned the commitments and impact of social design, posing the provocation "Is Humanitarian Design the New Imperialism?" (2010). Such questions about the commitments and capacities of design in relation to societal issues continue today, for instance in Mahmoud Keshavarz's (2020) scholarship exploring the limitations of design in addressing humanitarian issues such as migration and refugees.

At times, there seems to be a tension between the discourses and practices of critical and speculative, social and participatory design. At other times, and in curious ways, these discourses and practices seem to meld together. Arturo Escobar's (2018) concept of design for a pluriverse is one such example. Escobar articulates a pluriversal design that draws upon feminist and postcolonial theory, much of it from the Global South, calling for an approach to design that recognizes and strives for a multiplicity of worlds. Such a perspective is in stark contrast with the universalism that characterizes modernism and which continues to characterize much of contemporary design. Such a perspective also relies upon blending imagination with substantial and sustained commitments to politics, in order to participate in making other worlds possible. Ezio Manzini's (2015) long-standing research on design for social innovation also exemplifies an expanded practice of design, negotiating between expert and everyday practices, and the local and the global. In Manzini's work, the social is not a given but is rather a field of forms open to ongoing reinvention that design can contribute to. And design contributes not just through the making of things but through practices of collaborative and collective sense-making and meaning-making. Another example is Daniela Rosner's (2018) concept of critical fabulations, which draws upon the work of Donna Haraway (2016). Critical fabulations become a way of telling different stories about what design has been, what it is, and what it might be. Similarly, the work of Laura Forlano (Forlano 2016, 2017; Choi, Forlano, and Kera 2020) resists simplistic categorization and offers instead a robust and exciting approach to thinking and doing design that brings the critical, speculative, and social together. Deepa Butoliya (2020) offers yet another example as she draws on Indian practices of jugaad to develop a notion of critical jugaad as "a tool for resistance, subversion, and criticality against colonial powers of oppression" and "a nonviolent critique that provokes and questions the techno-utopian imaginaries in futures discourse." In such mingling of practices and discourses, the habits, values, and commitments of design change, and along with that, so too should change how we describe and judge design.

Participatory design offers an additional site of discourse and practice in which criticality, speculation, and politics meld together. Contemporary participatory design exceeds its original charter—collaborating with workers in the design of systems that structure their labor—to embrace discovering and expressing alternate presents and futures with a range of publics (Simonsen and Robertson 2012). What is particularly compelling about such work is that it retains a commitment to democratic conditions and experiences, while also recognizing that such conditions and experiences should be discovered anew through imaginative and collaborative making. We can also find connections between participatory design and design justice. What is notable about design justice, particularly as elaborated by Sasha Costanza-Chock (2020), is the commitment to communities and social movements. Design justice also questions the presumed authority of the designer. Rather than placing the agency of invention and action in the hands of designers, design justice privileges those who are most affected by the products of design and recognizes the existing creativity of people and institutions who do not necessarily call themselves designers. This approach echoes aspects of participatory design as it was initially envisioned, and then broadens and enriches those values and practices with contemporary theory and in the context of activism and advocacy. One particularly moving aspect of design justice is the breadth of theory and issues attended to. Costanza-Chock and others engaging in design justice draw from and combine Black feminism, queer theory, and disability studies to articulate perspectives that are boldly intersectional.

Across this range of approaches, there is a shared belief that the creative capacities of design can enable us to imagine and act in the world differently and can be used to propagate possibilities for engaging pressing social and political conditions. Furthermore, what is common across these practices and discourses is that, in varied ways, they are all experimental practices: they all involve forms of inquiry through making and use. The concept of design experiments in civics that I develop throughout this book is situated within these practices and discourses of design.

At the same time, it is important to acknowledge the shortcomings of design, in both intent and outcome, and how design can work *against* discovering and expressing alternate presents and futures, thwarting the making of other worlds. Lilly Irani's (2019) concept of entrepreneurial citizenship is crucial in this regard. Through her scholarship, Irani details how discourses and practices of design transform social and political conditions into opportunities to be capitalized upon through innovation. As Irani compellingly and thoroughly argues, "The function of entrepreneurial citizenship is to subsume hope and dissatisfaction, redirecting potential political contestation into economic productivity and experiment" (2019, 22). Throughout this inquiry, I wrestle with how not to fall into this trap, this tendency of design to reproduce and reinforce the status quo (Julier and Kimbell 2019), to assimilate and monetize difference, all the while claiming to be in some way empowering. Can an experimental practice of design contribute to other values and demonstrate other commitments? Rather than "foreclosing the slow work of democracy across difference" (2019, 22), as Irani notes design often does, can we articulate a practice of design that contributes to the resources and capacities needed for the often uncomfortable work of democracy?

An Engaged Practice-Based Research

The basis of this book is a series of projects, but I did not initially set out to assemble these projects into a book. Rather, I was interested in exploring design that straddled the critical and speculative, the social and participatory; I was interested in exploring—through reflective practice—how to think and do design as democratic inquiry. These projects developed from relationships with people, institutions, and ideas. They included organizing workshops to elicit participation in writing scenarios for so-called smart cities, collaborating with a collective that aims to address food insecurity, and assisting a resident in his use of data to advocate for resources for his neighborhood. Across these contexts and issues, three ideas united these projects: a commitment to those I was working with, the idea of design as inquiry, and a desire to support local activism. What I was attempting to do in each of these projects, individually and collectively, was articulate a practice of design that was engaged, imaginative, and political.

And yet, throughout these projects, what I encountered time and again were the complications and limitations of design. This included the inappropriateness of many methods and principles to community settings, the lack of frameworks and theories to account for the ad hoc qualities of this work, and the ambiguity of effect these projects had. This book emerged from struggling with projects that were fragile, partial, and compromised—characteristics that did not align with the standard discourses of design. But rather than trying to ignore those complications and limitations or write them out of the stories I told, I chose to accept those complications and limitations as the conditions and qualities of this work. In doing so, I wanted to find a different way of describing and appreciating practices of design. Rather than assert the authority of design—or, for that matter, democracy—I wanted to attend to its tenuousness. This casts design in a much different light from the heroic stories of innovation we have become accustomed to.

The work of these projects constitutes a mode of practice-based research, grounded in collaborations with communities. Throughout this book I use the terms "we" and "us." The "we" and "us" refers to those involved in these projects. That includes me and also an array of students, research staff, residents, organizers, advocates, activists, and government workers. While I will develop the interpretations that follow, this is not my work alone. These projects were and are collective affairs, and it is important to acknowledge that. Describing this work as collective and collaborative, attending to the labor of all involved, is part of what needs to be done to counter those stories that mythologize the individual maker and valorize the presumed expertise of the professional designer. The "we" and "us" also refers to those who are interested in the scholarly practice and study of design. And that is yet another way this work is situated.

Throughout this book I advocate for a reserved perspective on design. The projects in this book reveal numerous roles for designers in contemporary political life that benefit equity and justice. That is, I believe that people who design—who may or may not be formally recognized as designers— can aid the ongoing contestation and renewal that characterizes democracy. But I also believe those contributions are limited. By acknowledging the influence of design as limited, I hope to offer a theorization of design that recognizes how designers might aspire to participate in democracy, while remaining self-effacing about the effects of that participation. This does not mean such design is useless or token. Rather, I merely seek to recognize that such design is often modest. When we look to the realm of social and political action, the significance of design is difficult to discern, and its agencies are a challenge to untangle. This is true across the many modes of design practice. While there is evidence that support claims that critical and speculative design can prompt reflection, and that social and participatory design can increase the agency of those it engages, just as often the outcome of such work is a fog of affect and effect. Rather than disputing the ambiguity of design's effects, I accept its incompleteness and indeterminacy as a starting point for investigation. Indeed, questioning the efficacies of social and political design opens other interpretations and pathways.

While I do argue that the effects of social and political design are incomplete and indeterminate, I am not arguing for a rote instrumentalism or functionality that would make design seem to be more definite, to bring about certainty and closure. I am resistant to the idea that design should be operative and convenient in the ways we often expect of design.

It is notable, but perhaps not surprising, that so many of the practices and discourses of design that motivate this book are connected to academia. One reason may be that academia offers distinctive opportunities for inquiry. Without a doubt, the work described herein is academic, situated within academic institutions. Often, the term "academic" is wielded in a dismissive manner, as in "that's just academic." I take that to mean that whatever is being labeled as academic is seen as distanced, theoretical, or hypothetical. When the term is used so dismissively, whatever is labeled "academic" is often compared to industry. Many in government and civil society similarly deride academic pursuits as lacking. Throughout the projects that make up this book there were moments when the design work was dismissed as academic by people in government and civil society. Municipal employees, public officials, and foundation and philanthropy officers often wanted answers and solutions that fit their existing ideologies, agendas, and commitments. In these contexts, labeling work as academic cast it as hindering established modes of governmentality. In our contemporary condition in the United States, the role of government is increasingly managerial and fiduciary. It is focused on optimizing services and improving the capacity to manage capital. Accordingly, government and civil society often dismiss academic work because it does not meet their immediate needs to maintain the status quo of governing. I have no problem with that. In fact, I'll go further: it is often ethically appropriate and morally important to do design that does not align with the status quo of governing, or for that matter, with industry. It is a responsibility of academic designers to ask questions and pursue lines of thinking and doing that are at odds with our standard forms of government and governmentality and that are at odds with free-market ideologies. This is particularly true of work that seeks to support democracy beyond its current instantiations and institutions.

While I embrace the notion of "academic" as not beholden to the logics of industry or government, I reject the idea that academic work is universally distanced, inherently moot, or solely hypothetical. My position is that academic design, like all academic work, can be undertaken as a mode of engaged scholarship. The ability to be distanced from status quo forms of government, from a rote instrumentalism and functionalism that tends to define professional design, enables us to hew close to the lived experience of communities. Academic designers can take lived experiences seriously without needing to justify them in relation to market potentials or whether they adhere to formal modes of governance. One of the ways the work herein is so situated is in its closeness to the city of Atlanta.

Atlanta as an Ever-Emerging Smart City

This book is grounded in a time and place: a span of five years, from 2014 to 2019, in Atlanta, Georgia, in the southeastern United States. Throughout those years, and still ongoing, calls to create the smart city reverberated through governments, the tech industry, and academia. These messages made claims about the purported civic benefits of using data for decision-making. Across sectors, smart-city champions wanted to turn Atlanta into a testbed for ubiquitous sensors, autonomous vehicles, and open-data repositories.

The standard perspective was that smart-city technologies would improve our collective lives by making government and business services faster and more seamless. But I saw other reasons why Atlanta was an important place for rethinking how democratic pluralism might evolve in an age of algorithms and data.

Atlanta is the birthplace of the civil rights movement in the United States and a majority Black city. This rich cultural history defines Atlanta's identity, even as it remains haunted by the anti-Black legacy of the Jim Crow era and the racism and classism that continue to this day. Atlanta street names are a constant reminder of those who came before and fought for civil rights. They also attest to the divisiveness of that history and its persistence: street names change along a north-south line, demarking racist histories and racial divides. Many of those divisions remain. That demarcation did not occur by accident, nor is the gentrification that is displacing historically Black communities merely a matter of chance. To this day, the state of Georgia is renowned for its political activism, and Atlanta is still home to civil rights movement leaders and organizations that influence the city, region, and nation. In the 2020 US presidential and senate elections, the state of Georgia turned from red to blue for the first time in decades— the result of the tireless work of organizers, many of them Black and many of them women. At the same time, the opportunities for economic mobility for residents of Atlanta continue to be among the worst in the United States: those who are born into poverty are likely to remain in poverty throughout their lives (Chetty et al. 2014; Opportunity Atlas 2021).

The proud histories of civil rights and activism sit uncomfortably alongside present-day realities of blatant racism, voter suppression, and rampant inequality. The questions of how to do democratic inquiry, of how to contribute to diverse civics through design, were and are influenced by these legacies and their ongoing instantiations. Atlanta itself set the tone for this work far more than I did. All that being said, I need to acknowledge I am not from Atlanta, nor am I from the South. It means something to be a Southerner. As a white man from the North, my place here will always be somewhat of an interloper. And my position as faculty in a local institute of higher education is a privileged position.

Atlanta's foray into becoming a smart city was troubled and continues to sputter. Throughout the years these projects were undertaken, Atlanta had multiple chief information officers, chief resilience officers, chief equity officers, and two mayors. Each of these differently conceived of and shaped what a "smart Atlanta" might be. The Georgia Institute of Technology also played a role in the move toward a smart Atlanta. Several of the technology testbeds in the city were developed by Georgia Tech faculty and research scientists. In 2015, the city of Atlanta, in partnership with Georgia State University and the Georgia Institute of Technology, became part of the Metrolab Network—a national network of municipal and university partnerships exploring and advancing the technologies and services of smart cities. This connected Atlanta and its efforts toward becoming a smart city to other cities nationally and internationally. But Atlanta's data infrastructure remained limited and, moreover, vulnerable. In 2018, the city fell victim to a massive hack that brought down systems and services for weeks. Consultants were hired to rebuild and fortify these systems and services, though some remained offline for over a year.

Today, Atlanta is nowhere near other major US cities' use of data for municipal decision-making. The open data provided and maintained by the city of Atlanta is limited. There are no substantive and sustained municipal initiatives or offices or programs that are working to develop the data resources and capacities of city government, such as Boston's Office of New Urban Mechanics or Los Angeles's Innovation Team. There is, perhaps, a benefit to this. For the most part, the city has yet to move toward the kind of algorithmic automation and data surveillance that have proven so dangerous in other cities. Such conditions are important to note to make clear that the projects in this book were not undertaken under direction of existing civic enterprises. In fact, they were, for the most part, undertaken in response to or in the absence of municipal initiatives. Unlike the majority of technological testbeds and platforms being created and tested in Atlanta, these projects began with residents, with the neighborhood and community organizations of the city, within those very histories, presents, and futures of rights, activism, and inequality.

All these conditions are yet another way this inquiry is situated. Their entangled histories, relations, and aspirations are actors in the ongoing events of exploring what local democratic conditions and experiences are and might become. The projects in this inquiry emerge in relation to very particular happenings: to proposed sensor testbeds set within gentrifying neighborhoods, to collectives working to address food insecurity across the region, to residents attempting to figure out how to do the work of neighborhood advocacy when collecting data becomes part of that work. While these conditions situate this inquiry, much of the work is intentionally positioned in response to the prevailing discourses and techniques of smart cities and standard approaches of technology-driven research and development. Rather than presuming that government or industry—or academia, for that matter—should determine what a smart Atlanta should be, these projects look to residents to craft those futures. Rather than thinking that various technologies will help the city become entrepreneurial or resilient, this work begins with the recognition that the residents of Atlanta and its local organizations are *already* creative and resourceful, and that whatever technologies are introduced should work within and amplify those existing practices and desires. Moreover, there should always be an opportunity to refuse technologies: neither technology nor design should be assumed as destiny. Instead of the refrain of positivism that characterizes so much of technology-driven research and development, throughout this book I draw from reflexive modes of the humanities and social sciences, which offer critical perspectives of technology and design. Such critical perspectives are imperative for making democracy vibrant.

Toward Design Experiments in Civics

In a sense, this book is itself a design experiment. It gathers together values and experiences and orders them to produce a constellation of praxis. Another way to frame this inquiry is as aspirational design criticism. It draws together an assortment of theory and empirical accounts to consider both what is and what might be in regard to design and civics. I hope this book enriches our understanding of theories and practices of democracy as much as theories and practices of design. As Johan Redström (2017) notes, when making design theory we are constructing interpretations of design and also interpretations of something else. That "something else" is often the conditions of the work. In this case, that something else is civics and, more generally, democracy broadly construed. As such, an ambition of this inquiry is to inspire us toward thinking about and doing design differently, and also toward differently imagining our communal lives.

Throughout this book, I attempt to both describe and perform a way of thinking and doing design otherwise, inspired and informed by the work of others. Part of this is the stories I choose to tell, and part of this is *how*

I tell them. As mentioned, one characteristic of this approach is a reserved perspective on design, telling stories and theorizing in ways that eschew heroism and authority, to instead attend to the tenuousness of design and democracy. Another characteristic of this is in relation to academic discourse. It is standard in academic writing to push against something. To an extent, I'm doing just that; I'm contesting the usual narratives of design, familiar assumptions of what design achieves and how it should achieve it. At the same time, just as I'm resistant to the domineering narratives of design, I've become leery of critique that seems to presume a purity politics (Shotwell 2016). A move toward different modes of critical interpretation and engagement is emerging across the humanities and social sciences, and my approach to this inquiry is inspired by many others who are constructing a different kind of academic discourse, one that "gathers together" (see D'Ignazio and Klein 2020; Gibson-Graham 1996, 2006; Latour 2004; Liboiron 2021; Lindström and Ståhl 2014; Lury and Wakeford 2012a; Shotwell 2016). Of course, discernment and criticism are necessary. But more than pushing against something, my hope is to open design practice and discourse to other aspirations and affects. I want to articulate the potentials of design inquiry as engaged, committed, social, and political, *while also* fragile, contingent, partial, and compromised. What I've set out to do in this book is to tell and theorize stories that consider how practitioners and scholars might contribute to democracy through design in ways that are circumscribed and incomplete— and also hopeful. Design experiments in civics are one way to do so.

1 Design Experiments in Civics

Games and scenarios, sensors and maps, spreadsheets and apps—these are familiar design things. But their making and use can be put toward unexpected ends. They can be made and used to explore how our worlds are configured, and how they might be configured differently. In addition to providing us with entertainment and information, these familiar things can also provide us with insight and agency. They can be apparatuses in experimental practices of inquiry. My interest is how the making and use of such familiar design things can figure into inquiries about the conditions and experiences of democracy, through what I call design experiments in civics.

Design experiments in civics use creative practices to explore how we might make and experience our communal lives differently. They are a way of doing democratic inquiry through design. On the surface, they are a fairly typical way to bring design to bear on phenomena. They hold on to a belief that design can expand our possibilities for how we choose to structure and fulfill our lives. But at the same time, to appreciate these efforts requires taking different perspectives on the practices and potentials of design. Although familiar things like games and scenarios, sensors and maps, and spreadsheets and apps comprise these experiments, they are wielded unlike much of contemporary design. The commitments and purposes of democratic inquiry are distinctive. These design experiments in civics beget different narratives and theories of design.

My attempt to expand how we think and do democratic inquiry through design begins with making sense of the phrase "design experiments in civics." In this chapter, I introduce the concept, explain the terms that comprise the phrase, and discuss what they mean in tandem. Admittedly, "design experiments in civics" is clumsy. "Experiments in civics" and "design experiments" are more graceful, but both of those phrases lose an element of what is in play and what is at stake. When these three terms—design, experiment, and civics—mingle, significant themes and variations, potentials and consequences emerge. Such endeavors are experiments because they are crafted and performed in order to come to an understanding of the conditions they operate within and pose problems for further inquiry. They are civic because they are about forms of democracy "in the small." They are design experiments because imaginative making is employed to produce artifacts, systems, and services that are both sites and modes of inquiry. While the phrase can be quickly explained, more is needed to develop an appreciation of these design experiments in civics.

From Democracy in the Workplace to the Work of Democracy

Design experiments in civics blend imaginative making and politics. They are a way to envision, construct, and explore conditions and qualities of association between people. The term "making" has been in vogue over the past decade. Activities of making often involve material construction, but one could also speak of conceptual making or composing already existing things as making. Making is fundamental to design, but design is not reducible to making, nor are designers the only ones who make. And designers do more than make things; they also do things. One of the emerging topics in design is the relation between making and doing, which traditionally has been described as different realms of action (Lee 2020; Wang 2015). A theme that runs through this book is the interplay between making and doing. Making can be a way of doing inquiry and politics.

This practice of design experiments in civics springs from methods and philosophies of participatory design. Within participatory design, there is a history of blending making and politics that emerged from democratic concerns at work. The field of participatory design, as developed in Scandinavia in the late 1960s, was spurred by the introduction of computers into the workplace (Kensing and Greenbaum 2012). Practitioners, researchers, and activists asked, "How will these technologies affect democracy in the workplace?" They were troubled that the introduction of technologies of automation, monitoring, and information management would de-skill workers and lessen workers' voices in decision-making. Early participatory design practitioners were motivated to include people who would be affected by new technologies in the design of the technologies. These advocates believed that such inclusion would improve the design of systems. Better accounting for the practices and values of the workers through design could be democratizing.

Fifty years later, while some techniques of participatory design are found in mainstream design, it never caught on as a conventional practice. Lack of adoption may be because participatory design is as much a philosophy of design as a method. The origins of participatory design were influenced by Marxist thought (Kensing and Greenbaum 2012). While those Marxist perspectives have waned, there remains among many a fierce commitment to democracy, labor, and equity. And whether explicit or implicit, a Marxist philosophy runs counter to the dominant free-market agendas that most professional design today serves. Above all, participatory design was, and continues to be, political (Beck 2002). As part of those commitments and politics, the methods of participatory design push against the presumed authority of the designer and strive to create pluralistic and inclusive modes of making. Certainly participation is a theme often found in professional design, but it is often decidedly apolitical, limited to techniques merely intended to amplify a designer's creativity and impact. Much of what is touted as "participatory" involves simply enrolling potential users into facile activities of cocreation, without committing to the politics and values embedded in the philosophies of participatory design.

Without a doubt, there are issues with the histories and practices of participatory design. Participatory design originated in societies that were socially progressive, culturally homogeneous, and politically stable. Those conditions and our attentiveness to hegemony have changed, and so too must participatory design change. Much of the work of contemporary participatory design happens in shifting social, cultural, and political landscapes. This pluralism drives current debates about what constitutes participation and who is deemed able to participate (Harrington, Erete, and Piper 2019). There is also an urgent need to decolonize theory and practice in participatory design. The emergence of themes of justice and care in participatory design signals changes in our contemporary condition and the need to respond to those changes (Costanza-Chock 2020; Light and Akama 2014).

Contemporary participatory design remains committed to democracy, labor, and equity, and the scope of attention and action has broadened beyond traditional workplaces. Over the past several decades there has been a concerted move among designers to consider work in the public realm as a distinctive site of inquiry and practice (Bannon, Bardzell, and Bødker 2018; DiSalvo, Clement, and Pipek 2012; Huybrechts, Benesch, and Geib 2017a). In addition to examining how technologies affect work in factories, hospitals, and schools, the field of participatory design has expanded to examine how to sustain democracy in government offices, activist organizations, and neighborhoods. Whereas the origins of participatory design were concerned about democracy in the workplace, contemporary participatory design takes up the question "What is the work of democracy?"

Thomas Binder, Eva Brandt, Pelle Ehn, and Jochaim Halse (2015) offer the phrase "democratic design experiments" to characterize emerging practices of participatory design that retain a strong political agenda. As they state, "Democratic design experiments work by making issues experientially available to such an extent that 'the possible' becomes tangible, formable, and within reach of engaged yet diverse citizens" (163). These democratic design experiments emerge from participatory design, and they expand to become the basis for modes of designing that are profoundly collective, beyond the usual concerns of design. In the process they complicate our understandings and expectations of both design and democracy: "Democratic design experiments are, above all, committed to continuously finding new forms of emerging publics and aiming to enrich the repertoire of democratic forms of expression" (163). Undeniably, this book and the projects within are inspired by, and indebted to, their concept of democratic design experiments. The phrase "design experiments in civics" is my attempt to provide specificity to their concept, to focus it on and refract it through the contexts and events of the projects described herein.

The phrase "in the small" is often used to characterize these experiments as "democratic design experiments in the small" (Binder et al. 2015; Ehn 2017). Labeling work as "in the small" bounds design in a way that is at odds with most contemporary design discourse, which casts design as universal in method and scope. There seems to be no limit to how design is employed to solve problems or foster innovation. Global design consultancies regularly work with national governments and civil society organizations to develop programs, strategies, and policies. During an era of "big data"—when everything must occur "in the large"—the work of design and democracy can also be more modest; the context of the local and mundane is also important. At the same time, I am not claiming that working locally is preferable to working globally. Working "in the small" is not more desirable than operating "in the large."

Work at one scale or another, then, is not inherently more worthy. Rather, working at one scale or another is important because it focuses our attention on particular conditions, practices, and politics. The conditions, practices, and politics I am choosing to attend to are simply more local and mundane. My choice to work "in the small" was motivated by my belief that democracy occurs through our local actions and environments, just as much as national and global equivalents. I gravitated toward "the small" because I believed that design was not universal in method and scope, and it was important to identify and appreciate design's limitations and shortcomings. Perhaps most significantly, my choice to work "in the small" was motivated by my own desire for a more intimate practice and inquiry. Within this moment, particularly in the public realm, democratic participation is often co-opted as a strategy to feign engagement. Too often democracy is proffered as an ideal good without explication, meaning the very idea deserves inquiry and scrutiny. For me, that scrutiny took place within the closeness of civics.

Civics as Democracy in the Small

I use "civics" as shorthand for "democracy in the small," to describe situated experiences that strive toward forms of togetherness that enable collective agency and communal life. My understanding of both democracy and civics is informed by theories of agonistic pluralism and pragmatism, which conceptualize experimentation as an activity that cultivates and sustains democratic conditions and potentials. Democracies have always been fraught with inequity and injustice, disputes about rights and responsibilities, and challenges of collective action. One way to approach democracy is to consider these situations and the tensions they produce as defining the democratic condition. In such a view of democracy, what is important is not the resolution of problematic situations. Rather, what is important is the ongoing exploration of varied courses of action to address issues through the formal and informal institutions of our communal lives. Both theories of agonistic pluralism and pragmatism share this perspective and can productively meld together.

Agonism is based on the idea that democracy is characterized by the capacity to question, challenge, and refuse (Arendt 2013; Connolly 2002; Honig 1993; Mouffe 2013). In this way, agonism resists interpretations of democracy as consensus, because consensus is too often achieved through assimilation or the silencing of difference. Of course, there are practices of consensus that work in fair ways. But from an agonistic perspective, it is important to maintain the capacity for "perpetual contest" (Honig 1993). Contestation is perpetual because our social and cultural conditions are in constant flux. Amid ongoing change, beliefs and values shift, which affects our lived environments and experiences. The work of agonism is to continually identify and counter hegemony, which keeps open possibilities for differently configuring our communal lives.

In *Adversarial Design* (DiSalvo 2012) I explored how design might do the work of agonism by focusing on how the objects of design might express and enact agonism. In a sense, design experiments in civics continue an exploration of how design might participate in agonism. However, this current work broadens what is considered the activities and outcomes of designing as a situated practice, and takes a more humble approach to design. This move was informed by compelling critiques of the limitations of political design (Keshavarz 2018; Kiem 2013), shifts in my own practice, and the growth of work exploring agonism in the context of participatory design (Björgvinsson, Ehn, and Hillgren 2012; Hillgren, Seravalli, and Eriksen 2016; Kraff 2020; Sawhney and Tran 2020). In the context of participatory design in the public realm, some designers seek to create what Chantal Mouffe refers to as "agonistic spaces" (Björgvinsson, Ehn, and Hillgren 2010; Hernberg and Mazé 2018; Mouffe 2013). These agonistic spaces may be based in a physical space, but are better understood as an environment of material resources and social relations gathered together to prompt and sustain the exploration of the possibilities of difference. This bundling of resources and relations enables people to think and act toward diverse civics, even in constrained circumstances. The idea of contestation often brings to mind dramatic acts. But a notable characteristic of the work described herein is that contestation can also be subtle. This is not the same sort of contestation as street protests. Nor is it the same sort of contestation often expressed through political art. Many agonistic spaces foster a circumscribed, partial, provisional, often fragile contestation, akin to what Tau Ulv Lenskjold, Sissel Olander, and Joachim Halse refer to as "minor design activism" (2015). Within the scholarship and practice of making agonistic spaces we find projects occurring in community centers, neighborhood organizations, so-called hackerspaces and makerspaces, sometimes in collaboration with municipalities, sometimes in opposition to municipalities—in that realm that I label as civics.

Without a doubt, "civics" is a tricky term. Its traditional definition is bound to notions of citizenship that are often exclusionary and exercised to reproduce dominant ideologies. As children, we learned about civics in school to become responsible and productive members of our city and nation. Thus, civics is often directly connected to serving statehood and other formal institutions of government. But there is no need to capitulate to standard and stultified connotations of civics. We can reject impoverished notions of civics that demand we yield to the state and only encompass the presumed rights of those deemed citizens. Instead, we can embrace the concept as multifaceted, reflecting the complexity of contemporary conditions. There is value in "staying with the trouble" with civics (Haraway 2016). Design experiments contest civics as we know it. They envision and explore how we might refigure governance and governmentality. This endeavor of participating in and contributing to diverse civic imaginaries and practices is part of the work of democracy.

I use the word "diverse" to refer to varied conditions and experiences, not to groups of people. In other words, I am not using "diverse" as a shorthand for Black, Indigenous, or people of color. Nor am I using the term to label disabled people, women, or LGBTQ+ people. Such identities and subjectivities are crucial to my work, but I am not categorizing them under the label of "diverse." My striving toward diverse civics is informed and inspired by the work of J. K. Gibson-Graham and their engaged scholarship on diverse economies (1995, 1996, 2006, 2008). Gibson-Graham argued that too often we speak of "the economy" as if it were singular. We take the economy to be typified by contemporary free-market capitalism, mostly as we encounter it in Western industrialized and postindustrial nations. This is a problem for multiple reasons. First, it limits our thinking, making, and doing. Second, it is inaccurate; there is not one immutable economy. There are many kinds of markets, modes of labor and exchange, and nonmarket valuing practices. Examples of such diverse economies include worker cooperatives, consumer cooperatives, bartering, volunteering, informal lending, self-provisioning, and gifts. Gibson-Graham encourage us to recognize and appreciate this diversity of economies. Pertinent to this book's concern with civics, they locate possibilities in practices that could also be characterized as "in the small." Gibson-Graham turn their gaze to sites such as farmers' markets, foraging collectives, and community time banks as examples of diverse economies. These diverse economies depend on recognizing and appreciating diverse economic subjectivities—the multiple and distinctive ways of becoming and performing collective economic identities and practices.

This diverse approach to economies can be extended to civics. If we want to envision diverse civics, we must begin by understanding the myriad ways that individuals, groups, and communities cultivate, express, and participate in different social and political environments. At first glance, taking insights from work on economies and applying them to civics might seem dodgy. The confounding of the free-market ideologies with government is a destructive quality of our contemporary condition. But I am not arguing for a confounding of economies and civics. Instead, I follow Gibson-Graham's work methodologically. Gibson-Graham's work is compelling because it is based in a staunch refusal to yield our imagination to singular concepts of economic structure, action, and affect. We can follow Gibson-Graham's lead in refusing to acquiesce to a singular and domineering notion of civics. To resuscitate civics, we should purposively seek out, study, and engage with unfurling civic subjectivities and attendant practices. Rather than considering one dominant mode of civics, we should embrace a pluralistic perspective on how we might structure and experience our communal lives. This process of seeking and understanding diverse civics can be performed through experiments.

Experiments

So far, I have used the term "experiment" loosely. That is a problem, given the history of the term. Usually, "experiment" is used in relation to science. This might lead readers to wonder if I am making an argument that design experiments in civics are scientific, particularly given that there is a field of design science and decades of literature on the science of design. Design experiments in civics are not science, at least not in the way we tend to characterize science. This is not to denigrate science, only to recognize and appreciate a plurality of ways of knowing. Science is one way of knowing. Design, along with art, craft, writing, and other forms of imaginative making are other ways of knowing. All these fields have modes of inquiry that are experimental, which strive to understand "what might be" through investigative endeavors, the outcomes of which are not known. Experiments, then, are not limited to biology or physics or psychology; any intentional endeavor that trials ways of knowing and doing in order to produce knowledge and spur action might be called an experiment. At the same time, while design experiments are interpretive and exploratory in character, I am not suggesting that simply labeling something an experiment or experimental eschews commitments. Experiments do not evade consequences or excuse carelessness in thought or action.

Before going any further, it is crucial to acknowledge that experimentation can be grossly abusive. The history of experimentation is also a history of manipulation and exploitation. The Tuskegee experiment and the Stanford prison experiment are two well-known examples of how people can be horrifically harmed in the pursuit of knowledge. And most often, the people who are exploited are Black, Indigenous, people of color, neurodiverse, disabled, women, or LGBTQ+. In other words, experiments tend to be performed on those who are already subjugated by dominant and oppressive social and cultural norms, re-entrenching structural inequalities. Such manipulation and exploitation also occurs in the small; to this day, communities are beset upon by well-meaning researchers, designers, artists, and others who seek to study and even sometimes serve these communities. However, they do violence when they extract insights without ensuring enduring benefits to the community.

I recognize the problematic association of experiments with science and the potential violence of experiments. Other forms of experiment are possible, forms in which the experiment is undertaken as conjoint inquiry (Binder et al 2015; Dixon 2018; Steen 2013). As I develop this concept and practice of design experiments in civics, constant attention is given to issues of power and privilege, and the purported benefits of these design experiments are called into question. These are not experiments on people. They are collaborative explorations of the conditions and experiences of democracy, as those conditions and experiences are and as they might be. The inspiration for these design experiments in civics comes from pragmatism, in particular the work of Jane Addams.

Pragmatism provides a distinctive philosophical approach to experimentalism, oriented toward the social conditions and practices of democracy. In pragmatism, democracy and experimentation go hand in hand.

Furthermore, democracy and experimentation are experiential. Much of this thinking is usually credited to John Dewey, who believed democracy is always more than just a set of governmental structures. As he stated:

> Democracy is belief in the ability of human experience to generate the aims and methods by which further experience will grow in ordered richness. Every other form of moral and social faith rests upon the idea that experience must be subjugated at some point or another to some form of external control; to some "authority" alleged to exist outside the processes of experience. Democracy is faith that the process of experience is more important than any special result attained, so that special results achieved are of ultimate value only as they used to enrich and order the ongoing process. (1988b, 229)

The stipulation that experience is central to democracy aligns with work "in the small." In the closeness of local and commonplace encounters, experience comes to the fore. Democracy, then, is not an abstraction nor a set of formal organizations and procedures. Democracy is something we are involved in making, feeling, and doing. We encounter and construct democracy. And one way we do so is through experimentation. Continuing with Dewey, "The very foundation of democratic procedure is dependence upon experimental production of social change; an experimentation directed by working principles that are tested and developed in the very process of being tried out" (1988a, 273).

Pragmatism, and Dewey in particular, have long influenced design. The work of Brian Dixon (2018, 2020) and Marc Steen (2013) are especially important, as they weave together concepts central to this idea of design as democratic inquiry. Steen argues for understanding codesign as a practice of collaborative inquiry and imagination in which people come together to explore the possibilities for what could be, "so they can be creative and jointly bring about change" (2013, 29). Dixon offers a detailed and compelling interpretation of Dewey in relation to design research, drawing out how practices of design become practices of inquiry and how such practices of inquiry might be transformational. Through such work "we can contribute to knowledge on the basis of changing the situation and, consequently, changing the ontological baselines upon which we operate" (2020, 162). Pragmatism also runs throughout the concept of democratic design experiments (Binder et al. 2015), both in terms of the role of experimentation and that of publics (Le Dantec 2016; Lindström and Ståhl 2014), which is another point of connection between design and Dewey.

While Dewey provides a theoretical starting point to unite democracy, experimentation, and design, I do not want to dwell on Dewey (Rosner 2018: 26–27). Even more than Dewey, design experiments in civics are indebted to the work of Jane Addams and other feminist pragmatists. Addams worked together with Dewey and others who were members of the Department of Sociology at the University of Chicago and established what came to be known as the Chicago School of Sociology. Her work and writing are foundational to pragmatism. Addams, however, was not a traditional academic. Her pursuit of democracy took other forms. She put the concepts of pragmatism into action. In 1889, Addams and Ellen Gates Starr established Hull-House, a boarding house for immigrants in Chicago. It did more than just provide rooms; Addams developed ongoing programs of everyday learning for residents. Many of her programs revolved around what we would now call "making." For example, there were classes in bookbinding and crafting homemade soft drinks. She also pioneered experimental social services. As one of many cases of such experimental social services, in response to concerns of eviction for striking women, she created a boarding club—a kind of cooperative hostel.

> At a meeting of working girls held at Hull-House during a strike in a large shoe factory, the discussions made it clear that the strikers who had been most easily frightened, and therefore first to capitulate, were naturally those girls who were paying board and were afraid of being put out if they fell too far behind. After a recital of a case of peculiar hardship one of them exclaimed: "Wouldn't it be fine if we had a boarding club of our own, and then we could stand by each other in a time like this?" After that events moved quickly. We read aloud together Beatrice Potter's little book on "Coöperation," and discussed all the difficulties and fascinations of such an undertaking, and on the first of May, 1891, two comfortable apartments near Hull-House were rented and furnished. (Addams [1910] 1990, 110)

This brief example of the boarding club expresses the character of the work of Hull-House and Addams's feminist pragmatist approach to democracy. The boarding club was a caring collective. Not only was it situated in the lived experience and everyday challenges of women workers in late nineteenth-century Chicago, it was also responsive to those experiences and conditions. And that responsiveness was creative: through original and resourceful action, Addams, in collaboration with others, constructed an alternative institution and service.

Addams and residents of Hull-House also participated in extended and involved research, sharing that work as evidence of current conditions. One such example is *Hull-House Papers and Maps*, published in 1895. These maps depicted statistics of those who lived in the neighborhood of Hull-House and included data on the nationalities of residents and their wages. This data was collected by Florence Kelly, who was employed by the United States Bureau of Labor, together with residents of Hull-House. Taken together, this work is an early example of community-based participatory research and the use of community-collected data and maps for advocacy. The research took years for Kelly and the residents of Hull-House to complete, because it was conducted across multiple projects with different sources of funding. Once completed and the maps produced, they were later used in a Bureau of Labor Statistics report.

For Addams, projects such as the boarding club and maps were part of an experimental practice. As she stated, "The Settlement . . . is an experimental effort to aid in the solution of the social and industrial problems which are engendered by modern conditions of life in the great city" (Addams [1910] 1990, 98). As Charlene Haddock Seigfried notes, Addams's experimentation was distinctly collective; Addams sought to "make experience continuous beyond the individual" (Addams [1899] 1982, 186–187; Seigfried 1999). The work of the experiment, like the work of democracy, is not the isolated work of an individual but rather a communal endeavor. This communal characteristic of democracy and experiments continues to resonate in feminist pragmatism today. It is a characteristic that distinguishes feminist pragmatist democracy and experimental practices from other modes of action—including design—that all too often emphasize the allegedly epic efforts of a single person.

Though there was a strong and enduring collaboration between Jane Addams and the University of Chicago, Addams carefully managed this institutional relationship. She did not want Hull-House to become merely a laboratory for sociology, because she opposed "the detached view of knowledge that was gaining strength in universities seeking to emulate positivist models of science" (Seigfried 1999, 219). Addams believed that situated work in places like Hull-House set the standard for what we should understand as an experimental approach, not the work done in laboratories at universities (Gross 2009). I believe this tension with the university is productive for this inquiry. The connection between these design experiments in civics and academia are undeniable. In addition to explorations of what else civics might be, design experiments in civics are attempts at reconsidering what else academic design might be. Similar to Addams's push against reductive notions of science, I am resistant to positivist and universal notions of academic design.

Inspired by pragmatism, then, by democratic inquiry I mean the cooperative investigation of our communal conditions as they exist now and as they might be differently arranged and lived. To call this inquiry "democratic" is not to refer to specific mechanisms, such as voting, nor specific structures of government, such as a representative democracy. Rather, democracy is "primarily a mode of associated living, of conjoint communicated experience" (Dewey [1916], 1997, 93). Those associations are pluralistic and concerned with the welfare of the community. Bringing theories of agonism into this, those associations are also continuously disputed. Democratic inquiry thus works to cultivate and sustain pluralistic and caring associations, and does so in ways that are collaborative and just, while also nurturing contestation and dissent. How our lives and experiences are associated is not fixed; it is matter for experimentation. That is, experimentation is a way of doing democratic inquiry. This is where the work of Jane Addams becomes so important. Through Addams we can see a philosophy of democracy as it is lived out through experimentation: an experimental approach to democracy is performed throughout her life's work. My approach, inspired by Addams but with nowhere near her breadth of work, is to similarly explore how an experimental approach to democracy might be performed and lived out, as told from the perspective of contemporary design practice and discourse.

It is also important to acknowledge that experiential perspectives on democracy were not limited to those we think of as pragmatists. Ideas uniting democracy as experience were also present in the work of W. E. B. Du Bois, an originator of sociology who founded the Atlanta Sociological Laboratory and what became known as the Atlanta School of Sociology (Wright 2017). As Seigfried discussed, for Du Bois "'the real argument for democracy' is its recognition of the worth of each person's feelings and experiences as an invaluable resource for the community and consequent belief in the inherent capacity for learning of its members" (Seigfried 1999, 211; see also Du Bois 1975, 144). While the approach of the Atlanta Sociological Laboratory employed a more scientific model and was not situated in the same way as Hull-House, Du Bois's practices of data collection and representation are prescient. In the late 1800s and early 1900s, Du Bois collected extensive data on the lives of Black people in the United States, which he used to create stunning and compelling charts, diagrams, and maps. Shamefully, this first school of sociology has long been underrecognized (Wright 2017).

Contemporary philosophies of pragmatism continue to struggle to balance the limitations and potential of experimentalism. There is a persistent tension between pluralistic notions of experimentalism and regarding the experiment as a positivist endeavor that requires verification. In addressing the question "What Is a 'Democratic Experiment'?" Chris Ansell (2013) rejects the conclusion that what is meant by experiment and experimentalism in the context of pragmatism is a traditional positivist experiment. Rather, he situates pragmatic experimentation as "provisional, probative, creative, and jointly constructed" (165). Ansell's pragmatist experiment is strikingly similar to what I call a design experiment.

My concept of a design experiment brings Ansell's concept of a pragmatist experiment together with Jane Addams's Hull-House, as a prototype of sociopolitical experimentation through making. However, associating design and pragmatism requires returning to ongoing developments in design to enrich our working concept. When Ansell compares the pragmatist experiment to the design experiment, his point of reference is actually design science, drawn from the work of Herbert Simon. In *The Sciences of the Artificial* (1996), Simon asserted the role of design in the study and invention of the made world, as opposed to the discovery of the natural world. Simon was one of the foremost thinkers of the twentieth century and set the groundwork for design research. But Simon's reliance on positivist notions of science threatens to thwart more expansive conceptions of experimentation in and through design.

My thinking about experiments is also deeply informed by the work of sociologist Noortje Marres (2016), who studies "living experiments" with a keen eye toward design. Marres is similarly informed by pragmatism, and she approaches her scholarship into contemporary experiments in living as a mode of social research. That is, she believes that experiments can be studied from the perspective of social theory and that living experiments can be cast as a kind of social research. Marres's area of focus is sustainability, and the experiments she studies often prompt reflection on living sustainably, ranging from individual actions aimed at lessening one's carbon footprint through online communication to public engagement events such as eco-homes that model collective approaches to environmentally responsible dwelling. What is distinctive about the social experiment, according to

Marres, is that they provide "a format or 'protocol' for exploring and testing forms of life" (2012, 78). Marres states that "experiments in sustainable living can be said to undertake the modification of habits and habitats according to a fixed procedure; they are a way of implementing changes in everyday routines and living spaces according to a protocol" (78). As exemplified by the range of activities and things Marres studies, these "formats and protocols"—the devices of living experiments—can take many forms.

Marres is not alone in her scholarship on experiments in and as social science (see Gunn, Otto, and Smith 2013; Lezaun, Marres, and Tironi 2017; Lury and Wakeford 2012b). What seems to be emerging in the fields of the social studies of science and technology are hybrid practices of sociology, anthropology, and design. At times, these practices skew more toward one field or another, but there are commonalities across these evolving methods. As described by Xavier Lezaun, Noortje Marres, and Manuel Tironi (2017, 195), "Deploying settings, devices, and/or things experimentally makes it possible to curate novel forms of participation, eliciting expressions or accounts of public issues that would otherwise remain underarticulated or exist only *in potentia* (Lury and Wakeford 2012[a]; Marres 2012)." Such perspectives and practices at the overlap of the social sciences and design greatly inform my work. Indeed, we might consider design experiments in civics as akin to the material experimentation that Marres describes and that continues to be elaborated upon from within the social sciences, articulated in a complementary manner from within design.

While design experiments are not science strictly speaking, there are insights into the experiment that can be drawn from the philosophy of science. In particular, Isabelle Stengers's work on the experiment as event helps conceptualize the experiment as something made and experienced (2000). That is, Stengers's conceptualization of the experiment as event provides entrée to consider the experiment as a designed thing. Notably, Stengers also draws upon pragmatism in her philosophy—in particular, the work of William James. Stengers's explication of the experiment as event does not reduce the experiment to positivist conventions. Rather, she interprets it as a happening that prompts further inquiry. From this conception of the experiment as event, Mariam Fraser (2006) develops the idea of the event as "inventive problem-making." Fraser's idea of inventive problem-making is fundamental to design experiments in civics. As part of the work of democratic inquiry, what design experiments in civics do is construct problems within our democratic conditions and experiences. Design experiments—as inventive problem-making—identify and articulate problems that should be addressed, perhaps by people other than designers.

Imagination and Care

Design experiments are distinctive because they stimulate our imagination through practices of making and use. And imagination can vary and expand our repertoires of action, of how else we might configure and experience democratic conditions (Binder et al. 2015; Steen 2013). A rich history of scholarship exploring the relationship between the imagination, society, and politics forms the backdrop for this inquiry. C. Wright Mills (1959) famously described the sociological imagination as enabling "its possessor to understand the larger historical scene in terms of its meaning for the inner life and the external career of a variety of individuals" (5). To Mills, the imagination was activated based on the structure of society, "the mechanics by which it is changing" (6), and prevailing "varieties" of individuals of the period. Arjun Appadurai (1996) conceptualized the imagination as shaping both individual and collective identities, describing it as a "constitutive feature of modern subjectivity" (3). He saw the imagination's rise in relevance under modernity as being distinct from mere fantasy. To Appadurai, the imagination was a "staging ground for action" (7). Design experiments are just such a staging ground that help visions of society take form by activating the civic imagination through making and the use of made things.

Technology can play a powerful role in encouraging publics to imagine alternate presents and potential futures. The role of the technological imagination has historically been viewed with skepticism (Ames 2019; Barbrook and Cameron 1996), because scholars often think of the imagination as synonymous with technocracy or a way to describe the coercive aura of technology. There is substantive reason for such skepticism and concern, and such critique is important. I take a different route, treating the relationship between the imagination and technological practice as a way to imagine other ways of living together. Specifically, I draw on Sheila Jasanoff and Sang-Hyun Kim's (2009, 120) notion of "sociotechnical imaginaries," which they describe as "collectively imagined forms of social life and social order reflected in the design and fulfillment of nation-specific scientific and/or technological projects." They regard sociotechnical imaginaries as able to articulate differences, explaining why technologies are imagined to be useful for entirely different ends. Pushing back on earlier universal sociological visions for the imagination, they describe the sociotechnical imagination as "collective, durable, capable of being performed . . . [and] temporarily situated and culturally particular" (Jasanoff and Kim 2015, 19).

For pragmatists, imagination is essential to making democratic conditions and experiences vibrant. Erin McKenna's (2001, 83) feminist pragmatist approach to Utopia provides a compelling understanding of the role of imagination in striving toward other worlds. She argues that what distinguishes pragmatist politics is that it is process oriented—that is, "There is no end state at which we must work to arrive, but a multiple of possible future states which we seek and try out." Envisioning and trialing these future states requires imagination: creativity, inventiveness, and resourcefulness of thought and action. Furthermore, for McKenna the pursuit of Utopia as a feminist practice is also as an experimental practice. As she states, "We need to see life, and our visions of what could be possible, as an experimental process . . . of coping with conflict and difficulties" (3). It is no wonder, then, that McKenna draws upon writers such as Ursula Le Guin to exemplify the capacity of imagination to express and explore how we might differently configure our social and political relations.

Imagination is, of course, not new to design. There is a history of design that blends imaginative making and politics. Of particular interest and influence is the confluence of practices and discourses of participatory design and critical and speculative design. Melding together the artistic aspects of critical and speculative design with the engaged and political aspects of participatory design foments novel forms of inquiry (Sanders and Stappers 2008, 2012). Increasingly, designers are contesting and remaking these practices and discourses, articulating new practices and broadening discourse by engaging decolonization, Afrofuturism, feminism, and queer theory (S. Bardzell 2018; de Oliveira and de O. Martins 2019; de O. Martins and de Oliveria 2016; Harrington and Dillahunt 2021; Sengers, Williams, and Khovanskaya 2021; Winchester 2018). The issue for design, then, is not so much the limitations of imagination, nor a crisis of imagination, but rather the need for practices and discourses that are inclusive and expressive of more diverse subjectivities both within and beyond design. And, in fact, one way to cultivate and explore such diverse subjectivities is through imaginative making.

Other design theorists and practitioners have similarly explored the relationship between design, the imagination, and politics. Dan Lockton's (Lockton and Candy 2019; Lockton et al. 2019) work on imaginaries is essential in this domain, looking at how design can contribute to imaginaries that shape possibilities for change, even toward societal transition. Daniel Opazo, Matías Wolff, and María José Araya (2017) draw upon Cornelius Castoriadis (1997, 2007) to consider the political qualities of imagination and imaginaries in the context of designing public spaces in Chile, noting, "To think about design in terms of imagining the world otherwise—and act accordingly to change it—already involves an evident political edge" (Opazo, Wolff, and Araya 2017, 75). Recently, Paola Pierri (2020) has brought together the work of Cornelius Castoriadis and pragmatism to explore the role of the imagination in designing for democracy, proposing an idea of design for the radical imagination "which has—as its main ambition—the creation and the nurturing of a collective subject that can interpret and change the world politically" (5).

Imagination alone does not characterize these design experiments in civics. They are enacted; they are events that occur and that have effect. One of the reasons Jane Addams's work is so compelling is that experiments she pursued unfolded in the world. Not only is democracy experienced through such experiments, imagination is also experienced. In some cases, this imagination may be spectacular. For instance, Black Quantum Futurism, based in Philadelphia, has hosted a series of workshops that bring Afrofuturist themes into community settings, sparking radical imaginations of how alternative temporalities can be expressed and employed toward more just and equitable Black futures. Acts of imagination can also be events that tinker and differently attune our everyday conditions. The Creative Reaction Lab in St. Louis provides examples of just such efforts of grounded and engaged practices of imaginative democracy toward developing capacities in communities and across generations.

The design experiments in civics that I describe in this book find their place among these practices and discourses that blend imaginative making and politics. Imagination is essential to the ongoing renewal that democracy demands. And experimentation is a method for sparking the imagination. That is, experimental practices are imaginative *and* they incite our imagination. What distinguishes design experiments in civics is that imagination is given structure—at least momentarily—such that it might be experienced.

Finally, I want to bring care into this discussion. At this point, that may seem afield. But there is an argument that care is, or should be, fundamental to how we structure and experience our communal lives. Care provides a principle that gives purpose to these experiments. For Joan Tronto (2013), care is a way of conceiving democracy philosophically. Caring, according to Tronto, is how we should judge our formal and informal democratic institutions. The concern for Tronto is how care is allocated in society. Annemarie Mol (2008) offers a complementary perspective on care. Mol's perspective is ethnographic and situated in medicine rather than democracy, but it similarly offers care as an orientation toward others. For Mol, care is reflected in collaborative, relational processes of attunement. Both Tronto's and Mol's perspectives share a commitment to a way of ordering our relations that prioritizes communal life. They strive for a relationality that is attentive to and sustaining of togetherness. At the same time, both their perspectives recognize fluidity: whatever notion of "good" that care implies cannot be static or universal. Both perspectives, then, offer care as a value and an endeavor. Drawing these concepts together into a theme, one purpose of design experiments in civics is the care of the possible (Stengers 2011)—a practice of tending to diverse civic imaginaries and practices through the ongoing cultivation of possibilities.

Toward More Diverse Civics

It is tempting to claim that there is a particular urgency in thinking about civics and democracy in this historical moment. Such claims imbue writing with a sense of vital importance. But both pragmatist and agonistic theories of democracy stipulate we always and forever need to examine, contest, and renew our democratic conditions. Democracy is an ongoing endeavor. Whether or not we are in a moment of crisis, our democratic conditions and experiences require inquiry and experiment. The work of keeping democratic possibilities vibrant is constant and never complete. In the following chapters, I describe a series of design experiments in civics that blend democracy, imagination, and care. From these experiments I draw out themes, connect those themes to theory and practice, and elaborate on their implications. In doing so, my hope is to develop a shared appreciation for how such design experiments contribute to ongoing discourses of thinking and doing design otherwise, and also contribute to keeping democracy vibrant by contributing to diverse civic imaginaries and practices.

2 Stories

There was a buzz in Atlanta. The city was poised to become a so-called smart city, with environmental sensor corridors and autonomous vehicle testbeds. Statements were made about how robust data storage and sophisticated analytics would deliver computationally enabled insights into how the city works and might work better. Official announcements poured forth and press conferences were held. Members of various offices within city government spoke about their visions for a "smart Atlanta" at public events. While attending one of these public events, I heard an official from city government share this story:

> Imagine you're a mother living on Boulevard and you have a son who has severe asthma. Every morning he has to go and wait for the school bus at the corner of Boulevard and North Avenue. When the air quality is bad, it can trigger an asthma attack, which ruins his day at school; he can't learn because he's in the nurse's office, missing class. Now imagine you—you're the mother—you have an app that has access to some data from sensors along North Avenue that told you that the air quality was really bad this morning. And looking at this data you decide not to send your son out to wait at the corner for the bus because you don't want him to have an asthma attack. You decide instead to call into work to tell them you'll be late and then you drive your son into school that morning.

As I attended similar events over the next year, I kept hearing versions of this story, each one a bit different but essentially the same. In truth, there is nothing novel about this story. The idea of sensors informing decision-making is common in the stories told about smart cities. Air quality is a favorite theme, perhaps because air quality is an accessible concept and the technologies to monitor air quality work reasonably well. The story expresses a vision of a city rich in data, culled from an instrumented environment and made usable for everyday people. But the story is also questionable. The street mentioned—Boulevard—cuts through the center of the Old Fourth Ward, which is a neighborhood rapidly undergoing gentrification, displacing longtime residents. It is, or was, also a neighborhood with one of the highest concentrations of subsidized housing in the state of Georgia. Much of that subsidized housing stretches along Boulevard, the same street in the story. This story about a smart Atlanta, told through the characters of a mother and her asthmatic son, seemed profoundly absent of many of the everyday realities actual residents face.

Let's set aside for the moment questions about the technical capacities of these sensors and consider the characters in this story. On its surface, this story is supposed to tell us about how technology is useful to people. Who is the mother in this story? Is she a longtime resident or someone just moving into the neighborhood? How is she accessing this information? Does she have a smartphone? Is the access to this information free? What kind of job does she have, such that she's able to choose to come into work late? Not to mention, why is the care for the son so readily ascribed to being the mother's work? These details were curiously missing in the versions of this story that I heard told. Some might argue that this is just a vignette to proffer a compelling vision for what a so-called smart Atlanta might be—simply marketing to garner support for a suite of technologies. But stories such as these matter precisely because they market, promote, and encourage participation. They shape public understanding and expectations. Stories such as these influence procurement, engineering, and policy. Stories such as these are one way we collectively imagine the future.

These stories come from many sources, including design. In contemporary practice, stories are design things; stories are things purposefully made in different ways to do a variety of work (Erickson 1996; Lupton 2017; Quesenbery and Brooks 2010). Frequently, designers give form to what the use of technologies entails through stories. The kinds of design stories vary, from the fanciful tales of speculative design to the structured use-cases and personas of user experience design. Sometimes these stories inform engineering or become the basis of marketing. Other times stories function as counternarratives. Through stories, designers articulate imagined subjectivities. These imagined subjectivities are the individual and collective identities and practices of those who use, consume, manipulate, and resist these technologies. In the case of smart cities, through these stories designers construct and express ideas about who residents of the smart city of the future might be. The question of how one might shape those stories to express pluralistic subjectivities and correspondingly pluralistic imaginaries is a question I confront in this chapter.

The story of the mother and the air quality sensors at the corner of North Avenue and Boulevard is not a stand-alone tale. It is part of the grand narrative of a smart Atlanta. In the quest to establish itself as a smart city, in 2016 the mayor's office committed to developing an approximately 3.5-mile stretch of North Avenue as a smart-city testbed. The mayor proudly stated that by late 2017 this stretch of North Avenue would have the densest array of sensors in the United States. This would make it not just a smart corridor but the smartest corridor. Sensor boxes would be installed at intersections along this corridor. Many people in city government seemed certain that the bundles of technologies soon to be distributed along this corridor would provide an abundance of opportunities. And these opportunities were communicated in the form of stories.

Many stories of smart cities are influenced by vendors who wanted their infrastructure to imbue cities with computational capacities. Each vendor had their own storyline that situated their network, product, or service as most valuable to governing the smart city. For this reason, the stories from IBM were different from the stories from Cisco, AT&T, Intel, or GE. No single story presented a complete vision. But taken together, they promised residents that our modest urban life will be transformed into dynamic experiences. The legacy of smart cities has produced such durable stories about how technology will purportedly bring about new and improved forms of civics. Yet often lacking in these stories are the varied perspectives of people currently living in these neighborhoods. And when more varied perspectives are included, too often they are grossly simplified to advance already determined notions of who the residents of the smart city are, should be, or should become. Consequently, the forms of civic life that actual residents desire, as well as the civic futures the actual residents might wish to avoid, are absent. But other stories are possible.

The *PARSE* project was developed to elicit and share other stories of the smart city through activities of design, using familiar modes of making such as design games and scenarios. These scenarios, and the processes of constructing them, were meant to offer an alternative to the dominant and generic stories of a smart Atlanta. Such generic stories reproduce and reinforce subjectivities bound to hegemonic notions of what it means to be a resident of a smart city in the United States. Of course, those dominant stories held some appeal. Who wouldn't want to avoid an asthma attack? But although such stories are persuasive, they also restrict the pluralism that characterizes robust democratic conditions and experiences. The civic imaginary they foster is stunted, an impoverished vision of a city that serves sensor boxes and those who own them, rather than residents.

One way design experiments cultivate diverse civic imaginaries is by articulating pluralistic subjectivities: constellations of relational identities and practices. In this chapter, I explore how design might contribute to making and sharing such subjectivities through stories. These stories conceptualize and express ways of acting together, different from the standard stories about the smart city and its purported residents. Making and sharing stories about pluralistic subjectivities is a way of exploring possible roles and relations among and between residents, city government, and technical systems. Like all design experiments, this endeavor is provisional and fraught; but even so, it offers processes for collaborative creativity that thicken our imaginations. Through the making and telling of stories, design experiments help us explore what other civic worlds might, and might not, be desirable.

Smart Cities

The concept of the smart city is the latest historical instantiation of cities as sites of technological innovation. In many of these visions, urban areas are not merely places where technology is deployed; the place itself becomes technological. Design has long helped give these visions form. Throughout much of the twentieth century, architecture and urban planning, from the high modernism of Le Corbusier to the speculative work of Archigram and Archizoom, envisioned the interplay of technologies and cities. Architecture and urban planning still loom large in the smart city of the early twenty-first century. The fields of interaction and service design now join architecture and urban planning in creating visions and telling stories of the cities as sites of technological innovation.

The smart city, as we refer to it today, is portrayed as a collection of digital technologies that permeate the urban environment. Sensors are embedded in roads to count vehicles, digital cameras on traffic lights feed video into high-tech data centers, streetlamps monitor environmental conditions, and drones surveil traffic. Mobile and ubiquitous computing amplifies this data and compounds its value. It is not only buildings and roadways that are imbued with technology. People are turned into data collectors through the array of sensors and software in our phones that track our movements through the environment. We check in to locations on social media and take photos of events to share online. Even when we are not logging this data ourselves, it still exists in the background, ready to be called upon when needed. In some respects, the city has become a data machine. This data is vital material for computation. Analytics systems use this data to discern patterns and make predictions that, ostensibly, help set policies and improve residents' lives. But notably, there is nothing inherent in these technologies that make them about or for a city. As Jathan Sadowski and Roy Bendor (2019, 541) note, "Smart city technologies become smart city technologies only by association with the idea of the smart city and the narratives, logics, practices, and symbolisms of which it is constituted." In other words, smart cities are not defined by any particular suite of technologies or technical capacities but rather by their imaginaries.

Despite the fact that many of the discourses of the smart city tout a better life, it seems few services actually exist for use by residents. This does not mean that the smart city is not happening; it is just unfolding across different registers. Municipalities are tracking the use of roadways to understand traffic patterns to inform traffic planning. Cameras are being used to automatically ticket drivers and shame jaywalkers. Gunshots are detected by arrays of acoustic sensors, demanding police response. Some argue that these services are of value to residents, and perhaps they are. My concern is that they continue to reproduce the existing structures and processes of governing that operationalize and monetize civic life. The "actually existing" smart city seems to be less about enabling residents than about reinforcing neoliberal governmentality (Shelton, Zook, and Wiig 2015). Like so many technology discourses, the smart city is often implicitly colonialist, seeking to pervade all aspects of life (Dourish and Mainwaring 2012). Its air of universalism continues the modernist project of design in a different form.

There is also a growing body of interdisciplinary scholarship that pushes back against the prevailing discourses of the smart city (Green 2019; Greenfield 2013). These critiques recognize the potential for more diverse civics by finding and sharing spaces of possibility. For instance, scholars such as Catherine D'Ignazio, Eric Gordon, Paul Mihailidis, Andrew Schrock, and Benjamin Stokes probe the capacities and limitations of new modes of mediated action in the local politics of smart cities through civic media and civic tech (D'Ignazio, Gordon, and Christoforetti 2019; Gordon and Mihailidis 2016; Gordon and Mugar 2020; Schrock 2018; Stokes 2020). Laura Forlano and Nassim Parvin draw together feminist technoscience and design to both scrutinize and shape possibilities for emergent forms of participation in the smart city (Forlano 2016; Parvin 2018). Allison Powell (2021) looks to communities and activists to offer alternative models of data citizenship that resist rigid and controlling notions of smart cities. Much of the pushback against the smart city is not an outright rejection of computation and data in civic life writ large. Rather, it is a call to work toward different configurations and reconfigurations of technologies, people, organizations, and institutions (Suchman 2002, 2007). It is in these spaces of possibilities—as small and constrained as they might be—that democratic inquiry can gain a foothold, through what Sheila Jasanoff refers to as the "publicly performed visions of desirable futures" (Jasanoff and Kim 2015, 4).

Stories and Subjectivities

In their discussion of community economies and postcapitalism, feminist geographers J. K. Gibson-Graham (1995, 1996, 2006, 2008) emphasize the importance of acknowledging and developing diverse economic subjectivities. These diverse economic subjectivities provide the potential to conceptualize, describe, and enact ever more varied forms of economic activity. In order to envision more diverse markets and labor, we have to be open to more varied ways of being and becoming economic actors. This effort of acknowledging and developing subjectivities extends beyond the field of "the economy." Gibson-Graham notes that their thinking of subjectivities was inspired and informed by the work of political theorist Chantal Mouffe and her discussions of political subjectivities (Gibson-Graham 1995; Mouffe 1992). Just as there is a need to acknowledge and develop diverse economic subjectivities, so too should we acknowledge and develop diverse civic subjectivities.

Activities of designing and the uses of designed things are entangled with the formation and expression of subjectivities. What it means to be a designer, who is considered a designer, and what activities are considered to be designing are central questions to design. Such questions challenge the presumed authority of the professional designer and were a basis for the emergence of participatory design in the 1960s and 1970s, driving lively debates to this day (Harrington, Erete, and Piper 2019; Kensing and Greenbaum 2012). These questions also trouble how designers construct and express the subjectivity of "the user"—that ubiquitous person upon whom design depends for its valuation. Despite its pervasiveness in design, the user is a contested figure. Of late, numerous scholars have probed the subjectivities of design, expanding and enriching concepts of both the designer and user. For example, Silvia Lindtner (2020) has explored how technological platforms and culture combine in the subjectivities of so-called makers, and Lilly Irani (2019) has investigated how practices of innovation contribute to the development of "entrepreneurial citizenship," fusing design and national identity. Both Lindtner and Irani offer us crucial perspectives on how the subjectivities of designers, broadly construed, are influenced by market logics. Jeffrey Bardzell and Shaowen Bardzell (2015) and, with Guo Freeman (Freeman, Bardzell, and Bardzell 2017, 2019), have also explored how the very categories of designer and user are troubled in contemporary creative and critical practices that sit outside of the usual discourses and contexts of professional design. Bardzell and Bardzell point us to ever more varied critical practices informed by ever more varied subjectivities, opening new perspectives on both the capacities and limits of design. Such scholarship broadens our understanding of the complex interplay between design and subjectivities.

Daniela Rosner's (2018) work on critical fabulations also highlights the importance of stories to the subjectivities of design. Rosner argues that it is crucial to recognize those stories that have been excluded from the histories of design and designing, because exclusion reinforces and reproduces oppressive structures within the practice of design and its study. Rosner's creative scholarship takes seriously Donna Haraway's (2016, 12) assertion that "It matters what stories make worlds, what worlds make stories." Rosner's work brings the importance of varied stories of making, using, and resisting to our understanding of design. Such varied stories are inhabited by and subsequently produce different subjectivities of design, enabling us to tell different accounts about what design is and might be and expanding our appreciation of who is designing. Following from Rosner and Haraway, the stories we tell matter because they are how we imagine other worlds and the subjectivities that inhabit and comprise those worlds. My interest is how activities of designing might contribute to the imagination and articulation of pluralistic subjectivities through stories. And subsequently, how we might approach the making and telling of those storied subjectivities as part of a practice of design experiments in civics.

There are many ways that design and storytelling are entwined. Where I will begin is with a particular form of storytelling in design: the scenario. Scenarios are written descriptions of the envisioned use of a product or service, with sufficient detail to give context to that use. Often scenarios include information about when and where a design is intended to be used and by whom. As a distinct design thing, the scenario is regularly used for early-stage conceptualization of a product or service. Scenarios are commonplace when technologies are nascent or otherwise unfamiliar because scenarios give a semblance of form to a concept. When there are few systems to interact with, we discuss and debate technologies and their perceived potentials and consequences through such stories of possibilities. Scenarios are currently used by smart-city advocates to tell stories across government, industry, and academia. In a sense, the scenario functions as a sort of narrative prototype—a device that sets a horizon while also immediately serving as a boundary object (Star and Griesemer 1989).

Scenarios do important work in making a case for technology, and thereby design. The imagined users within these stories and their encounters with technology function as what Alex Wilkie and Mike Michael (2009) refer to as a "narrative joint"—a means of connecting the technical and the social. Wilkie and Michael describe a pattern to these joints. First, a social situation is portrayed in such a way that a problem is posed or conveyed, like the child who suffers from asthma and must wait at the bus stop where he will be exposed to poor air quality. Second, a technology is introduced and a future imagined user makes use of that technology to alleviate the social situation. The cleanness and austerity of such a joint is what makes it compelling as both a strategic and tactical form in product, service, and even policy development. But the entanglement of the social and the technical is, in fact, a mess.

There are aesthetic, political, and practical reasons for making simple narrative joints and corresponding scenarios. But when overly simplified, they deny the complexity of lived experience through one-dimensional narratives. Certainly, it is possible to multiply and reconfigure the narrative joints of the stories we tell about smart cities. As experiments, these scenarios and their narrative joints should not merely reproduce established patterns. Instead, they should articulate varied constellations of identities and practices. It should be possible to use activities of designing to purposefully cultivate divergent, contrasting, and contrary subjectivities. Such a practice would entail eliciting, articulating, and sharing pluralistic subjectivities as a mode of democratic inquiry into how we might differently conceive our civic conditions and experiences. To achieve such pluralistic subjectivities involves alternate practices of joinery, in addition to different kinds of joints.

PARSE

Participatory Approaches to Researching Sensing Environments (PARSE) was developed in response to hearing stories about smart cities like the one told at the start of this chapter. The goal of *PARSE* was to create a series of scenarios that would articulate pluralistic subjectivities. These pluralistic subjectivities would offer alternatives to the dominant and generic narratives of smart cities, in the hopes of expanding the collective imagination of what a smart city—and specifically what a smart Atlanta—might be. To achieve this goal, we wanted to use methods of participatory design that would bring together residents to contribute to those stories. We were also aware that representational practices such as scenarios are suspect because, as Sasha Costanza-Chock (2020, 81) notes, these practices often rely on "creating abstractions about communities that are not really at the table in the design process." And we were conscious that storytelling can be an extractive practice and that design can be paternalistic, claiming to "give voice" but doing harm in the process (Parvin 2018). So care had to be taken.

The *PARSE* project was initially supported by federal grant funding with the aim of exploring the potentials of smart and connected technologies for public life. It was primarily composed of myself and graduate student Cookie Nguyen, who brought additional skills in communication design and writing to the project. Together, we conceptualized a workshop to engage participants in codesigning local services that would leverage sensors, data, and analytics for purposes that the participants envisioned. Cookie took the lead in designing the workshop materials and the events of the workshops themselves. From the start, we intended to take the outcomes of the workshop and transform them into materials that could be circulated through government and civil society. Along the way, we received additional funding for the project from both the university and industry. We consciously directed the industry funding toward creating new understandings of the smart city beyond (and in some cases counter to) the familiar frames and narratives of industry.

Gathering Together

It's a Wednesday night about 6:00 p.m., and we are hosting our first *PARSE* workshop at the Atlanta City Studio. Cookie and I are attending, along with a handful of other students who volunteered to help. The Atlanta City Studio is a satellite of sorts for the Department of City Planning, set up in a public place for about eighteen months to put their work on display and make themselves available for comments and questions from residents. For the first installment of this program, the Atlanta City Studio was set up in Ponce City Market—a former warehouse turned into a mixed-use development. Depending on whom you ask, Ponce City Market is either an exciting transformation that energized an underused city block, or it is a marker of gentrification at the edge of the Old Fourth Ward. Ponce City Market is on North Avenue, right in the midst of what was to become the North Avenue smart corridor. As the workshop is about to get underway, people start to arrive, mostly young to middle-aged professionals. There is a mix of genders, ethnicities, and racial identities. Many work close by. There is also a handful of professional planners who work for private firms, as well as municipal employees. Activists and advocates and civil society organizations rub shoulders with designers. There are, however, very few residents.

At 6:05 p.m., the workshop begins with two introductions. A colleague in the Department of City Planning gives a general overview of what city planning is, to set the context of how cities are designed. She explains how planning works to shape the urban environment and the role of the Atlanta City Studio as an organization committed to public engagement. People ask questions about what planning does and doesn't do, which quickly transitions to people asking questions about their own particular matters of concern. The second introduction comes from a research engineer at the Georgia Tech Research Institute involved in the development of a smart-city sensing platform to be deployed along North Avenue. He's brought a prototype with him—a version of one of the sensor boxes. The gray utility box, about the size of a plastic milk crate, lies open on a table at the front of the room to reveal a series of circuit boards, ribbon cables, and sensors. Once again, people ask questions, this time about the technology. They are curious about what it can do, what it can't do, and who owns it.

After the introductions, we ask attendees to self-organize around six tables placed about the room. In most cases, everyone knows someone else at their table. At each table, a six-foot-by-two-and-a-half-foot map covers most of the table and displays the streets just outside the window, going about two blocks in either direction. In addition to the maps, there are four five-inch by seven-inch photographs on stands, each depicting a street-level view. Then there is a white cardboard box about the size of a shoebox, labeled "Smart Cities Toolkit." Inside there is an instruction packet, about six individual scenario packets, and five sets of cards: Scenario cards, Weather cards, Temperature cards, Stakeholder cards, and Stump cards. There are also about a dozen plastic baggies, each with different physical icons made of translucent acrylic, each with a sticker depicting the icon on the outside of the baggie. Icons of things found in a cityscape are black (Ambulance, Car, Bus, Person, Bike) while the sensor icons are orange (Air, Sound, Temperature). Unpacking it all and laying it out, it looks like a board game is about to begin, and that was the intention (see figure 2.1).

Figure 2.1
Room setup prior to the start of the workshop.

Eliciting Concepts

Kits such as these are well known in design and draw from practices of participatory planning and participatory technology design (Brandt, Binder, and Sanders 2012; Kensing and Greenbaum 2012; Sanders and Stappers 2012; Sanoff 2000). Within planning, the notion of the design charette is a familiar activity where stakeholders come together to discuss and debate planning potentials through making representations. Maps are common to the charette because they serve as one of the most basic forms for expressing planning. Often what is being examined are issues such as zoning, placement of bicycle lanes, and traffic flow. Within technology design, the use of cards as framing and elicitation devices is also familiar. What we find in the smart city is a mixture of planning, technology production, and service design. In a broad sense, public goods and services are manifested and experienced through objects more common to media than to architecture. Design kits foster hybrid forms of engagement for participation—what Eva Brandt, Pelle Ehn, and other designers have long called "design games" (Brandt 2006; Ehn 1988, 2008). Drawing from Wittgenstein's (1953) "language games," design games are a way for participants to, at the same time, make and make sense of emergent contexts of the artificial that may manifest through play.

After the kits are unpacked, Cookie provides a brief overview of this design game. Each person at the table first draws a Scenario card. The Scenario cards represent moments, such as New Year's Eve or the Thanksgiving half-marathon. Some Scenario cards request that you also pick a Time card and a Weather card. From these cards, a concrete situation emerges, such as "New Year's Eve, 9:00 p.m., 55F, Raining." Each person is then asked to describe the scene from their perspective and to make note of the setting in their workbook, writing a short description of what is happening (see figure 2.2).

Participants then use the acrylic icons to build their scene on the map. Along the way, they add specifics, such as whether there is traffic or how many people are out and about. Each participant builds their own scene, and over time a confluence of scenes emerges on the map. Once the liveliness of the activity becomes apparent, and everyone has chuckled at various scenario combinations ("New Year's Eve at 3:00 a.m." or "Ice Storm in April"), there seems to be a contagious willingness to play along. Without a doubt, the scenes confound one another. But it is in this mingling and confusion that conversation develops, and through that conversation,

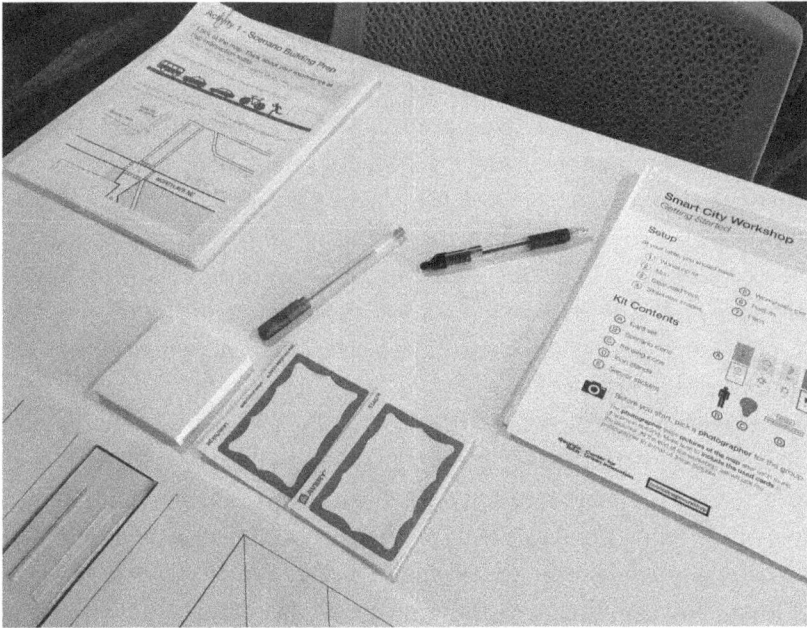

Figure 2.2
Some of the components of the toolkit.

perspectives and concepts that reflect diverse subjectivities are fostered and shared.

Once the first round of scenario development is done, participants are asked to draw one or more Stakeholder cards. The Stakeholder cards represent roles for people who use the city: commuters, runners, the visually impaired, the homeless, those in wheelchairs, bus drivers, street vendors, and so on. Participants are then asked to describe the scene from the perspectives of the stakeholders. They begin discussing variations, such as "Monday, 6:00 p.m., Commuter" or "New Year's Eve, 55F, Raining, Unlicensed Street Vendor." The Stump cards are optional, but many choose them to add even more variety. One Stump card reads, "Imagine all the cars in the scenario are self-driving." Others read, "There is a citywide power outage" or "A light pole has fallen across the intersection."

In designing this game, we sought to keep an openness to the play, to provide the space for the creativity and distinctiveness of those participating. For instance, the scenario prompts were concrete without overly scripting outcomes. We included only a few specifics of identities because we hoped that participants would project those qualities into the scenario as a way of expressing themselves and making themselves present in the moment. We wanted to keep the activity open so participants could customize the scenario to be more compelling for them. As a simple example, they could choose to attend (or not) to weather or time. Of course, there were no real rules, so people could sift through the cards, comparing and composing possible scenarios, often in collaboration with those seated around them. Design decisions such as these were intended to create a structure for imagination that supported participants, but without requiring a singular, prescribed mode of participation or outcome.

An hour into the evening, the room is loud with lively chatter and laughter as various scenarios are discussed over a mess of cards and icons scattered on the maps (see figures 2.3 and 2.4). From these constructed scenes, we move to envisioning the potentials of sensors and data. But thinking of smart cities is not a common thing to do. To scaffold this leap of imagination we borrowed the structure of Mad Libs: a children's game where a framework for a story is given and you fill in the blanks with nouns and verbs and adjectives and adverbs to construct the story, often to hilarious result. Our goal was not hilarity but to provide just enough structure to support envisioning smart-city services. Participants are asked, "What information is in this space: noise, light, dust, heat, moisture, etc.?" and "What do you sense around you, things you see, hear, smell, touch, etc.?" as ways to prompt them to think of the space of the scenario as a place rich with cues. From these questions, they are walked through a series of further prompts like "What do you want to know?" "What does your stakeholder want to know?" and "Why do you and your stakeholder want to know this?" Finally, they are given a set of stickers representing sensors such as "Air Quality" and "Sound" and "Temperature" as well as a blank sensor, and asked to consider how these technologies might contribute to their and their stakeholder's experiences in the space.

Bits and Pieces

Using their cards, participants quickly craft fragments of scenarios by filling in the template that led from a collection of circumstances and desires to a description of a smart-city service. Some in attendance simply talk during the entire workshop, never putting pen to paper with their ideas; a few

Figure 2.3
Design game in session, constructing a scene.

Figure 2.4
Design game detail.

make sketches, and this is fine. There was no demand to participate in one way or another. All of these modes of participation, whether they fit our structure or not, contribute to making an environment for imagination. As the story fragments start to take form, we pause to share and talk through the scenes. Each group presents their bits of narrative. For example, one group's emergent narrative is about a certain sound that might indicate dangerous driving conditions on the hill outside of the building we were in: "Right outside, up North Avenue, that hill is undriveable when it ices over, and there's that sound of tires when Atlanta drivers think they can 'gun it' up the hill. We thought maybe we would listen for that sound and use it as an alert of sorts." Another group gravitated to events in the park nearby: "There's all these festivals here now that the park is done and the Beltline and all that, but not everyone wants that, so we were thinking of ways you might be able to know not just where things are happening, which is what all this stuff tells us, but also know where things aren't happening, because maybe that's really what you want to know."

While discussing their emergent stories, people chime in with comparisons, suggestions, questions, and the occasional challenge. For instance, one group is interested in how smart-city technologies might respond to traffic, both automobile and pedestrian. They pose a hypothetical question:

"What if traffic lights changed as walkers, cyclists, and runners approached the intersection, so they could keep the flow, making it more about the people, not the cars?" Still others are skeptical of the economics of the situation, asking, "Who owns this data about where we're going and when?" and "If we're making data by doing things in the city, and the city is making money from it, shouldn't we make money from it too?" Some professionals see planning the smart city as separate from their domain, saying, "I don't know if this is really a thing for planning or design. I mean, it's not like we are talking about bike lanes or bus benches, this is all different stuff, not the stuff we're responsible for."

At this point in the evening we've been together for almost two hours. It's time to wrap up. Each group returns their attention to their maps and story sheets to add any bits and pieces they want to add before the evening's end. As they do so, we share our plans for more workshops, and our plans to draft these worksheets into scenarios. We thank folks for coming and the Atlanta City Studio for hosting, and then the room begins to empty. Some of us start to clean up the space, stacking the chairs and rearranging the tables. Others photograph the maps and all the materials as best and as quickly as we can; the maps are jumbles of cards, icons, and post-it notes with scrawls of addendums and ideas that escaped the worksheets (see figure 2.5). The messiness of joining the social and technical together through stories is evident across the materials from the workshop.

Residential Narratives

PARSE was intended to differently envision smart-city technologies by encouraging residents to craft stories from their perspectives. The workshop at Ponce City Market was useful for gathering together people with varied experiences of the neighborhood, attachments, and commitments. Yet, only a few attendees lived in the neighborhood. What was missing was the perspective of those who called a neighborhood home: residents who could imagine the ongoing lived experience of a place and its communities from the perspective of actually living there. And so we held another workshop in another neighborhood. It took place at Good Kupa Koffie, a coffee shop on the border of the English Avenue and Vine City neighborhoods in Atlanta. There are similarities and differences between the settings of Good Kupa Koffie and the Atlanta City Studio at Ponce City Market. Both are in historically Black neighborhoods in Atlanta. Whereas the Old Fourth Ward was rapidly

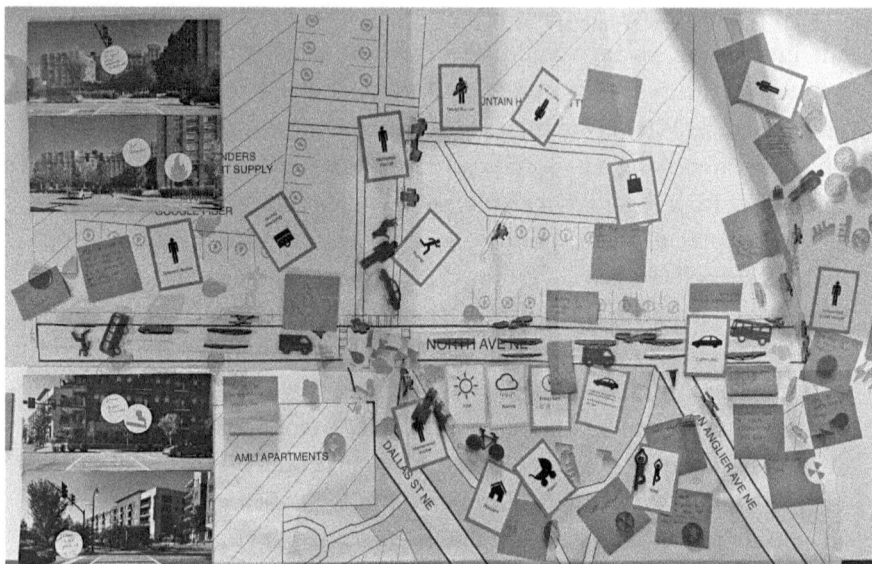

Figure 2.5
Fragments of stories at the end of the evening.

gentrifying at the time of the first workshop, English Avenue and Vine City had yet to face those pressures, though there were signs of impending gentrification and residents were concerned. This concern was well founded, as today the neighborhoods of English Avenue and Vine City are now undergoing gentrification and displacement.

Good Kupa Koffie is in an urban strip mall—a common place for businesses in Atlanta. Like the Atlanta City Studio, Good Kupa Koffie was a civic gathering place of sorts—a place where residents came together to talk about things going on in the neighborhood. But it was not a formal community center, it was a commercial space. To distribute invitations to this workshop we used some of the same channels we used for the first workshop. We also relied upon community partners, residents that we had been working with on other projects in these neighborhoods over the past several years. They were activists in the community who trusted us, at least as much as any activist should trust an academic. Through their standing in the community they could entice others to participate. Still, encouraging participation was tenuous; this workshop was almost a workshop that wasn't.

The workshop was planned to begin at 6:00 p.m., and we had received confirmations from about twenty residents that they would be participating. Yet by 5:50, no one had arrived other than us. At 5:55, one guest arrives: Ms. P., one of the partners on many of our projects, a resident of the neighborhood and a community organizer. She says not to worry and steps outside to get better reception on her phone. She types out text messages to residents she knows, neighbors, and folks she works with. A few minutes later, she comes back inside. By 6:25, the coffee shop is filled with residents—younger and older, families, single people, a local real-estate developer, a bus driver, a few community organizers—mostly attending at the encouragement of Ms. P.

This workshop follows the same structure and flow as the event at Atlanta City Studio. We begin with Cookie providing an overview to the workshop activities, and we use the same kits, although the maps reflect the specificity of this location. These maps extend out from a major intersection a block away from the coffee shop, an intersection that was to be the end point of the sensor deployment. Good Kupa Koffie and this neighborhood are just outside of Atlanta's smart corridor—itself a telling fact. Just as before, the participants build out scenes on the maps with the icons, working through the prompts and sharing stories among themselves. They compare experiences and wonder whether or not these sensors and drones and all this data might be good for them, and if so, how. One marked difference is that most of the participants at this workshop can locate their homes on the map. They live in this neighborhood and walk these streets daily. There's also a greater diversity of socioeconomic backgrounds. Most of the adults work, but some are working class while others are middle class. There are also several adults who are retired. As residents, their knowledge of the neighborhood is informed by lived experiences: everyday encounters and perspectives developed over time as neighbors in these communities.

Different from the rapidly gentrifying location of the first workshop, this neighborhood has not yet seen an influx of spending from the city and investors. One result of this is worn infrastructure, common in most neighborhoods of the city, actually. One participant notes discrepancies in sidewalk and road conditions block to block, saying, "The problem is that you don't know things two streets over. Maybe the sidewalk here is fine and I'm out walking, but after a rain, a few blocks away the street drain is broken again, it's all flooded and you can't walk through it. I'd want to know about that." Others reflected on existing patterns of surveillance, wondering what civic value these so-called smart technologies might actually bring: "There's already cameras on every other corner. But only a few of them are turned on. And it seems like no one's looking at them anyway, so why put more cameras up?" Another member of their group chimes in, saying, "True. And we don't need to listen to find out where things are going off—we know, and the police know too." They shared a wariness of the hazards of already-existing urban technologies.

Just as before, over the course of the evening the conversations are animated. We've also ordered food for this event from a local who runs a catering business out of her home, and people take breaks from talking about sensors and data to refill their plates. Since many of these attendees know each other, there are inside jokes woven into the conversations, personal stories being referenced in the telling of these emergent stories. Just as before, at the end of the evening we have a jumbled abundance of ideas and fragments of stories. And so, about 8:00 p.m., we find ourselves once again taking pictures of maps and story sheets, rearranging tables and chairs, and thanking attendees for spending their evening with us.

What these workshops achieved was modest but nonetheless meaningful. Over the span of a couple evenings, people came together to learn, create, reflect, and share their thoughts on what a smart Atlanta might be. That endeavor was facilitated and shaped by design activities that assembled scribbles and notes into the barest of outlines. What was important was that these ideas were not the same as those made up by corporations looking to sell their infrastructures and services. Nor did they simply reproduce stories espoused by government officials and staff looking to advance the interests of city hall. They were not vague expressions of just any city. These were stories driven by people who worked and lived in these neighborhoods, in this city. They were influenced by city hall and corporate visions, of course, but they were not bound to them.

From Design Games to Design Fictions

From these workshops emerged dozens of compelling and inspiring concepts of what a smart Atlanta might be, expressed in the fragments of stories that the workshop attendees generated and shared. These bits and pieces were to be the basis for ideas that would be interpreted and constituted together as scenarios, which would contribute to the imagination and articulation of pluralistic subjectivities, different from the standard stories about the smart city and its residents.

Care was taken in this process, and it is important to express care in interpretation when we explain what these stories were and were not. As Nasim Parvin (2018) so compellingly describes, practices of storytelling common to design, even those oriented toward just outcomes, have ethical concerns and can do violence. To be clear, this was not a community storytelling project where residents shared their personal narratives. This was a project in which the participants of the workshops generated ideas toward smart-city services, which we wove together into scenarios. Our intention was not to "give voice" to others, although amplifying voices can be a way to empower residents. Our intention was not to speak "on behalf of" others. We did not claim that we were conveying a raw, distilled reality. These stories were fiction, informed by the perspective of those who participated in the workshops. In this sense, they were neither biographical nor ethnographic. This distinction is crucial. Asserting these stories as fictions acknowledges and accepts our own roles, subjectivities, and accountabilities in this endeavor (Parvin 2018, 526). Our role was to combine, edit, and extend the bits and pieces of concepts expressed in the workshops into scenarios. Our subjectivities were those of designers, of researchers from a technical institute, perceived and treated as experts by colleagues in city government, industry, and civil society. Our accountabilities were to those who participated and to those who might have to bear the futures described in these scenarios.

After the workshops, we gathered fragments from worksheets, fieldnotes, and maps to discuss and share. In some cases, we combined multiple fragments. In other cases, a single phrase sparked a narrative that was then developed, drawing in and refracting questions, comments, and conversations from the workshops. The writing process was more difficult than other attempts at writing scenarios because there was a commitment to be respectful to what had been expressed, while also working toward stories that would open spaces for exploring different practices and desires. Cookie took the lead throughout this process, sifting through the fragments and assembling them into narratives. She would share them weekly, sometimes twice a week, and we would meet to discuss them. We constructed them attentive to the possibilities, consequences, and implications that would spill forth from each scenario as it was drafted. The process was iterative, going through drafts of scenarios, drawing out themes, and developing a complexity that would eschew quick-fix perspectives—seeking to multiply and reconfigure the narrative joints of the stories we tell about smart cities. Our intent was to construct scenarios that would describe situations, potentials, and implications that were appropriately intricate.

Fictions of a Smart Atlanta

What emerged at the end of the process was *Fictions of a Smart Atlanta*, a collection of thirteen scenarios developed from the concepts in the workshops. These are neither exhaustive nor conclusive. Some concepts from the design games were not developed, while others were overdetermined. Put another way, these fictions were not mere translations. They were crafted from the wants, needs, interests, and curiosities expressed in the workshops, blended together with the real and imagined infrastructures, data, devices, and services of smart cities. We reworked them to appeal to and affect a set of audiences. That is to say, the stories in *Fictions of a Smart Atlanta* were objects of design. As an example, what follows is a summary of one of the fictions:

> Game day brings tens of thousands of people into downtown Atlanta, and with them, the need to park tens of thousands of cars. Leveraging new smart parking systems, the EventPark app directs drivers to open spaces in municipal and private garages and lots. But sometimes those garages and lots fill, and sometimes people want a bargain, and so they venture into the neighborhoods next to the stadium looking for parking. In these neighborhoods it's common for residents to sell people parking in their front lawns or driveways. Rich, a resident of one of these neighborhoods, created the ParkingLawn service—a service similar to what the municipal and private lots use, but for residents of the neighborhoods surrounding the stadium. Using the ParkingLawn service, residents in these neighborhoods can list their lawns or driveways as available for parking. Rather than each neighbor having to go out Northside Drive with a sign to advertise their lawn or driveway, residents combine the listings in a single directory. A suggested rate is provided as a default, but by accessing the real-time data from the city service, residents can also choose to set dynamic pricing. As there are fewer and fewer spaces available downtown, the cost of their lawns and driveways increases proportionately. Rich explains, "Say the Dome lots are packed, and the other ones around the stadium are filling up. Well, Ms. Bernice's house is way closer to the stadium than those other lots. People are going to pay more for that convenience."

When I share this story with residents, it elicits a chuckle. When the story is shared with folks in city government, they often laugh too, but uncomfortably. The concept of surge pricing is a familiar feature in car services and parking. The very parking lots that are charging $40 for Sunday game day parking are often only charging $10 for parking on a Wednesday afternoon. Industry vendors as well as start-ups for adaptive parking systems already have submitted proposals for systems that would function in similar ways. The difference in Rich's story is that the protagonist isn't quite working within the system. What Rich is proposing in this scenario imagines smart-city services as an informal economy, to be used in service of what has historically been a gray-market enterprise: selling access to park on lawns and in empty lots. This concept is not radical. Frankly, it may not even be desirable, even for Rich and his neighbors. What is of interest, however, is not the novelty or desirability of this concept. What is of interest is how this scenario expresses a story of the appropriation of smart-city technologies by residents in support of their current practices. This appropriation carries a meaningful difference from the usual stories of innovation that resonate through city hall.

In writing these scenarios, we worked to tell stories of the smart city from multiple perspectives and express multiple imagined subjectivities. Rather than telling only the familiar stories of success, we also crafted scenarios that told of the shortcomings and failings of the smart city. The fiction that follows "Game Day Parking" is called "Sensor Maintenance" and begins with the callout "Atlanta has a sensor problem." This scenario tells of sensor errors and breakdowns, things that occur with any public infrastructure and most certainly will occur with public technologies in a smart city. In the workshops, participants raised concerns about what new infrastructures would be put in place, but even more so, *who* would tend to those infrastructures. A sentiment expressed more than once by residents was that if the city was unable to maintain its current infrastructure, how would it maintain the infrastructure needed for smart services? If the sidewalks and sewers are broken, how long until the "smart" is broken too? Will neighborhoods already suffering from poor infrastructure now also suffer from poor smart services? For instance, whereas the location of the first workshop was set within a stretch of North Avenue that received massive infrastructural upgrades, the location of the second workshop quite visibly had not.

The fiction "Sensor Maintenance" addresses these issues. In this scenario, residents become engaged in tending to the smart infrastructure. They are enrolled into the processes of maintenance and compensated for reporting on the conditions of the sensors in the streets and surrounding areas. These scenarios emerged from combining questions from the workshop about who would be responsible for these technologies and services with themes of maintenance and repair in contemporary research and practice. Steve Jackson (2014, 221) refers to this as a sort of "broken world thinking," in which we recognize the inevitable breakdown of technology and develop "an appreciation of the real limits and fragility of the worlds we inhabit." This focus on repair, and also maintenance, shifts our attention away from innovation as we commonly think of it and demands that we recognize a wider range of labor necessary to make technology work—or continue to work, as the case might be (Russell and Vinsel 2018). This scenario is also not alone in its attentiveness to maintenance. The next fiction, titled "Data Stewards," includes the perspectives of both municipal employees and residents, who express a desire for collective agency with data in the smart city. In "Data Stewards," residents again become city employees, paid for collecting data on behalf of the neighborhood. But this scenario is not presented as a naïve embrace of civic duty. The fiction ends with a reflection by a resident character: "Really, we just need jobs."

There are also stories of using smart services to streamline time spent at summer festivals and negotiate the frustrations of commuting—narratives that are familiar in the prevailing discourses of smart cities. The repeating of such familiar smart-cities tropes speaks to how deeply this rhetoric has pervaded community discourse, such that they become expectations. Even with these other fictions, however, residents attempted to open spaces of possibility. So, in assembling the collection, we sought to balance narratives that would serve as provocations, those that would garner a quizzical response, and those that would be read with ease. Some stories went with the grain of established smart-cities discourses, while others went against it, as unexpected narrative joints.

Once the stories were completed, Cookie compiled them into a booklet to be distributed electronically and read onscreen or printed on a standard office printer. Her design is strong but unassuming, with clear typography and composition. For each fiction there is a set of Key Ideas and Key Assumptions. The Key Assumptions map to concerns in engineering, design, and policy. Each story is one to two pages long. Altogether, *Fictions of a Smart Atlanta* is an accessible collection of stories for an audience of people who use such stories in their own work of constructing visions of what a smart Atlanta might be. These stories were shared with people in local municipal government and industry. While the readership for *Fictions of a Smart Atlanta* is limited, they did circulate. As we met with municipal council members or staff in the various offices working to implement a smart Atlanta, we told the stories and spoke of the collection.

Discursive Experiments

The work of *PARSE* is twofold. First, there is the work of developing a tool for eliciting concepts about how an unfamiliar suite of technologies might be made useful, usable, and desirable . . . or not. Second, there is the work of developing ideas and insights from the uses of that tool into a representational artifact (scenarios) that can be shared. Both kinds of work are familiar to design. There are histories and traditions of participation in design that use a slew of techniques, including design games. The use of scenarios is common in engineering, planning, and even policy. As design experiments, the making and telling of stories are both sites and modes of democratic inquiry: events through which we collectively explore how our civic worlds might be different. But as Parvin (2018, 524) calls our attention to, stories are "not ready-made commodities of exchange. They are contingent social processes and emergent accounts that depend on the nature and quality of the encounters that bring them to life." In these encounters, inquiry is not "downstream" in a prototype or technical implementation. Inquiry unfolds through the play of the design game and the articulation of story fragments, which are those "contingent social processes and emergent accounts."

The design game is a way of experimenting through play (Gordon and Mugar 2020). Yes, it is fun (maybe), but it is also play in the sense of enabling performance. Within the design game, one is invited to entertain and compose a future of one's own interests and desires, as common, hopeful, desperate, or frivolous as those interests and desires might be. For one or two hours, participants share their current routines and envision new ones. Through the prompts of the game they establish and explore new positions within the city. From these positions unfold orientations and perspectives, which give way to observations, interpretations, and imagined capacities. Through the scenarios and stakeholders, participants project a set of possibilities for what a smart city might be. What's more, this is not just any smart city; it is *their* smart city, Atlanta. Even more accurately, it is a specific neighborhood in Atlanta, a set of blocks with parks, businesses, churches, and residents. Through the situated event, otherwise generic discourses of the smart city are made particular. The design game then became a way to purposefully cultivate divergent, contrasting, and contrary subjectivities.

Through the design game, participants create and investigate subjectivities—constructing ways of being in a smart Atlanta. This construction is inventive because some of these ways of being have yet to be conceived. These subjectivities are collective and intersectional; as participants work to envision and explain how these scenarios and their characters fit together, their matters of concern and care overlap, and their routines and wants converge. At the tables, around the maps, with the cards and acrylic icons and worksheets, common worlds are imagined and inhabited. These worlds draw from and privilege the individual and collective lived experiences of participants. These worlds bring to the fore ways that residents and communities are already creative and resourceful, putting their experience as foundational to democratic conditions. Admittedly, these worlds are constrained, and the time for imagination is brief. But even such brief moments provide the opportunity for collective inquiry and imagination (Steen 2013): a happening that is "provisional, probative, creative, and jointly constructed" (Ansell 2013, 165), in which people gather together to trial assemblies of what a smart city might be and to what effects.

Productive Frictions

Returning to Wilkie and Michael's (2009, 516–517) discussion of enacting future users through narrative joints, what commonly occurs is that "the imagined user serves as a joint between the social and the technological that allows the connections to be reconfigured and permits movement from existing to future use." Reconfiguration happens by way of "imaginative tinkering of emergent connections between specific social and technological entities and relations to provide a novel account of use" (516). The purpose of the design game was to enable and support precisely this imaginative tinkering. But rather than articulating narrative joints to create stories that fit or amplify the prevailing visions of cities and technologies, our intent was to elicit stories that produce friction (Korn and Voida 2015; Tsing 2011). The narrative joint that Wilkie and Michael refer to as basic to the scenario as a genre is still present. There is still an articulation between the technical and the social. But the movement of that joint is not singular nor necessarily smooth—it's multifaceted and allows for twists and turns, sometimes getting tangled.

The site of that friction is important. The friction is not technological, or at least it is not reducible to the technological. The friction is not utilitarian; it is not that a given technology does not work. Nor, for that matter, is the friction reducible to a sequestered notion of the social, existing in isolation and deficient, and thereby potentially "fixable" by the technological. The friction appears precisely when and where the social and technological are joined in the narrative. When the technological is introduced to fix the social, it breaks the social. Perhaps the break occurs at the site of articulation or elsewhere, but that elsewhere is not written out of the narrative. That elsewhere becomes significant within the story, a purposefully awkward moment. The role of design in these moments is not to relax the awkwardness, and not to fix things. That would be the expected narrative joint: some product of design would resolve the situation. Instead, in the absence of a fix, the concept at play can foment. The story is staged and told, but there is no heroic or innovative moment that announces a set of props to resolve the situation. That space of resolution is left intentionally empty for others to attempt to occupy.

Rich and the ParkingLawn service scenario prompts uncomfortable laughter among municipal employees because it flouts and dodges regulations and procedures. At the same time, it is also obvious, technically feasible, and compelling. Following the nervous laughter, it is in the discussions considering how it might be made—or as the case might be, why not—that politics and the political unfurl. These stories and their consideration become agonistic spaces—circumscribed moments in which divergent, contrasting, and contrary subjectivities are expressed. For Mouffe (2013, 105), the activity of creating these agonistic spaces, of "constructing new practices and new subjectivities" is a role that artists—and I would extend to designers and other makers—can take up. The questioning of conventions and presumed conditions *together with* the consideration of how those conditions might be otherwise is necessary for the ongoing renewal of democratic conditions. What the activities and outcomes of design offer are experiential and material means for questioning and considering democratic conditions as they are and as they might be.

After the ParkingLawn service scenario was shared, colleagues from the Office of Information Management wondered aloud how to make the APIs support such a use of data. Their colleagues from the same office, who are involved in writing data-sharing agreements, were quick to point out that such a use of the data would be a violation of terms and services. Staff in the mayor's office realized that either way, if this idea became real, it could be a public relations issue. Colleagues from philanthropic foundations trying to support social innovation who heard the scenario argued for precisely such uses of data by residents. The ensuing discussions bring to the fore issues of race and class. Why is it that some forms of civic innovation are lauded and others not? Everyone in the city knows that the neighborhoods that abut the stadium are historically Black, working-class neighborhoods. These discussions confront racist and classist assumptions concerning who is considered to be an innovator or entrepreneur in the smart city and who is not.

Design Experiments as Discursive Design

The term "discursive design" is a broad label for work that prompts reflection, in which an object fosters consideration, discussion, questioning, and perhaps dissensus (Tharp and Tharp 2019). The term is useful because it encapsulates a range of methods and styles and focuses on the purpose of the work: to facilitate and contribute to dialogue by means of provocation. This provocation could be direct and confrontational, or it might be subtle, quizzical, and even playful. The term eludes any single strategy for prompting reflection, and thereby sidesteps the various debates about those modes and strategies—such as what it means to be critical in and through design, or the limits of speculation. Instead, attention and appreciation in discursive design are directed to how the activities of designing and the objects of design are themselves both forms of discourse and means of participating in discourse. One might consider the *PARSE* project to be a project of discursive design with a distinctive tone and texture. The discursiveness of the project is literal; the project employs speaking, writing, media, and communication as the material, means, and purposes of the work. Even more specifically, we might cast *Fictions of a Smart Atlanta* as a form of design fiction (Bleeker 2009; Sterling 2009).

Within discursive modes of making, the designer develops and expresses a point of view (Dunne 2008; Dunne and Raby 2013; Tharp and Tharp 2019). Often in the practices and products of discursive design, the designer is the sole author, and authorship is claimed as a way for the designer to assert a position of authority. In the processes of *PARSE*, that was not exactly the case because the entanglements of the workshops complicated the idea of authorship. Without a doubt, we were present as designers, shaping the activities through their structure and materials, and giving form to fragments of concepts as stories. In this sense, we were authors, and we take responsibility for these scenarios. The project was driven by our responsibility as designers to convene and distribute stories and subjectivities. And yet, authorship of the *PARSE* scenarios is expressive of points of views that are not ours alone. The very framing of the project was meant as an alternative to singular framings of the smart city that dominate public discussions and municipal planning. Instead, we hope to bring forth narratives that are multiple and entwined. To achieve this goal requires a different approach to authorship, one in which the designer both acknowledges their presence, directions, and authority and at the same time works to cede power by inviting others into the endeavors of imagination and making.

The work of *PARSE* is also distinctive as discursive design because it is so local and mundane. Much of discursive design uses striking images that prompt defamiliarization and reflection by way of spectacle. Spectacle certainly has its place in design and in social and political discourse, but so too does the ordinary. One way to appreciate both the design game and the narratives of the *PARSE* project is to interpret them as attempts to stitch the unknown aspects of emerging technologies with the ordinary and often overlooked activities of the city. Pelle Ehn (1988) refers to this need as holding dual orientations or commitments to tradition and transcendence. In such an endeavor of imagination, we acknowledge and respect existing routines, beliefs, and desires in processes of change. As we work together to explore futures, the conditions of the in-the-now must be accounted for. Rather than imagining futures (or for that matter, alternate presents) where there are no side hustles or gray markets, no breakdown or need for repair, and all data is collected and maintained effortlessly, we should be accountable to and appreciative of the social and political complexity of the present. Rather than the exceptional, what the design game elicits and the stories express are the everyday as it intersects with imaginaries of the smart city. The very ordinariness of the stories and their form of sharing is a tactic to engender engagement.

Constructing Subjectivities

In their 2019 article "Actually Existing Smart Citizens," Taylor Shelton and Thomas Lodato (a former student and himself an attendee of one of the *PARSE* workshops) analyze participation and nonparticipation in smart-city planning in Atlanta. In that article, Shelton and Lodato examine another set of workshops hosted by the city of Atlanta and the Georgia Institute of Technology, which occurred about the same time as *PARSE*. They frame their analysis in relation to notions of the so-called smart citizen, which was imagined to be a counterpoint to the top-down government-centric discourses of the smart city. It is not so much that Shelton and Lodato are against the concept of the smart citizen. Rather, they find the smart citizen elusive, noting that, "the 'actually existing' smart citizen might not *actually* exist at all" (48). They suggest two alternatives drawn from their ethnographic work: the general citizen and the absent citizen. The description of the mother and son that opens this chapter is emblematic of the general citizen—a generic figure mobilized to express the needs that the smart city will supposedly fulfill. The absent citizen marks the lack of true inclusion of citizens in the substantive planning initiatives undertaken in Atlanta, and more broadly, in smart-city planning globally. The people invoked, and more significantly those people to be affected, by smart-city discourse are simply not present. Shelton and Lodato's critical analysis is astute, and all the more important because it sets the complicated conditions for work bringing civics together with design practice. *PARSE*, and other cooperative smart-city projects, sit in relation to the realities of such conditions, to the limitations of participation and hegemonies of smart-cities discourse and practice. Our intention with *PARSE* was to counter what Shelton and Lodato refer to as the general citizen and the absent citizen, as well as to offer an alternative to the corporatized stories and imaginaries that Sadowski and Bendor (2019) call to our attention. Yet, we must admit that the design games and emergent stories and subjectivities were enmeshed with these very discourses and settings. This raises concerns regarding the capacities and limits of design experiments in civics.

It is fair to ask whether these stories write residents, municipal employees, professional planners, and community leaders into subjectivities in which the agencies to resist and refuse are lacking. By casting and then projecting participants as actors in the smart city, making use of corporate systems and infrastructures and taking on the role of the entrepreneur or repair technician, are we not crafting an idealized neoliberal subject through design? These concepts of the parking services informed by gray markets, of sensor maintenance and data stewardship that enroll residents, are akin to Irani's formulation of entrepreneurial citizenship and threaten the same capitalization of peoples and weakening of politics that Irani (2019) warns of.

Let's again examine the abbreviated story of Rich and his game day parking concept. A critical perspective might claim that all we have done is enroll Rich and his neighbors into the all-encompassing fold of the smart city. Perhaps worse, design could be seen as providing a means for Rich to enroll himself without opportunity for reflection or resistance. Rich previously had his parking hustle, relatively unencumbered from the economic and policy machinery of government. In the smart city, he would be enmeshed in a set of services, applications, data, and legal regulations.

Of course, there were regulations before. But these digital services produce different streams and connections; they are more traceable and have dependencies that did not exist before. If those services, applications, and data fail due to some error in the system, does Rich and his neighbors' hustle also fail? Or imagine that Rich subscribes to or builds a service that taps into a smart parking data feed, which requires a digital token of some sort. Without knowing it, Rich may have just revealed his hustle to authorities. There is now a data trail from the smart parking system to Rich's phone. Will the informal hustle now be forced to become a formal business? Is that really to Rich and his neighbors' benefit? Will he have to pay taxes or insurance? Such implications are real for the lives of Rich and other Atlanta residents.

A critical perspective would also level similar critiques at the other two fictions shared. In both "Sensor Maintenance" and "Data Stewards," residents are enrolled into maintaining city services. They become contract employees that the city outsources work to. While one way to interpret this is as manifesting notions of repair and maintenance into our civic imaginaries, at the same time the concept of outsourcing such work to citizens fits the most prominent and pernicious themes and patterns of confounding civics and capitalism. Services once the responsibility of the government are dispersed and assigned to citizens. These scenarios could be read as emblematic of the accusation that design is simply a means of enabling neoliberal caring.

Such critiques are fair. Undeniably, the processes of participation we used to generate these scenarios, and the scenarios themselves, were entangled with neoliberal governmentality. Rather than trying to argue these conditions away, I maintain these are the actually existing circumstances of design experiments in civics. Rather than trying to write them out of the stories, I maintain that acknowledging these conditions *and imagining within them* is a necessary part of the work of democratic inquiry. If we want to understand and probe the possible roles and relations among and between residents, city government, and technical systems we must acknowledge how those structures and agencies are currently manifested. To craft a narrative in which some product, service, or policy suddenly and seamlessly undoes dominant modes of power would be just as reductive as the more familiar scenarios of design. The civic imaginary proffered would be just as stilted. What's needed is a situated imagination—an imagination informed and influenced by, but not restrained to, contemporary conditions.

In her discussion of the role and importance of imagination in democracy, philosopher Charlene Haddock Seigfried (1999, 208) states, "Imagination is the capacity to creatively explore inherited structures from past experience, in light of the future as a horizon of possible actions, and so, of possible meanings." In the work of the design games and the subsequent writing of the scenarios, the inherited structures of the contemporary city and its forms of governmentality remain present. They comprise the problematic conditions within which we, collectively, work. They are the situations from and with which we envision how a smart Atlanta might be different. In other words, these structures and experiences are intentionally part of the multiplicity of narrative joints that are configured together and from which pluralistic subjectivities emerge. So, we imagine the gray-market entrepreneur and the resident on the payroll of the city. We might foresee our neighbor as a data steward, tending to civic information in order to make ends meet. Are these the civics we want on the horizon? Are these possible actions we want to enable, meanings we want to pursue? Perhaps, or perhaps not— and that is part of the point. These scenarios offer pluralistic subjectivities for our consideration as possibilities, subjectivities that are expressive of the perspectives of those who would actually inhabit these worlds. In this sense, through activities like design games and storytelling, these experiments in civics put into effect and elaborate our capacities for imagination. The point of this work is not to hasten a bias to action that is endemic to design nor to evade political awareness (Irani 2019, 111, 158), but rather the opposite: to provide a prompt to pause and center the political qualities of these technologies and their possible uses.

Returning to Haraway and Rosner, it matters what stories we tell (Haraway 2016; Rosner 2018). It also matters where those stories came from, from whom, and under what conditions. Making and telling stories can be ways of contributing to the imagination and articulation of pluralistic civic subjectivities. Activities of designing can offer creative means of eliciting and expressing those stories. Such work becomes part of a practice of design experiments in civics not because it brings about new products or services, but because it constructs opportunities through which we collectively envision and reflect upon diverse civics, upon what our associations with one another might be. And it attempts to do so in ways that are just (Costanza-Chock 2020), through engagements with those who live, work, and play in these neighborhoods, privileging their experiences and practices. Without a doubt, this is difficult. It is an endeavor of telling stories that dwell in the complications of contemporary civics, as residents, government, and industry mingle together, sometimes in uncomfortable ways. A challenge for designers in these conditions is to resist the urge to offer the quick or clever fix. Stories are not equations; they are not meant to be solved.

Design Appendix

PARSE Project

Design Concept: Cookie Nguyen and Carl DiSalvo

Design Lead: Cookie Nguyen

Design of workshop activities, visual design and production of workshop materials, analysis and interpretation of content produced through workshops, development of stories from workshop materials, design and production of *Fictions of a Smart Atlanta*.

Workshop Assistants: Caroline Foster, Karl Kim, Amanda Meng, Sandjar Kozubaev, Firaz Peer

Workshop Hosts: Atlanta City Studio, Good Kupa Koffie

3 Devices

On a warm Saturday afternoon in early September, a group of people begin arriving in Candler Park to forage persimmons. Off to the side of the playground stands a grove of trees that will be the site of our first pick of the day. Some of us have driven, while others have biked. A few walked over from their homes in the neighborhood that surrounds the park. Katherine— the executive director of Concrete Jungle and our lead for this pick—arrives in her truck and waves us over. We grab a few large, well-worn blue bags made of woven plastic, two ladders, and two fruit pickers from the back of her truck. As we gather under the trees, seeking a break from the heat, we introduce ourselves. Altogether, there's about ten of us here to pick fruit. Katherine describes how to pick persimmons. She reminds us to be careful not to rip them from the branches, since the fruit or the tree could be damaged. Then we set about picking.

Two people immediately begin scaling up a tree, giggling as they climb, racing to reach the highest fruit. Several others set ladders against the trees. While one person ascends each ladder, another stays on the ground, doing their best to steady the ladder as it wobbles precariously. Others gather persimmons immediately in reach from the lower branches. As the tree climbers begin shaking branches up top, those on the ladders dodge falling fruit, while ground-dwellers scurry to grab the persimmons bouncing off the grass. The swarm of smiling people reaching, jumping, and swaying to fill the bags with persimmons looks like a slapstick routine. The climbers are just a slip away from a fall, and laughter rings out across the park. Katherine suggests we sample the persimmons, though they are not quite ripe. Our faces pucker tasting the tart fruit.

The bags quickly begin to bulge, and within an hour this grove has been picked clean of fruit. Katherine tells us where the next set of trees are, and we discuss how to best get there. We carry three surprisingly heavy bags of fruit back to the truck. By the time we arrive at the next set of trees, a few more participants join us. Others bid farewell, deciding it's getting late or they had their fill of excitement. We're all a bit sweaty and stinky now. Unlike the last trees, which were off to the side of a neighborhood park, this grove stands along a roadway at the end of a walking path. The location is iconic Atlanta; just to the east we see a Martin Luther King Jr. statue, while gazing across a street serves a view of the city often used in television and films. Underscoring the view's allure, as we're picking these trees, a tour bus pulls up and parks. Tourists file out and walk over to the bridge, taking selfies and recreating scenes from some television series. As often happens, a few of them stop, curious about what we are doing. "Is that real fruit? Is that safe to eat?" they ask, with a doubtful, almost incredulous tone, followed by, "Is that even allowed?" clearly suspicious of both us and the fruit. We assure them it's real, safe, and allowed, and invite them to join us or sample a persimmon, but none of them do. Soon enough the second pick is done. It's now late in the afternoon. We carry these bags back to the truck bed, now filled with over three hundred pounds of fruit. Before dispersing, some of the volunteers discuss going for a beer, while others share plans for later in the evening.

I've collaborated with members of Concrete Jungle for almost a decade. The organization emerged from a group of friends who enjoyed climbing trees and shaking fruit out of them. They quickly realized there was an abundance of fruit in the city, matched by the persistent need of residents suffering from rampant food insecurity. Rather than consuming the fruit themselves, they collect it and then give it to homeless shelters, women's shelters, and other social service providers. In the early years, they picked and donated fruit as opportunities arose. In 2010, there were a few dozen volunteers, who picked and donated about two thousand pounds of fruit. In 2019, there were more than two hundred volunteers scrambling up trees and pulling up vegetables, and Concrete Jungle donated more than thirty-six thousand pounds of produce. Picks are now scheduled about six months out of the year. During the height of the fruit season in summer and early fall, Concrete Jungle hosts multiple picks a week in different locations. Though it is still primarily a volunteer organization, in 2016 Concrete Jungle registered as a nonprofit, added a paid executive director, and established an active board of directors. Their small organization had grown on the produce of Atlanta's overlooked and forgotten fruit trees.

In this chapter, I discuss a series of projects that explore how technologies might be appropriated to support the work of foraging. Foraging is a canonical practice of commoning: creating, sustaining access to, and using shared resources. As such, I approach foraging as another site of democratic inquiry because foraging offers a way to shape and perform our communal lives. Designing to support the work of foraging is both an experiment in the making and use of tools for foraging and an experiment in commoning. These projects, then, provide another opportunity to explore the many facets of design experiments in civics: as explorations of what to make, of how made things might influence practice, and of how we might organize our communal lives differently.

Within these experiments in civics, the activities and outcomes of designing help us collectively conceive and instantiate diverse civic imaginaries and practices. These things made and used work as devices of inquiry (Lezaun, Marres, and Tironi 2017; Marres and Lezaun 2011), enabling us to engage in rehearsing futures (Halse et al. 2010). Such rehearsals are part and parcel of an experimental method of democratic inquiry, through which we participate in and contribute to the ongoing exploration and reinvention of democratic experiences and conditions. Philosopher Erin McKenna (2001, 89) describes how "imagination helps us envision alternative social orders, which we might want to try out." Devices of inquiry contribute to this envisioning of alternative social orders, in material and experiential form. Such devices are different from prototypes intended to lead designers progressively toward a finished product or service. Rather, these devices of inquiry serve to query possible futures. And they do so through forms and functions that are partial (Suchman 1993, 2002), embracing an incompleteness that is characteristic of the design experiment.

Through our extended and ongoing collaborations with Concrete Jungle, I trace the idea of devices of inquiry through the making and use of material objects to support the work of foraging. These objects guide designers and participants in discovering and appreciating how technologies might support imaginative civic practices. In such design experiments, the object is not the subject of the design experiment. Rather, design experiments elicit and nurture our consideration of the potentials and consequences of refiguring civics practices. While these devices are inherently partial, they nonetheless help us notice and care for existing and possible relationships. They also help us continue the collective work of exploring pluralistic subjectivities through activities of making and use. Such design experiments in civics are part of an ongoing endeavor of democratic inquiry that aims to enlarge our understanding of what is possible and desirable and what is not (Binder et al. 2015). And in the case of the grassroots organization Concrete Jungle, these devices of inquiry also help grow practices of commoning.

Foraging

Foraging involves collecting naturally occurring foodstuffs from sites other than farms and orchards. They might be apples from trees in city parks or figs from a neighbor's tree. They could be serviceberries from bushes on a roadway median or mustard greens from an abandoned lot. In each case, the produce is growing "wild" because the soil, plants, and surroundings are not cultivated to grow food. In this sense, foraging is the antithesis of commercial agriculture. Foraging is an affair that relies upon accident and exploits the abundance of the incidental and unplanned. These foodstuffs grow regardless of human intentions. Foraging reclaims the forgotten and overlooked as sustenance.

People engage in foraging for many reasons. For some, foraging is a cultural heritage. Fruits, fungi, herbs, leaves, and roots may be collected and used for medicinal or ceremonial purposes. For others, foraging is simply what one does at certain times of the year—collecting berries at the height of summer or hunting mushrooms after a rain. The berries might make it into a tart, or perhaps the mushrooms become part of a salad. Still others engage in foraging as a business. The berries foraged and mushrooms hunted might end up at a farmer's market. Flying dragon fruit might be found, collected, and sold to a bartender as an ornate garnish or an ingredient in boutique syrup. In such cases, enterprising locals use foraging to create products. The foraged fruits and fungi become proto-artisanal goods, infused with the nostalgia and the expense that such goods often demand.

There are also laws, regulations, and customs that structure and govern the gathering, consuming, and distribution of wild foodstuffs. In Scandinavia there is a tradition known as *allemansrätten* (Swedish, translated as "everyone's right"), which gives the right to forage on private property. In contrast, in many cities in the United States, fruits, herbs, and other edible plants growing in public spaces are protected by the same regulations that make it unlawful to pick flowers from a city park. Roses and apples are often governed by the same municipal rules and regulations, despite their obvious differences.

The type of foraging discussed in this chapter is distinctive because its purpose is to provide for others. Concrete Jungle forages large amounts of wild-growing foodstuffs to distribute, free of cost, to those in need. The fruits and vegetables they collect go to homeless shelters, women's shelters, and other social service providers. In these situations, foraging takes on the contours of a civic practice. Foraging becomes a way of participating in what philosopher Joan Tronto (2013, xi) characterizes as a caring democracy: a way of collective caregiving. In her description of care as a basis for democracy, Tronto notes that "we have lost sight of the other side of human existence besides the world of the 'economy.'" As a prototypical postcapitalist practice, foraging offers an alternative model of exchange, while also exemplifying an alternative model of democracy.

Concrete Jungle's practices of foraging are mostly set within Atlanta. As urban practices, foraging also provides an opportunity to creatively reframe and remake the dominant discourses and technologies of smart cities. As previously discussed, the notion of an instrumented environment is foundational to stories of smart cities. These stories imply that cities will soon be saturated with data-capturing devices that will deliver actionable information to government and residents. These are some of the very same stories that motivated the design experiments in the previous chapter. As such, similar potentials, complications, and subjectivities weave through these projects. In these collaborations with Concrete Jungle we can reimagine what the services of the smart city might be and whom they might be for, and contemplate how such technologies might be appropriated. At the same time, there is still also a danger of enrolling those engaged in such alternative practices into regimes of technological citizenship, Fordist labor, and hyperrationalization.

The design experiments described in this chapter extend into activities of making and use, which is a distinction from the earlier discussions about scenarios. The activities of making and use provide material and experiential situations for our reflection on the potentials and complications of refiguring practices of foraging. To be sure, designing for foraging is about the construction of stories and subjectivities. But these stories and subjectivities are materialized in the worlds they are working toward—worlds of mutual aid and the redistribution of resources, worlds of commons and commoning.

Commons and Commoning

Most often, we talk about the commons as a set of shared resources. Historically, that shared resource was land that was public, distinct from land that was privately held. Today the commons can still refer to land, but it can also refer to any set of shared resources: bodies of water and the fish that inhabit them, encyclopedias, open-data collections, computer software, and digital platforms. According to the United Nations, the oceans, outer space, the atmosphere, and Antarctica are commons. In some cases, resources that are not formally held in common can be transformed into commons through activity. For instance, when people use city squares for direct action—whether that action is protest or celebration—they become commons. By collectively occupying and making use of the city square it becomes an informal, temporary commons (Harvey 2012). Foraging begets a similar space and practice of commons; the fruit foraged from trees and bushes is transformed into a common good through communal appropriation that complicates claims to private or commercial ownership. Trees, bushes, and their fruits are not intrinsically a shared resource—they are *made* into a shared resource by practices of foraging.

Commons are often haunted by failures. The "tragedy of the commons" is a familiar (if overwrought) narrative of the outcomes of a commons (Hardin 1968). To be sure, commons have failed time and again, wrecked by greed, malice, and ignorance. But commons are not destined to failure. Elinor Ostrom (2015) demonstrates in her Nobel Prize–winning work how the commons can be productively governed. However, just as we should not naïvely resign the commons to tragedy, we also should not presume that the commons are necessarily progressive or emancipatory. In the twenty-first century, even the World Bank embraces discourses of the commons. Although the commons are suggestive of communal ownership—evoking concepts of community economies—they are also regularly co-opted back into global capital, transmuted and absorbed into the market economy (Caffentzis and Federici 2014; De Angelis 2010a). Too often what was held in common is enclosed, made into an exclusive resource. Gated communities provide an example of a perverse notion of the commons: a shared resource enclosed to bar others from entry. But even the specter of enclosure, which is taken to threaten the commons, must be called into question. As David Harvey (2012, 71) points out, "A common demand on the left for 'local autonomy' is actually a demand for some kind of enclosure." In other words, throughout theory and practice the idea of the commons is contested. While it is at times co-opted, it also suggests other modes of togetherness through alternative desires and practices.

Of late, the ideas and practices of the commons have sparked the interest of designers (Franz and Elzenbaumer 2016; Manzini 2015; Marttila, Botero, and Saad-Sulonen 2014; Seravalli 2014; Teli 2015; and Teli et al. 2020, among others). For designers committed to themes of participation, communities, labor, and politics, the commons are understandably enticing. What the commons provide to design is aspirational—the concept proffers hope and potential for employing design toward ends other than commodities for the free market (Teli 2015). As designers search for new work domains and ways of working, the concept and a practice of the commons offers an alternative. Without much effort, we can find examples of design being applied to commons projects like open making and manufacturing (Seravalli 2014), various forms of peer-to-peer practices and institutions (Franz and Elzenbaumer 2016; Sciannamblo et al. 2021; Teli, Di Fiore, and D'Andrea 2016; Teli, Lyle, and Sciannamblo 2018), and the use of public space and community centers (Seravalli, Hillgren, and Agger-Eriksen 2015).

The commons, however, are not static or stable. Like democracy and design, they are an ongoing endeavor. "Commoning" has evolved as a term of art in both economic and political discourses, referring to the activities of creating and sustaining the commons (Linebaugh 2014). Its existence as a verb signals that members of a community continually remake and maintain the commons. Ideally, these activities are "social practices of constant democratic and horizontal negotiation" (De Angelis 2010a; Franz and Elzenbaumer 2016, 3). What is significant about the term "commoning" is that it labels—and thereby recognizes—the relational qualities of the commons (Gibson-Graham, Cameron, and Healy 2016). The commons do not simply appear and then continue to exist. Commoning requires work, and the work of commoning is evident in foraging.

Foraging demands volunteer labor precisely because it is not agriculture—there is no farm or orchard that is professionally tended. The plants and trees the forager watches and picks are spread across the city, and fruit ripens at different times, even among a single species. There is no formal supply chain to become a part of in order to streamline the distribution. The many efficiencies brought about by agriculture are lost in practices of foraging. All the forms of work that make foraging possible—managing, organizing, and maintaining—are also the work of commoning: the labor needed to foster, cultivate, and sustain a commons.

These design experiments in civics begin by exploring the design of tools for foraging, with the question, "How might technologies be designed or redesigned to relieve some of the work of foraging?" Neither technologies nor design are neutral; they shape and are shaped by practice and discourse. And so, throughout this process of designing tools for foraging we give persistent attention to how those technologies and design might affect the practices of foraging. These projects, then, also become experiments that ask a suite of related questions: "What might the practices of foraging become when imbued with computation, and, consequently, how might such new tools affect foraging as a practice of commoning?" Designing for foraging is thus a way to explore designing for the commons—an experiment in a different mode of democratic living.

The Work of Foraging

When I helped Concrete Jungle pick persimmons that day in September, picking was just the beginning of the afterlife of the fruit. Katherine drove the fruit back to her house a few neighborhoods over. There, other volunteers and board members helped her carry the heavy bags inside. She weighed them and recorded how much fruit was collected. Then she made calls to the food pantries and shelters that the persimmons were promised to. And before this batch was distributed, Concrete Jungle was off on their next pick to manage the seemingly endless supply of fruit. This was the pace of work for Concrete Jungle throughout the long growing season in Atlanta.

As the organization grew, Concrete Jungle made sure their picks stayed playful. People still climbed trees and joyously shook the branches to clear them of apples, pears, and persimmons. But it became a challenge to sustain the work. Every season new trees and bushes were found by chance or following a rumor: "My cousin told me about a pomegranate tree in East Lake that no one picks." Sometimes an owner called to ask Concrete Jungle for help: "Could you please come get these figs? They're falling everywhere and making a mess; you can have it, all of it." And every season some trees and bushes disappeared. They would die or stop bearing fruit. Or a house was built and the new owners cut the trees down. Or the city put in a sidewalk and pulled out the bushes. Volunteers also come and go. Long-term volunteers participate year after year, but many help once and move on.

As the collection of the produce has grown, distribution required more effort. There is often a delay between when the fruit is collected and when it can be distributed. There is only so long fruit can be stored on someone's porch or in their living room before the fruit begins to spoil or attract pests. Moving hundreds of pounds of fruit is also a strenuous challenge that requires sizeble cars or pickup trucks. There is the constant work of meeting the conditions of those in need and organizations who provide for them. Food pantries and shelters need to have some idea of when food is arriving and how much. To meet the needs of their partners, Concrete Jungle has diversified beyond foraging in the strict sense. They operate a small urban farm, and a portion of their annual collection comes from gleaning—retrieving the leftovers from fields and orchards. They collect the fruit and vegetables once planted to be harvested by conventional means that, for one reason or another, are no longer wanted. This diversification in collection methods adds to their ability to contribute to the local food system. It also adds to their work.

One logistical challenge is that all this food needs to be taken account of—literally counted and calculated. Although there is often a romance that accompanies discussions of foraging, groups that forage at a larger scale encounter logistics problems. To organize a pick, they need to know when the fruit is ripe. If they arrive too soon, volunteers will pick fruit that cannot be distributed or needs to be stored for too long. Too late and the fruit will have fallen to the ground, been eaten by insects, or trampled. Should any of this mistiming occur, valuable volunteer labor will be squandered. While foraging evokes a carefree image of pleasurable afternoons spent gathering fruits and vegetables, that belies the tedious work of planning picks, managing distribution, sustaining relationships with social services providers, and monitoring trees and bushes. None of this is truly crucial, and herein lies one of the conundrums of foraging: a bushel of apples or even five hundred pounds of pears is not going to end hunger. And yet, it does matter. For those who receive that apple or pear, foraging matters.

Designing to Support Foraging as Civics

Over the past several years, an ensemble of students and I have collaborated with Concrete Jungle to develop a series of devices to imagine how we might differently support the work of foraging. Together with the founders, executive director, board members, and volunteers of Concrete Jungle, we have explored ways to support the work of monitoring fruit trees to better know when the fruit is ripe in order to plan picks. Our blended cohort used practices of codesign to conceptualize, make, and use these systems. This work was funded in myriad ways, sometimes as sponsored research, other times as self-supported efforts. In some instances, designers were paid for their work. At other times, they volunteered or integrated the project into their studies.

This mix of improvisational configurations of working, studying, and making is a characteristic of doing design experiments in civics, because the structure of the design experiment is often irregular. Some of the work with Concrete Jungle was supported through federal grants and industry gifts that enabled multiple designers to work on the projects over multiple years. Other times, the project ran on entirely volunteer labor. While the designers on these projects shifted over the years, the engagement with Concrete Jungle remained constant, and ideas came from our ongoing collaboration with them. Our partnership began when a graduate student named Beth Schechter, who was friends with members of Concrete Jungle, built the first prototype of a mobile mapping application for the organization. The project lay fallow for a couple of years, lacking resources to sustain it, but it was prescient of work to come; two years later Concrete Jungle approached us about borrowing a drone to use for fruit monitoring. And since then, for more than a decade now, we have worked together in a consistent and ongoing partnership.

In our foraging projects, the technologies and stories of smart cities and precision agriculture overlap. Accordingly, our approach to developing devices of inquiry was to creatively reframe and reread the discourses and technologies of precision agriculture in the service of foraging (Gibson-Graham 2008). So-called precision agriculture is data intensive, driven by a vast field of products and services to provide farmers and others with information to improve their practices and maximize yield. More farmers are now employing drones, distributed sensor networks, and geographic information systems. They use these technologies to track environmental information such as air temperature, ground temperature, humidity, and soil moisture. Drones are used to collect aerial views of fields, feeding images into software to reveal soil and crop health through computational analytics. The data is aggregated in reports, displays, and interactive maps, which, combined with external data and models, guide decision-making.

Overwhelmingly, precision agriculture technologies, products, and services have been designed for the context of industrial production. These systems are costly and require expertise to install and use. Through them, the farm is no longer just a landscape to be tended—it has become a datascape to be analyzed, interpreted, and acted upon. In contrast, foraging is often romanticized for its very lack of precision, for the ways it is different from (and even counter to) industrialized agriculture. But might we take inspiration from the precision technologies of industrial agriculture to better support the imprecise practices of urban foraging?

Reimagining Foraging through Making

Our use of design to support the work of foraging as civics enabled us to collectively reimagine the activities of foraging, and also the concepts of commons and commoning that characterized those practices. As devices of inquiry, the things we made are both motivated by practical questions and serve as creative apparatus—they enable us to probe current conditions and glimpse what might be possible. Over the past decade, through ongoing collaboration with Concrete Jungle, we designed a series of devices for monitoring the ripeness of fruit. One of those devices was a sensor; another was a digital map. These devices facilitated the work of foraging, which in turn expanded our understanding of foraging as a civic practice and prompted consideration of different figurations of commoning.

Fruit Are Heavy

Knowing when fruit is ripe and ready to be picked is a perennial problem for many foragers. There are simply too many distant trees to keep track of them all. Craig Durkin, one of the founders of Concrete Jungle, wondered if we might be able to devise a sensor to better estimate when fruit would be ready to pick. An earlier collaboration with Concrete Jungle explored the use of drones to monitor fruit from a distance. For a variety of reasons, this proved not to be viable. After the drones, Craig suggested that perhaps we might monitor the trees directly. One afternoon we were sitting around a table discussing various fruit-sensing technologies (as one does, of course). We were trying to think through what was and wasn't actually possible, when Craig offhandedly mentioned that on his way to our meeting he happened to notice a pear tree in midtown ready to pick. "What do you mean you happened to notice it? You weren't out actually checking it?" I asked. "Oh, no, with apples and pears it's easy enough to tell as you just pass by," Craig replied. "The branches were nearly touching the ground." This simple insight sparked *Fruit Are Heavy*: a system to detect the ripeness of fruit by monitoring the relative droop of a fruit tree branch.

The general concept of using sensors to detect the ripeness of fruit is commonplace in research labs. Systems have been deployed for use in the industrial food system and use a variety of methods to detect ripeness. One way that industrial engineers detect the ripeness of fruit is by monitoring the gases they emit. Many fruits exude ethylene as they ripen, which can be detected and measured by electronic noses—sensors that are engineered to register the presence and amount of the gaseous chemical. While this off-gassing process can be accurate when measured in a closed container, it is difficult to deploy in the field. We considered the idea of wrapping individual fruit in Tyvek bags when the fruit was still young, but this seemed unlikely to succeed because wrapping the fruit could affect its growth, and attaching the bag around the young fruit was difficult. Moreover, the price of the gas sensors would make the platform too expensive. Other ripeness-detection methods use visual inspection strategies, such as analyzing the size or color of fruit. This process too has promise but is similarly difficult to deploy in the field and is expensive in terms of monetary and computational costs.

Compared with these more sophisticated options, monitoring how much a tree branch bends is simple and inexpensive. Bend sensors cost less than a dollar and function as variable resistors. The more the bend, the more the flow is restricted. Reading data from the sensor is easy; a number goes out, a number returns, and the difference between those two numbers tell us about the extent of the bend (see figures 3.1 and 3.2). As the fruit grows and becomes heavier, the branch begins to bend under the weight, changing the sensor's reading.

In collaboration with Craig, we came up with the idea to attach a bend sensor to a branch of a tree when its fruit was young and small. As the fruits grow and ripen, we would be able to detect the branch's bend. In other words, the bend in the branch serves as a proxy for the ripeness of the fruit. We did not need to know the exactness of the bend. The numbers were unimportant in any absolute sense. What was important was being able to detect relative difference—that the tree branch was bending much more at

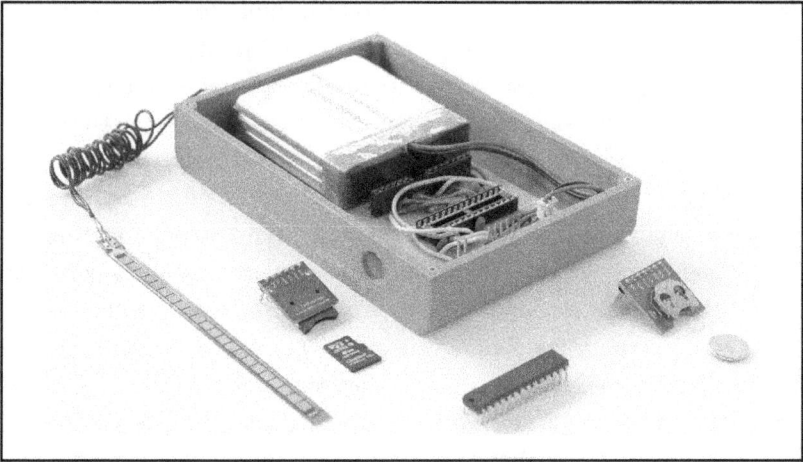

Figure 3.1
Components of the *Fruit Are Heavy* platform.

Figure 3.2
The *Fruit Are Heavy* platform assembled.

some point in time than at an earlier point in time. Tom Jenkins, then a PhD student, set about constructing a series of technical prototypes.

The sensing platform we were building also brought more familiar product design challenges, such as how to encase and attach the sensor. The sensor does not simply rest in the tree; it needs to be attached to the tree and able to withstand the torrential rains of an Atlanta summer. We hired an industrial design student, Catherine Meeschia, to join us and develop a housing and strap system for the device. The electronics and battery were placed within a 3-D printed box, and a set of wires protruded from the box, with the bend sensor attached to the end. But how to attach the box to the tree? Catherine designed and created a small backpack, just big enough to snugly hold the plastic box, which strapped the device to the tree limb or trunk. One advantage of the backpack was that it could easily accommodate variations in the girth of the branches or trunks and attach or detach with ease. The backpack was constructed from material used in DIY diaper making—water-repellent materials that were easy to cut and sew (see figure 3.3).

While we developed something that looked product-like and addressed the sensing challenge, we faced significant issues with power and connectivity.

Figure 3.3
The *Fruit Are Heavy* platform in its backpack.

For the platform to be useful, it would need to be deployed for four to six weeks at minimum, ideally two or three times that. Providing power for that timespan was no easy matter. Tom developed a shrewd approach: a two-tiered system in which one lower-powered circuit operated a clock that would "wake up" the other circuit every twenty-four hours to take a reading, effectively turning on and then turning off the sensor. This allowed us to streamline the power needed, making it possible for us to build something that we could deploy with a battery pack to run in the field for over a month.

Connectivity became our Achilles' heel. The *Fruit Are Heavy* project is premised on the idea that data would be collected remotely. Despite the popular discourses of smart cities, networks are not free, open, or ubiquitous. At the time of the project it was difficult to get real-time data from the device in a cost-effective way. Atlanta does not have a municipal Wi-Fi. If it did, that would have solved this problem. Short of that, the two most viable options were to subscribe to an existing network or build our own network. Subscribing to an existing network would have more than doubled the cost of the hardware for the platform and added the price of a subscription plan. The second option—building a network ourselves—was simply beyond what we could consider in terms of our technological capabilities. Tom and Craig explored ad hoc networking models, such as piggybacking onto a nearby home network, using a drone to broadcast a network that could retrieve the data, or using Bluetooth from mobile phones to collect the data—but the complexity of implementing these concepts was prohibitive. Instead, Tom arrived at a creative solution that met our needs to explore the capacities of the sensor and the practices around sensing.

Tom developed the ability for the devices to record data locally. Data was taken from the sensor and written to a memory card that we connected to the sensor board. Checking the memory over time allowed us to test whether the sensor was working. While this did not provide us with the functionality needed for full deployment, it let us determine that the sensing system was viable for our goals.

We deployed the sensor for two consecutive summers in a pear tree Craig selected. It was away from busy thoroughfares and next to a cohousing community that would not be concerned with us climbing their trees. Craig scurried up the pear tree and bent branches to find a supple one. As Tom and I handed the sensor platform up to him, he strapped the backpack to the tree trunk and zip-tied the sensor and wires along the branch (see figure 3.4). To

Figure 3.4
Installing the *Fruit Are Heavy* platform.

everyone's satisfaction, the sensor registered the relative droop of the branch over time as the fruit grew during both summers.

The trials and errors of making and using this platform brought to our collective attention a set of potentials and complications. As a device of inquiry, *Fruit Are Heavy* expanded and changed the constitution of the commons and the practices of commoning in conspicuous ways. If commoning attunes us to more-than-human relations (Gibson-Graham, Cameron, and Healy 2016), then the *Fruit Are Heavy* experiments fold an unusual device into those relations. During this process of making and using sensors to monitor the relative ripeness of fruit in trees, we became differently attentive to people and objects around us. In this emerging imaginary of foraging, it is not just the fruit and trees we attended to, but also the devices. They too became part of the more-than-human landscape, as part of the work of foraging became about scrambling up trees and leaning across branches to strap the sensors in place. The knowledge about what's needed to participate in foraging changes too; now it also involves understanding these devices and what's needed from a tree for them to work. Notably, then, these devices did not really do away with labor; they only reconfigured the labor that was demanded by foraging.

Sensors are things that need to be maintained and repaired—a problem also on the minds of residents in the last chapter. The first summer the sensors were deployed, we checked them weekly to confirm they were still in the tree, the sensor was still attached to the branch, and the housing didn't appear damaged. While the intention was for the device to displace or delegate work, what happened instead was that new forms of work were introduced to, and then understood as, foraging. There is a history of introducing technology and automation into work practices—and as feminist scholarship has documented, often into the work practices of care and domesticity—with the allure of alleviating work, only to create more work (Cowan 1983). In this experiment of exploring the possibilities of using sensors to support the work of foraging, the activities and outcomes of design demanded new labor practices and brought about new problems. One effect of making and using these devices, then, was to instantiate a potential consequence of sensing. This instantiation—these constructed material conditions—prompted us to collectively consider whether this was a practice of foraging and commoning that we actually wanted to pursue.

Fruit Are Here

Geographic information systems (GIS) are a cornerstone of precision agri-culture and smart cities. More than just recording locations and routing, GIS has the capacity to present space as data and examine data within space. What GIS provides is both a set of tools and techniques for spatial analysis and an orientation that attunes us to space as a site of information that can be gathered to shape understanding and action. In the context of precision agriculture, GIS is often the platform through which other data is organized and presented to be transformed into actionable insights. Just as maps are not new to farming or cities, maps are not new to foraging. Foragers com-monly use maps to keep track of the locations of fruit trees, bushes, and vacant lots where wild greens grow. A handful of foraging collectives have constructed and maintained digital maps for their cities. In addition, there are efforts to create conglomerate maps. For example, the *Falling Fruit* proj-ect is constructing a global map of forage-able food.

Almost since they began, Concrete Jungle used digital maps to commu-nicate what they do. There may be no better visual form than a map to show the distribution and abundance of fruit in Atlanta. Years ago, Concrete Jungle created a map using Google Maps, placing colored pins to mark the location of fruit trees and bushes around Atlanta. The colors of the pins differentiated the kinds of fruit, and checkboxes allowed users to select and deselect different fruits to be displayed. The map had all the basic properties of an interactive map that you would expect, such as the ability to zoom, pan, and navigate visual space. It was featured prominently on the Con-crete Jungle website and was used extensively to set the context for their story of urban foraging: the map was dense with colored pins, making clear just how much fruit was available across the metro region.

This original map displayed most of the fruit. The qualifier "most" hints at the complexity of data in this civic context. Much of the fruit that was on public land and safe to pick was displayed on the map. Fruit trees or bushes that were on public land but located in dangerous settings, such as in roadway medians or next to the highway, were hidden. Fruit trees that were on private land that Concrete Jungle had been given access to, such as trees in people's yards, were also hidden. What fruit trees to share or hide are decisions about the governance and maintenance of the commons. In both theory and prac-tice, the commons are never a free-for-all; what resources are shared and on what grounds characterizes a commons. Decisions are made about access and exchange, and these decisions enact beliefs and desires, tactics, and strategies.

Such decisions are expressed through formal and informal processes and made things. In the case of Concrete Jungle, the foraging map takes a particular role in enacting decisions about the governance and maintenance of the commons. Like all maps, it is made to display some things and hide others—this is a foundation of cartography and the political quality of maps and mapping (Wood 1992). Constructing maps allows access to some knowledge, places, and resources, and not others. Any map is as much performative as it is representational (Crampton 2009).

The question to be asked of the map, thus, is not only "Where is the forage-able fruit?" An additional question is—at least from the perspective of designing for the commons and design as commoning—"How might *this* representation enable and participate in the work of governing *this* commons?" As with *Fruit Are Heavy*, this experiment becomes an event through which to explore the potentials and consequences of reimagining foraging and the commons, an event through which to experiment with different configurations of work in supporting foraging as a civic practice.

How the map works and shapes the commons and commoning instigated a multiyear project to redesign Concrete Jungle's digital map. As with other projects, it was undertaken collaboratively. Members of Concrete Jungle served as designers and programmers, making aesthetic and technical decisions throughout the project's lifespan, sometimes as paid contractors on the project, sometimes through their roles within the organization. Karl Kim, an undergraduate, took on the technical development of the map together with Craig Durkin from Concrete Jungle. Karl worked on the project—in the summer for hourly pay, during the school year for credit—over a span of three years. The project looked to explore and broaden the potential of the map for Concrete Jungle's organizing. The basic goal of the map remained to display the type of fruit available at specific locations. However, the purpose of the project evolved to demand features that might amplify the value of data to Concrete Jungle. Exactly what the value of data was or might be to Concrete Jungle was not known at the outset. The redesign was an attempt to consider and trial what functionalities might be needed and developed to support enhanced practices of foraging.

The *Fruit Are Here* project foremost raised the question of whether data from the map might assist in the most basic of activities: scheduling picks. Rather than relying upon either weekly visits by volunteers or sensors to monitor the relative ripeness of fruit trees, the hope was to use data and analytics to track when fruit was picked in the past to predict future pick dates.

Custom features were designed and implemented to enable volunteers to contribute various forms of data to the map, and to analyze and display that data over time. This would allow Concrete Jungle to track and compare trees and their fruit over multiple years. Functionally, the features enabled volunteers to upload pictures of the trees and the fruit and add ratings of the size and quality of the fruit throughout the year, alongside the dates of picks and pick yields. Across and through these multiple data points, a data set emerged that expressed when a given tree ripens (see figure 3.5).

As the redesign progressed, other ideas emerged for how data from the map might be used. These ideas expanded our vision for how practices of foraging might intersect with other civic concerns through the collection of spatial data. One such idea built upon phenology: the study of cyclical phenomena in nature. The timing of the ripening of the fruit could be correlated with other data to provide additional insights. The ripening of fruit becomes a proxy for other environmental conditions and can be combined with other data to detect other issues. Correlating data about when fruit trees ripen with aggregate data (temperature, rainfall, pests, and other environmental factors) becomes an expression of climate in local settings. Over time, these analytics could detect changes in microclimates and perhaps even patterns of climate change in the region. Data from the picks might also be merged with data that serves as a proxy for urban development, such as demolition and building permits. That is, as new homes, offices, and strip malls are built, trees are felled and disappear from the data set. The absence of these trees and their yield could serve as a marker of changes in the built environment, which in turn might be markers for gentrification and other patterns in the city. Through such envisioned uses, the map becomes a device for constructing imaginaries of *what else* foraging might be, and also *what else*, in addition to fruit, might be gathered from foraging.

The redesign of the map also became an opportunity to explore organizational possibilities—how Concrete Jungle might change their management of collective foraging. In so doing, it aligns with a long lineage of scholarship that sees information systems in relation to organizational structures and labor. For instance, the map contains basic functionality to associate volunteers with trees and then to communicate directly with those volunteers. Specific volunteers would become stewards of specific trees. Simple features built into the map remind volunteers when to check on their trees and pick the fruit. The volunteers can also contribute back to the work of data collection. As volunteers check their trees, they can submit images of the trees and fruit and rate the ripeness, enabling tracking the current status of a tree and hopefully informing predictions of future picks. The map thus serves as a conduit between the organization and its constitution by hundreds of volunteers, each with different levels of engagement and attachment. Over time, this conduit might become an amplifier, generating yet another value to the work of foraging through emergent practices of gathering fruit and data, now linked through collective practices. As with the scenarios that use foraging data for other goals—tracking phenology, the conditions of climate change, and the effects of urban development—these new organizational practices are creative extrapolations of the present.

It is important to note that these features, functionalities, and uses of the map emerged in response to the expressed desires, frustrations, and reflections of Concrete Jungle board members and volunteers. These are not simply the ideas of designers projected on an organization and its practices. They came about through conversations, through demonstrations of the map as it was being built that prompted board members and volunteers to ask, "What if . . . ?" They also came about after the map was functional and put into use. Board members and volunteers would share their experiences of using the map, good and bad, and ways they would like or could envision using the map.

The map thus performs along multiple registers and suggests multiple pathways. It continues the representational purpose of the original map in an updated visual form. It displays the locations and kinds of fruits, and allows for the usual features of panning and zooming, selecting and deselecting that we have grown accustomed to with digital maps. The map is also designed to enable the orchestration of the collective that is Concrete Jungle. It serves as an interface between volunteers and trees, and a platform for practices of collecting and sharing data that signify more than just apples and pears. In addition to supporting the work of foraging as it is done now, the map charts what Concrete Jungle might become: it is a site of collective imagination, a way to materially explore how Concrete Jungle as an organization might act differently. The features, functionalities, and uses are expressions of how the organization might additionally perform the work that defines it: of caring, of being grassroots, and of earnest commitment to those among us who are in need.

Figure 3.5
The *Fruit Are Here* map for Concrete Jungle, basic map view.

The Object Is Not the Subject of Design Experiments in Civics

By some conventional measures, *Fruit Are Heavy* and *Fruit Are Here* are relatively well designed. They are aesthetically pleasing and usable. From a process perspective, they emerge from identifying and understanding the practices of foragers, and they were developed cooperatively; they embody and reflect the logics and ethos of a participatory approach to designing. And yet, in some other respects, these things do not work. They may be usable and desirable, but their usefulness is complicated. They are weighed down with limitations. Through these limitations we encounter a characteristic of making and made things in the context of design experiments: the value of the device lies in its capacity to contribute to the conditions of inquiry. That capacity is not the same as its immediate or presumed functionality. This sets the design experiment and these devices apart from more familiar modes of design and ways of judging making and made things.

Neither *Fruit Are Heavy* nor *Fruit Are Here* fully achieves the aspirations that motivated making them. As tools to reduce labor, both come up short. The sensor can detect the bend in a tree branch with enough accuracy, but there is no way to transmit the data to the foragers who need it. Instead, the data remains on the device, written to a local memory card like those used in so many digital cameras, recording data snapshots as proxies of the ripening fruit. But the snapshots remain unseen until the data is downloaded. With *Fruit Are Heavy*, the problem encountered was an engineering problem. Considering the actual cost in dollars, the cost of power from battery draws, and the limits of our collective knowledge as designers-not-engineers, there was no feasible way to wirelessly collect the data from the sensors. Cellular was too expensive, and building a bespoke network was beyond our resources. Over time, these problems may solve themselves as networking becomes simpler, cellular becomes cheaper, or municipal Wi-Fi becomes pervasive. But for the time being, the promise of *Fruit Are Heavy* to lessen the work of foraging remains hypothetical.

Fruit Are Here has greater use value. It still functions as a compelling visual representation of the abundance and diversity of fruit across Atlanta. As of this writing, Concrete Jungle still features it prominently on their website, a valuable piece of publicity for the organization. Arguably, some of the aspects of the visual representation were improved through our work, such as the ability to search for and home in on fruit that is nearly at peak ripeness. *Fruit Are Here* can collect and store data, then produce charts and diagrams from that data. But only a few volunteers use it for that. As software, it is slow—not optimized for the speedy display or data processing that is expected today. Sluggish performance frustrates some members of Concrete Jungle, who are leery of using it for more than marketing. Accordingly, there are few images being uploaded, little data being collected, and minimal planning occurring that involves the map.

While we must acknowledge the incompleteness of these devices, we must also resist simplistically labeling them as failures. The incompleteness of these devices is a characteristic of the design experiment. Within design experiments, the object is not the subject of the experiment. Different from so much of design, the purpose of this experiment is not to expertly produce a product or service for sale. The purpose of the device is to contribute to the conditions of inquiry: to make possible the constitution of settings and situations that express civic imaginaries and to try out diverse civic practices. Consequently, we should not describe or judge the devices of design experiments by their immediate or presumed functionality. Rather, we should evaluate them by their capacity to enable inquiry and imagination.

Other scholars have explored the idea of devices and developed nuanced understandings of the roles of design in and as experimentation. In particular, Noortje Marres's (2016) work is foundational to this concept of designing devices and practices of experimentation. For Marres, things such as eco-homes serve as devices of public engagement. They attract and enable participation in the issues of science and technology and broad discourses of environmentalism. In the process, such devices produce new knowledge about an issue. They also involve "the reconfiguration of the social-material relations among which new entities are to be accommodated" (117). Marres's description of the "reconfiguration of the social-material relations" deeply influenced my thinking about devices and design experiments in civics.

Following from Marres, as devices of inquiry, these things work to inform us about the material and social conditions of the practices they are made to enable. One of the things design experiments can do is inform us about what might be needed to enable the futures that the experiment queries. Put another way, design experiments in civics ask the question: What tools, capacities, and processes are basic to the civic imaginaries and practices we are exploring? (DiSalvo, Jenkins, and Lodato 2016). The question is then answered through making and use, through processes of codesign that Marc Steen describes as "joint inquiry and imagination" (Steen 2013).

The devices of inquiry created together with Concrete Jungle let us ask what sorts of artifacts and systems might assist emergent practices of foraging. With *Fruit Are Heavy* and *Fruit Are Here*, after trialing these artifacts and systems, we collectively know more about both these devices and the world around them. We can point to the limitations in accessible networking technologies as a need. We could make an argument for the value of municipal Wi-Fi to support the endeavors of community groups interested in using sensing technologies toward their own ends, harkening back to narratives of sensing in smart cities. We know what features of the mapping platform are easy to use and which are more difficult. We know what data is desirable or extraneous. Importantly, Concrete Jungle remains interested in and committed to exploring these options; discussions about sensors, maps, and data continue among members of the organization, even though the role of academic designers has lessened. Moreover, these experiments have informed Concrete Jungle's awareness of what the organization might need to change to support future data practices. All these learnings reflect on the devices and also the practices surrounding them—important lessons for designers and the organizations they partner with.

But these devices do not need to function well to inform us. James Pierce (2015) provocatively suggests that designed things work as reflexive devices precisely because they do *not* work as we expect products to. What they offer is a semblance of function. They present material and social conditions as unresolved. Rather than being fixed, these situations are now open to interpretation (Jenkins 2014, 2015; Sengers and Gaver 2006). As devices of inquiry, *Fruit Are Heavy* and *Fruit Are Here* construct a world in which unstable, emergent practices of foraging are made present for consideration. In this setting, what we might describe or judge as a "good" or "well-made" device of inquiry unsettles the practice, but without breaking it.

This move of providing a semblance of function (Pierce 2015), just enough to manifest conditions for consideration, is similar to the previously discussed techniques of scenarios and storytelling that work to twist the narrative joints of progress. With devices of inquiry, however, that unsettling unfolds through making and use, interrupting some small part of the world while trying to shape it differently. Similar to scenarios, this work also manifests subjectivities in the context of possible futures: stories are told through the making and use of these devices, which elicit pluralistic civic subjectivities. But the material making of these devices and the opportunities they afford for partial use brings about additional insights beyond what is possible from scenarios alone. This is the value of rehearsing the future, described by Joachim Halse as "rehearsing the relationships and practices that follow with a new artifact" (in Halse et al. 2010, 17). Through these devices, the activities of foraging change in practice, if only momentarily.

In this imaginary of foraging appropriating the techniques and technologies of precision agriculture, in addition to tending to the trees and bushes, the forager or other some member of the collective must tend to the sensors. In this imaginary of foraging, knowledge of fruit is mediated. In this imaginary of foraging, the foraging collective is doing more than just gathering and distributing fruit—it is also managing and sharing data. Foraging, as a civic practice and institution, is thus differently constituted. In each of these situations, the subjectivities of being a forager and being a foraging collective shift. As with the scenarios previously discussed, the purpose of this making is not to determine and chart a course of action. Rather, we now have new instantiations—artifacts and experiences—through which we might consider possible futures with an understanding of their potentials and consequences in action.

Refiguring the Assemblages of Commoning

In addition to offering insights into what sorts of artifacts and systems might assist the work of foraging, these design experiments in civics offer lessons about commons and commoning. That is, in addition to enabling explorations of what to make and how made things might influence practices, design experiments also enable dialogue on theories about how we might organize our lives. This echoes Johan Redström's (2017) assertion that when making design theory, we are producing empirical understandings about the processes of making and the qualities of made things, while also producing theoretical perspectives on the social, cultural, and political contexts in which that making and use occur. As design experiments, making to support the work of foraging as civics simultaneously enables inquiry into what sorts of artifacts and systems might assist that work, how those artifacts and systems might affect the practices of foraging, and how those nascent practices might fit, clash, or refigure theories of commons and commoning.

Appropriating discourses and technologies is risky because they carry politics with them. These politics, even if not deterministic, may have lingering influence. Gathering together the techniques and practices of precision agriculture, smart cities, and foraging offers opportunities for exploration and invention, but it is also an awkward affair. Precision agriculture is an endeavor of efficiency achieved through automation, intended to mitigate risk and amplify productivity to increase yield. The techniques and services of precision agriculture are advanced by industries that provide the infrastructure, hardware, and software to transform fields of corn and pastures of cattle into landscapes of data. Make no mistake, precision agriculture is driven by a market logic that prioritizes a hyperrationalization of farming. However, that is not to say it is without value. Agriculture is laborious, and efficiency is often welcomed by farmers. The problem is that discourses of progress achieved through technology are often overbearing, if not oppressive, and design tends to serve those in power. We should indeed be suspicious of the values and implications of precision agriculture (see Miles 2019). When performing the work of shifting perspectives through mixing discourses, techniques, and practices, it is important to recognize how those discourses, techniques, and practices can continue to manifest a presence and leave traces upon successive inventions and use.

The concerns about precision agriculture echo concerns raised previously about the smart city because they have similar (at times identical) discourses and technology. Both precision agriculture and smart cities claim to enhance capacities and services by imbuing environments with computation. Both are driven by market forces and should be historically recognized as continuing long-standing regimes of Western rationalization. Just as we should be concerned that participation in the smart city enrolls residents into practices of neoliberal governance and citizenship, so too should we be concerned that participation in precision agriculture enrolls foragers into practices that may run counter to the values that undergird their work. Glibly importing these practices could threaten to disrupt the conditions that give foraging its character. Foraging is decidedly imprecise. To optimize the work of foraging seems paradoxical; foraging is only made possible due to the excess produced by circumstance or accident—a fruit tree happens to be planted here, or berries happen to grow there. Strapping sensors to a tree branch and monitoring the relative ripeness of fruit precludes certain modes of engaging with that tree and its environs. Using maps and data analytics to plan and manage picks directs foragers toward certain modes of coordinating volunteer time and effort. By the very activities of making and using these devices, new actors and associations are introduced into the assemblage of foraging, including those corporations that provide the mapping technologies, databases, servers, networks, and sensors. These actors and associations are material and ideological intrusions, meddling in the commons and practices of commoning.

How do we, as designers, make the claim that such meddling is sensible and democratic, not just reckless, self-serving cleverness? We do so by holding ourselves accountable to naming these entanglements, by attempting to answer the questions they raise, and by questioning the normativities of technology and progress they originate from. To pursue democratic inquiry in these conditions requires confronting the complications that design introduces. Democratic inquiry requires a reflection on our practices of making, the things made, and their use in relation to how those activities and outcomes will affect the practices and communities we work with. The materiality and performance of the design experiment provides an opportunity to ask and answer these questions directly.

The issue at hand is how these particular devices contribute to or thwart forms of togetherness, and what that might tell us about commoning more generally. The purpose of the sensors is to provide knowledge at a distance that would lessen the amount of time volunteers put into monitoring the ripeness of fruit and increase the ability of organizers to schedule picks. The map provides additional capabilities to track data over time that might then be useful for future analytics and planning. In both cases, mediation occurs: the work done by people is augmented and even replaced by work delegated to machines. We should question whenever human labor is delegated to machines. With foraging, we should ask how this delegation of labor changes what it means to participate in this endeavor. The potential harm is that introducing such artifacts and systems displaces a collaborative endeavor.

Do such artifacts and systems subvert qualities of the experience of foraging, changing its character to the detriment of volunteers' perspectives on commoning? They certainly change some activities of foraging, and they require new work, new volunteer roles. Whether or not this is to the detriment of commoning is unclear—but nonetheless, we must address these questions as best we can through reflection. To do so requires understanding and appreciating the different points of attachment in the endeavor of foraging. It seems to me that in the gathering and sharing of fruit, moments of commoning come to the fore. In these moments, there is a sense of "doing together," much more so than in the monitoring of the trees or bushes. Perhaps this is obvious; the activities of gathering and sharing are the collective moments of foraging, whereas monitoring the fruit is more often done individually.

But there was also a different sort of experience of "doing together" that emerged from using these devices. Working with Natalie Larkins—another industrial design student who contributed to these projects—we explored how the introduction of sensors and sensing might affect foraging from the perspective of a service. The sensors need to be installed, which takes knowledge, skill, and effort while also requiring certain physical capacities. A person climbs a tree, finds a suitable branch, and stretches their body out across the branch to strap on the sensor. In its fully envisioned functioning instantiation, the sensor is not making a determination; it is conveying digital impressions of conditions. It is a loose distribution of agency—a casual delegation.

With the map, there is less direct engagement between people. But still, the map enables at least two capacities of note. First, the maps enable us to appreciate the commons in ways that would otherwise be difficult. We can view the distribution of trees and bushes across the entire metropolitan region of Atlanta. Through these maps, we can come to appreciate the scope of the foraging commons. We might discern the variety of fruits that fall within *this* commons—the apples, pears, and berries of Atlanta—and see where they are and when they ripen. Second, the map might enable us to construct and consider representations from the past and project them into the future. That is, through the data collected and rendered as a map, a previously unseen temporal aspect of the commons emerges. We can see what the commons were last year or the year before. We can also envision the state of the commons in the near future—what might be gathered here and there next year.

Without a doubt, my generous readings of *Fruit Are Heavy* and *Fruit Are Here* are disposed toward a desire that these devices provide benefit, rather than do harm, to the commons and commoning. Such generosity of interpretation is, or at least should be, a quality of such design experiments in civics. As the same time, part of this is work is taking seriously so-called unintended consequences (see Parvin and Pollock 2020). Imagination is not a carte blanche. As McKenna states with regard to the role of the imagination in democracy, "As the horizon expands, the possibilities of the future become more numerous. While we must critically select and act on particular goals, at least now we realize these decisions have wide ranging consequences. What we select makes a difference. As our possibilities increase, so too do our responsibilities" (2001, 9). The making and use of devices of inquiry in the context of design experiments provides a way of realizing, through experience, what some of those consequences might be. As part of this practice, it is incumbent on designers, together with those they are collaborating with, to name and consider those consequences—this is a responsibility mandatory for an ethical practice of design experiments in civics.

Contributing to What Commons and Commoning Might Be

As I previously discussed, design experiments in civics are enmeshed with neoliberal logics. This was the case for the projects in the prior chapter that reimagined the stories of smart cities. This is also true for the projects in this chapter that reimagine the work of foraging. While we can talk of pushing back against technological citizenship, hyperrationalization, and market imperatives, we must also acknowledge that design experiments in civics operate within those conditions. Once again, these are the conditions of contemporary democratic inquiry. *Fruit Are Heavy* and *Fruit Are Here*— and the work of Concrete Jungle more generally—are not examples of a "commons against and beyond capitalism" (Caffentzis and Federici 2014). Concrete Jungle's commoning is woven together with the materialities, discourses, and practices of capital, the state, and technological innovation. But democratic conditions are not somehow devoid of entanglements. Our conditions of making and using always are compromised (Liboiron 2017).

When the state comes to rely on civil society, advocates, and activists to provide social services and care, there is reason for concern. This may signal an abdication of responsibility by the state, and practices of commoning may be exploited. Harvey (2012, 87) argues that this is not the death of commons, but that it does require new approaches to commoning. He states that it "requires a double-pronged political attack, through which the state is forced to supply more and more in the way of public goods for public purposes, along with the self-organizations of whole populations to appropriate, use, and supplement those goods in ways that extend and enhance the qualities of the non-commodified reproductive and environmental concerns." Such an approach recognizes the inevitability of interleaving institutions and makes use of their resources. At the same time, such an approach also contributes to a cultural and intellectual commons—another way of conceptualizing our collective imaginaries and practices.

The approaches suggested by Harvey can be glimpsed in these design experiments. Following from Harvey, one way to continue with these devices of inquiry would be to turn the insights from them into claims for resources. That is, the knowledge gleaned from design experiments can be the basis for requests made to the state. For instance, one might make use of *Fruit Are Heavy* as a real and immediate exemplar in support of claims for municipal Wi-Fi. With *Fruit Are Here*, we have seen appropriation and supplementation in action, using existing commercial mapping and data platforms in unintended ways, as tools for the commons and employed toward commoning. Such a move is an example of using the goods of the state and corporations—satellites, software, databases, APIs, and interfaces—toward commoning. Such everyday assemblages can act in ways that individuals or technologies alone might not. This, in turn, leads to a greater awareness and appreciation of the hybridity of the commons in theory and practice. As Gibson-Graham, Cameron, and Healy (2016, 207) put it,

> The agent of change, the commoner, is no longer (and perhaps never was) a person or a category such as the working class but an assemblage. Certainly these assemblages include humans, but they also include non-humans; they may include class but also non-class alignments; they may include social movements and grass-roots organisations but also governments, institutions, and firms; they may include non-market mechanisms but also markets; they may include animate beings who have nothing in common except breathing and living, but also inanimate entities that share an existence on this planet.

Stepping back from the immediacy of foraging as a practice of commoning, we might also cast endeavors of designing in *Fruit Are Heavy* and *Fruit Are Here* as contributing to cultural and intellectual commons. This approach opens an even more expansive notion of commoning, and of designing as a way to contribute to diverse civic imaginaries and practices. Drawing from Hardt and Negri (2009, 350), the field of cultural and intellectual commons "is dynamic, involving both the product of labor and the means of future production. This common is not only the earth we share but also the languages we create, the social practices we establish, [and] the modes of sociality that define our relationship." In this space of the cultural and intellectual commons, the endeavor of designing to support the work of foraging as civics reimagines those "means of future production." In this case, those means are collaborative, collective, and oriented toward care. All the capacities of these artifacts and systems are conceived and made with the hope of enabling the work of foraging and enabling the work of providing fresh food to those in need. The cultural and intellectual commons are relational resources, shared for all to use in fomenting desire and action. Contributing to the cultural and intellectual commons is another way to consider how design contributes to the production of imaginaries that animate us toward democratic conditions.

Hardt and Negri (2009) talk about the creation of languages for these cultural and intellectual commons, akin to Gibson-Graham's (1996, 2006) need for new vocabularies to envision and describe diverse practices. Accompanying the languages and vocabularies of the cultural and intellectual commons, we designers might bring into the world devices of inquiry that contribute to our collective capacities to imagine, express, and trial possibilities. In the context of democratic inquiry, such devices become props in new collaborative practices and set the stage for more diverse democratic conditions and experiences. These props can also contribute to theoretical discourses. For instance, in developing a concept of "caring democracy," Tronto (2013) stops short of providing examples of how a caring democracy might manifest. This is perfectly reasonable; not everyone needs to design, and theory is itself a meaningful contribution. To such concepts we designers can contribute material and experiential things that allow us, collectively, to begin to express and explore how these theories and constructs might be lived out. As many designers and design theorists remind us, the commons and commoning are socio-material practices; they involve making (e.g., Marttila, Botero, and Saad-Sulonen 2014; Seravalli 2014). What the commons and commoning are and might be is open to ongoing interpretation, adjustment, and change. This line of thinking and doing inquiry extends to civics and democratic conditions more broadly because the democratic experience is constantly undergoing making, unmaking, and remaking.

Design Appendix

Fruit Are Heavy

Design Concept: Tom Jenkins, Craig Durkin, and Carl DiSalvo

Design Lead: Tom Jenkins
Design of sensing platform, including custom electronics. Field deployment and testing of sensing platform in collaboration with Craig Durkin.

Engineering Design: Craig Durkin
Consulting on issues related to the engineering of the sensing platform, including power and connectivity. Consulting on use. Field deployment in collaboration with Tom Jenkins.

Product Design: Catherine Meeschia
Concept, design, and production of housing for sensing platform (the backpack).

Service Design: Natalie Larkins
Development of touchpoints and volunteer journeys to describe and support foraging with the sensing platform.

Design Documentation: Sean Mackey
Photo documentation of sensor platform, housing, and deployments.

Fruit Are Here

Design Concept: Karl Kim, Craig Durkin, and Carl DiSalvo

Design Lead: Karl Kim
Design of mapping platform. Field deployment and testing of mapping platform in collaboration with Craig Durkin and Katherine Kennedy.

Engineering Design: Craig Durkin
Consulting on issues related to the software engineering of the mapping platform, including database structure and strategies for display. Consulting on use. Field deployment in collaboration with Karl Kim.

Service Design: Natalie Larkins
Development of touchpoints and volunteer journeys to describe and support foraging with the mapping platform.

In addition: Early research into designs for foraging, not reported on in this chapter but that influenced *Fruit Are Here* and *Fruit Are Heavy*, was conducted by Beth Schechter, Caroline Foster, and Tasmia Alam.

4 Institutions

It's a Thursday afternoon in late April, and we're meeting Les at the Promise Center to canvass his neighborhood again. Two high school students will be joining us, similar to the last few weeks. They're part of a credit-recovery program in which they're required to make up school credits to graduate, and volunteering is one way to do so. When Les heard about the credit-recovery program, he seized the opportunity to recruit residents who could help with data collection. It was a way for him to build his "Block by Block" initiative while helping neighborhood students.

There are five of us canvassing today: Les, students Kevin and Tanya, and Amanda and me from the university. Les has charted a route out the door of the Promise Center that circles a few blocks. Along the route there are houses, apartment buildings, several lots, and a warehouse. Kevin and Tanya each carry a small tablet computer. As Les, Amanda, and I head down the first street, he asks Kevin and Tanya to go a few houses ahead, one on each side of the street, looking for code violations. Les knocks on the door of the first house on the street. He's talked to the woman who lives there once or twice before.

"Hi, do you remember me? I'm Les. I asked you about your neighbors a while back—the ones staying in that house. Remember? Are they still there? Are people still staying in that house?" Les points to a boarded-up house across the street. Looking closely, a board on one of the first-floor windows on the side of the house is missing. There's a crate pushed against the wall underneath it. The front porch is littered with bags from a nearby fast-food restaurant.

"Yes, they're still there, I see 'em at night," she says.

"Are they bothering you?" asks Les.

"No, not really," she replies.

"Okay, you let me know if they start becoming a bother." Les wishes her a good day before he walks back down to the street. After we start walking, Les makes it clear that this conversation won't be part of the official record. "We're not going to record that," Les tells me. "I'll remember, but no one needs to know about that if they aren't being a bother."

A few doors down the street, Kevin has stopped in front of an abandoned apartment building. The structure appears solid, but its lot is overgrown and its walls are covered with graffiti. "It's been like this for a while," Kevin says. He lives nearby, so he would know. Using the tablet, he takes a picture of the front of the building, and then he opens the app. A series of checkboxes appear, which he begins ticking: Abandoned, check. Overgrown, check. "I can't see the address . . . what's the address of this apartment?" he calls out.

Amanda walks over to help. She opens her phone and navigates to Google Maps to get their position. Then she opens a parcel map from the city of Atlanta in another browser tab, and searches for the street address of the parcel. Once Amanda finds it, Kevin enters the correct address into the form on the tablet. I jot down a note about the difficulty of finding addresses. There are as many abandoned buildings and vacant lots as those that are occupied. Many house numbers have fallen off or are worn away. And, of course, vacant lots don't have houses or mailboxes to attach numbers to. Missing information is just one factor that makes collecting this data difficult.

Around the corner there's an older man sleeping on the front porch of another boarded-up house. Les says, "Don't mark this house down either," as the five of us walk over to the older man and start chatting with him. "So, seeing anything? Seeing any rats?" asks Les.

"Rats, yes, I see rats. There're rats everywhere. There're rats in there," the older man says, pointing to a trash-strewn lot across the street. "There're rats that come out of that basement," he says, pointing to the boarded-up house next door, "and then there're rats going in and out of that sewer all day and night. There're rats everywhere."

"Mark down that lot and that house," Les says, pointing at the lot filled with trash and the vacant house next door. Tanya marks down the vacant house, while Kevin notes the lot filled with debris. Looking at the addresses of occupied houses on either side of the lot, Kevin figures out the lot's address. We thank the man for the information and keep walking (see figure 4.1).

We've canvassed six streets, logging twelve code violations and five rat sightings, before returning to the Promise Center an hour and a half later.

Figure 4.1
Collecting data on code violations in the neighborhood.

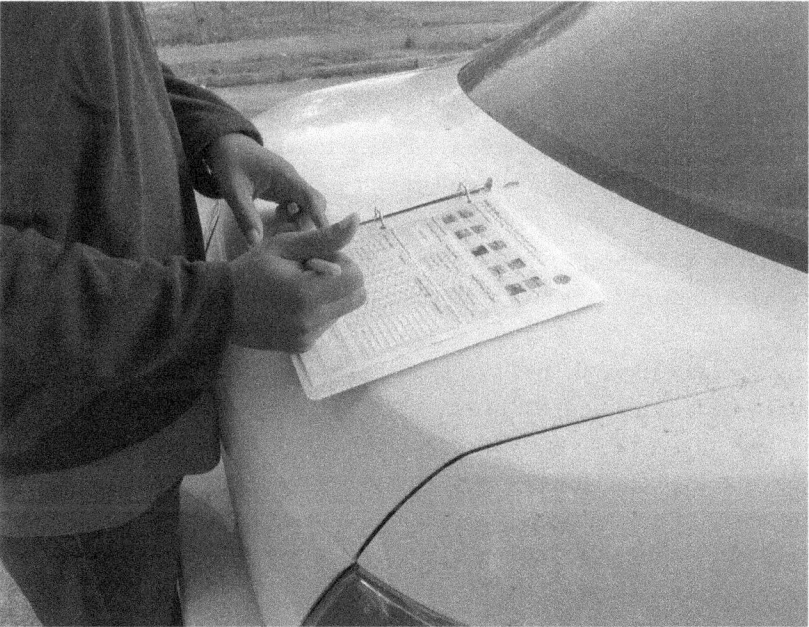

Figure 4.2
Marking out streets where we've collected data on code violations.

Kevin and Tanya are tired and hand over their tablets. Next week we'll review the data together. Today has demanded enough effort just to collect the data. Les pulls out a rolled-up map from behind his desk and spreads it out on a table. With a highlighter, he marks the streets we covered today. Each week, as he and the volunteers collect more data, Les can highlight more streets (see figure 4.2).

Amanda and I return the tablets to the university to recharge them for next week's data collection. Tomorrow we'll copy the data from the app to a spreadsheet, adding twelve rows, one for each code violation collected. But our work won't yet be done. We'll still need to match the photos with each spreadsheet entry. Matching the photos to the records takes time, since our tool doesn't automatically geocode photos or allow us to upload them in the field. Once the data has been wrangled, we'll compare it to the database of code violations maintained by the city of Atlanta. Then we can see which violations we found were already known by the city. Comparing the data sets will also take work, because the structure of the city of Atlanta's public database inhibits us from automating the process. There will also be a chance that the city's data isn't up to date, or that some of the code violations have already been resolved. Our hope is that we'll soon have enough code violations to convince a code enforcement officer to meet to discuss how to process these violations and increase attention to neighborhood issues.

In this chapter, I discuss how designing tools and processes for data collection offers a way to explore and shape institutional relations between residents and city government. The *Careful Coding* project, an ongoing collaboration with Les and his organization, Block by Block, uses data to draw attention and bring resources to his neighborhood, while attempting to retain the collective agency of residents in determining what gets acted upon. I argue that this work is a kind of institutioning—coupling dialogic and material practices in civic processes and politics. Institutioning puts the explorations of diverse subjectivities and devices of inquiry discussed in previous chapters into situated and ongoing practice. These activities are not only rehearsals of what might be, they are experiments in real time, enacted through the work of on-the-ground data collection, meetings with government officials, and conversations with and among residents, municipal workers, and designers. As such, they demonstrate the importance of lived experience to democracy, particularly as espoused by feminist pragmatists (Addams [1910] 1990; McKenna 2001; Seigfried 1999). This work of democratic inquiry develops through a series of encounters, in which we collaboratively probe configurations of action and authority within, across, and between institutions, thereby contributing to diverse civic imaginaries and practices.

Institutioning brings design into the world of municipal policy and procedures, and this requires understanding institutions. If, as part of the work of democratic inquiry, designers want to experiment with relations between civic constituencies, we should understand the cultures and procedures of institutions—"the rules of the game" (North 1990). If we do not understand those rules, we risk engaging in the most selfish sort of play—casually participating in a contest that matters deeply for others.

Careful Coding

Careful Coding is a community-based project where designers work with residents to collect, manage, and share data on code violations in their neighborhood. Such violations include overgrown lots, trash, squatters, and rodent infestations. In Atlanta, code violations are handled by the Code Enforcement Section of the Atlanta Police Department. Placing code violations within the police department means that enforcement tends to emphasize reporting and responding to violations that most directly affect public safety. There are multiple regulations that guide how a code violation might be reported and acted upon. These include the Atlanta Housing Code, the Graffiti Ordinance, and the Commercial Maintenance and Industrial Code.

Code infractions are often the result of underlying issues. Absentee or delinquent owners and landlords are a common problem, for example. Empty lots become overgrown and used for dumping tires when the owner is negligent or complicit. Occupied buildings with rodent infestations and open roofs tend to persist when landlords don't maintain the property. These situations can fester, due to even deeper structural inequalities. Like many cities in the United States, multiple neighborhoods in Atlanta suffer from the long-term systemic neglect characteristic of endemic racism and classism. Abusive financial practices have enabled properties to be purchased based on financial speculation and left to rot in anticipation of rising real estate value. One reason to document and track code violations is to hold absentee and negligent landlords accountable. Data ostensibly helps residents request action from a city government tasked with addressing issues of safety and well-being.

Yet, documenting and tracking code violations is a form of surveillance. Methodically observing and inspecting a neighborhood or community of people, particularly a Black neighborhood, is deeply problematic due to the ongoing oppression and abuses brought about by the surveillance of Black and Brown peoples and the ways data can amplify that oppression and those abuses (Benjamin 2019; Browne 2015; Crooks and Currie 2021; Milner 2020). The fact that code enforcement is part of the police department adds an additional layer of complexity, given the history of oppression and abuse by police in communities of color. Furthermore, the correlation of environmental factors with social phenomena can lead to racist policies. Consider broken-window policing, which justifies enforcing minor infractions in communities of color (Harcourt 2009). This policing method is driven by the idea that minor maintenance problems in a neighborhood promote criminal behavior. Such logics neglects more community-engaged strategies. It is a challenge to consider how practices of collecting and sharing data on code violations might be infused with care.

A code violation is like a traffic ticket for an infraction against regulations of the built environment. When a code enforcement officer observes a code violation, such as a house with a collapsed roof, they write a citation. If there is a structure present, the officer affixes a code violation sticker to the front door to notify the owners and area residents that a citation has been issued. Once the citation has been issued, the owner of the property receives a summons to court. In court, the conditions of the structure or lot are discussed and the owner may be fined and required to remedy the violation, depending on the circumstances. Locating the owner is not always an easy task due to incomplete records or discrepancies in records. These difficulties are exacerbated when dealing with holding companies or other legal and corporate configurations of ownership often used for real estate investing. Even when the owner is located, there is no guarantee they will appear in court. It is not uncommon for violations to accrue, leading to properties deteriorating.

In cities like Atlanta there are more reports from residents about violations than there are officers to field them. This disparity has spurred efforts to encourage residents to directly report issues to the city, either by calling or sending an email to the Code Enforcement Section or by using the city's

311 system (a system for reporting nonemergency events to city government). Once a resident's report is logged, if it is deemed to fall within the various categories of code violations, an officer is sent to investigate. In the best of cases, code enforcement officers develop relationships with neighborhood organizations and residents over time, and they work together to document issues to be improved in the built environment.

The *Careful Coding* project grew from our ongoing collaborations in the neighborhood. Les, a middle-aged Black man, works as a counselor for a local nonprofit for youth and families. For some time, Les had been collecting data about his neighborhood and trying to organize residents to take action, such as cleaning up lots and reporting broken infrastructure to the city. As we began working with Les, we came up with the name *Careful Coding* to provide an umbrella to our collective efforts. We wanted to call attention to the aspect of this work that was most distinctive—that the work was performed with care. Collecting data is not Les's day job. However, his day job provides him with the flexibility and opportunity to work on *Careful Coding*. The nonprofit where he works has an office in the English Avenue neighborhood where he lives, which is also where he's collecting data.

English Avenue is a historically Black neighborhood in Atlanta, long known for its activism. It has also suffered from the massive withdrawal of resources that occurred in the 1960s. Decades later, many houses, apartment buildings, and lots remain vacant. At the same time, English Avenue has a strong working- and middle-class community that supports a vibrant neighborhood culture of churches, neighborhood associations, community gardens, and small businesses. This is a neighborhood to be celebrated. Disturbingly, gentrification is now encroaching, bringing more affluent white people back. After decades of being overlooked, real estate investors have started speculating in English Avenue and nearby neighborhoods. Long-time residents are concerned about displacement.

Atlanta is similar to many cities; the municipality is investing in databases and data-driven platforms. Increasingly, data services are used by government agencies to streamline their work and structure new relations with residents. Some of these systems are sophisticated, employing machine learning and "big data" to derive insights and direct action. Other systems are simpler. The catchphrase "There's an app for that!" has become a punchline that applies to all aspects of governance. Want to contact your councilmember, sign a petition, or report a pothole? There's an app for that! SeeClickFix is the canonical example of a "civic tech" app that lets residents report on local conditions, which are then routed through municipal government and attended to (Berkowitz and Gagnon 2017; O'Brien et al. 2017). The ubiquity of these systems and the use of data becomes a conundrum. While these systems and their data tend to reinforce and reproduce existing hegemonies and their institutions, for neighborhood residents, advocacy groups, and activists, having data is also increasingly necessary to influence government officials: they use it to contest policies, drive new practices, and campaign for action (Schrock 2016).

But data as an end unto itself has not been Les's motivation; his interest in data is more pragmatic. Data is an evidentiary currency, documenting a set of conditions in a form that can be used to broker attention and resources. He wants his neighbors' homes and their surroundings to be safer. Les would like to hold absentee landlords and negligent owners accountable and make them tend to the properties they manage. If Les wants to campaign for better living conditions for his neighbors, data can influence stakeholders to change how they operate. Les also wants the city to do its jobs regularly, by cleaning lots and fixing broken sewers. At the same time, Les wants to promote a shared understanding and acceptance of the precarity of his neighborhood's residents. He is aware that for some people, being served a citation could start a chain of harmful, compounding consequences. They would have to go to court and pay a fine. If they couldn't pay it, the fine would likely increase, and they would have to go to court again. And perhaps again. Sometimes the conditions that cause a violation can be addressed among neighbors, given the chance. As reasonable as Les's stance might seem, it's complicated to both care for residents and track conditions in the built environment. City government works by way of formal procedures. Technocratic systems and policies that use data tend to enforce formal procedures and rules with little sympathy for neighborhood context and lived experience.

Given the significance of data in civic contexts, it should come as no surprise that there are many tools available to help residents collect and analyze data. A more complex challenge is how to align data processes and practices across organizations, institutions, cultures, and communities. This requires the imagination and trialing of modes of engagement between civic constituencies that characterize design experiments in civics. Recalling Jasanoff and Kim (2009, 120), civic imaginaries are "collectively imagined forms of social life and social order reflected in the design and fulfillment of nation-specific scientific and/or technological projects." But projects like *Careful Coding* differ from Jasanoff and Kim's level of analysis; they don't involve the whole nation, only a neighborhood. Such projects are not an examination of democracy in the abstract, but rather an examination of the lived experiences of democracy. These imaginaries, then, are not speculative. These imaginaries unfold through situated practices of doing, through ongoing practice. Increasingly, data is a medium through which such doing occurs. But while these modes of engagement between civic constituencies depend upon and are mediated by data, they are more than data alone. For these engagements to come into being and cohere, relationships need to be established and sustained.

Design as a Relational Practice

The idea of design as a relational practice—that is, a practice that is social in character and contributes to shaping associations—is not new, but it is receiving renewed attention (Agid and Chin 2019; Blauvelt 2008; Montuori et al. 2019). The questions of how design activities and outcomes contribute to forms of organization and collective action can be vexing, because historically the practices and discourses of design have focused on individuals and small-group interactions. As design meets the civic realms of law, policy, and government, there is a need to refigure activities and theories of design (Crivellaro et al. 2019; Del Gaudio, Franzato, and de Oliveira 2016). After all, these experiments are woven into fabrics of residents, communities, corporations, and government agencies that include but also exceed individuals and small groups. Considering design as a relational practice also affects how we understand our roles and actions as designers, in concert with those we partner with. As Shana Agid and Elizabeth Chin (2019, 81) describe this relationality, "Designers do not produce value by *creating* or *instigating* political or social change as outsiders, we do with others through joining in, when invited, and finding our way." In the civic context, we are often "joining in" with established institutions, and their cultures and practices. One useful line of thinking comes from discourses and practices of participatory design: How do "democratic design experiments in the small" engage the "in the large" contexts they are situated within? (Binder et al. 2015; Huybrechts, Benesch, and Geib 2017b). This line of thinking begins with commitments to individuals and groups, and then swells to develop an appreciation of how design contributes to existing and ongoing assemblages of meaning and action.

The term "publics" has guided some conversations about how design might gather and cohere diverse constituencies (DiSalvo 2009; Le Dantec 2016; Lindström & Ståhl 2014; Venturini et al. 2015). In much of this work, designers are informed by the work of John Dewey (1927) and inspired by his description of why people organize: publics are formed by those who are concerned about an issue and its consequences. In contrast to notions of a "public sphere," there is not a single unified and generic public. Rather, a plethora of publics constantly form and dissipate in relation to issues. A public, then, is a distinctive form of organization because it is issue-oriented, temporary, and contingent. Through various tactics and practices of making, designers can bring together those affected by an issue and produce resources for taking action on that issue. Those resources—and the practices of their making and use—are occasions for infrastructuring.

Infrastructuring refers to processes of making supports and connections that enable future action. In her groundbreaking work on infrastructure, Susan Leigh Star (1999) explains that infrastructure is more than technical components. To her, infrastructure is inextricably social and involves ongoing coordination work. Like infrastructure, processes of infrastructuring collapse distinctions between the technical and the social. Infrastructuring involves changing arrangements of assets and means, both human and nonhuman actors. One way to think about infrastructuring is in relation to prototyping. If prototyping creates sample artifacts to learn from through making and use, infrastructuring assembles collections of resources for ongoing learning through making and use. Some of these resources are prototypes—bespoke made things. Others are already existing artifacts and systems enrolled into the collection of resources. The ongoing and layered quality of infrastructuring opens the ability to establish assets and means for participation over time and across sites. As such, infrastructuring is more than simply prototyping at a different scale. Infrastructuring is making with the purpose of enabling future action. "Infrastructuring, then, is the work of creating socio-technical resources that intentionally enable adoption and appropriation beyond the initial scope of the design, a process that might include participants not present during the initial design" (Le Dantec and DiSalvo 2013). What is put in place through infrastructuring is used by those who might not be traditionally considered in design processes, and who may not even call themselves designers.

Concepts of publics and infrastructuring have been developed in relation to projects that tend to exist "in the small": local, lived conditions of workers and residents. But there is often a mismatch between the grassroots and the government, which challenges moving from the micro to the meso (or macro) scale of politics. Liesbeth Huybrechts, Henric Benesch, and Jon Geib (2017b) offer the term "institutioning" to sensitize designers involved in micro-scale politics to the broader contexts of their work. Institutioning delineates a practice of design that works within and with institutions. They use the term "institution" to encompass an assortment of structures, procedures, and cultures. In other words, institutioning is a shorthand for a swath of activities, "a practice of navigating in a structured yet highly porous institutional landscape, through attentiveness to dependencies but also by canalising synergies and serendipities. It involves a practice of interweaving between—as well as producing—various insides and outsides in participatory processes, by consolidating and challenging existing institutional frames as well as forming new ones" (Huybrechts, Benesch, and Geib 2017b, 158).

The concept of institutioning, then, expands the perspective of design to relations between organizations and collective action. Whereas "infrastructuring" is a label for practices and materialities that supported participation over time within publics, "institutioning" is a label for practices and materialities that construct and align associations extending beyond what we commonly consider a public (Dixon 2018).

Huybrechts and her colleagues' focus is on institutional frames. In this chapter, I expand their concept and practice of institutioning to include a range of activities and outcomes. Institutioning suggests that designers should consider how institutions might be sites and means of making, unmaking, and remaking. The concept of institutioning is compelling because design experiments in civics work across an array of settings: nonprofits, municipal agencies, local, state, and federal programs, small businesses, multinational corporations, universities, and the courts. The structures, procedures, and cultures of these settings profoundly matter. But what does this institutioning look like in practice? How do these endeavors of making synergies and serendipities, of interweaving and producing insides and outsides, actually happen? How should we appreciate these efforts? Answering these questions will produce the descriptions needed to understand institutioning as a relational design practice and to begin to meet the ethical and political importance of understanding institutions. Institutioning also helps designers perceive and value organizational, policy, and legal contexts not as an inscrutable tangle of knots but as replete with possibilities.

Returning to *Careful Coding*, it is both a civic data project and a project exploring civic relations as they are made possible by data. It explores the making and use of data for local advocacy, taking up Yanni Loukissas's charge that "all data are local" (2019) and probing the qualities, potentials, and limitations of data in a particular setting. That making and use works, in turn, as a design practice concerned with imagining and instantiating different probative associations between civic institutions. In this project, artifacts and systems are made with residents who assert their values and desires through the collection of data, in dialogue with the practices of municipal workers and governmental structures and processes. Through institutioning, data becomes a medium for cultivating relations. It enables people to create synergies and serendipities for weaving between and together new insides and outsides through participatory processes. The *Careful Coding* project thus straddles the worlds it is engaging with and tentatively composing; it is both a grassroots effort led by residents to address pressing issues and a project through which we collaboratively explore how we might affect our civic institutions.

Designing for Data Collection and Interpretation

Les had been tracking various issues in the neighborhood for over a year before we met and started working together. He mostly documented problems with neglected and abandoned buildings and lots. He also tracked the conditions of the streets and sidewalks. When there was a stream of water down the street for over a week, Les knew there was a water main break or a clogged sewer somewhere nearby. He found the source of the water and contacted the Code Enforcement Section, which arranged for the Office of Watershed Management to fix it. Les also kept track of what changed for the better when problems were fixed or resolved. He called his effort the Block by Block initiative because he wanted to create an organization that improved the living conditions for himself and his neighbors one block at a time.

Dr. Amanda Meng and I had been working with another community organization in this same neighborhood for several years. After Les saw Amanda present another data project in the neighborhood, Les approached her about collecting code violations together. Together, Les, Amanda, and I started *Careful Coding*, a project that attempted to use data to mediate and enact new political relations in Les's neighborhood. Over time, Les's desire to track code violations expanded into enabling strategic encounters among researchers, residents, and city employees. Throughout the course of the project, we collaborated with Les to develop and use a series of processes and tools for collecting, wrangling, and sharing the data. Because it never received direct funding, supporting this work has always been difficult. It has involved making time, finding resources, and maintaining commitments to each other, unbound by a formal research proposal or defined deliverables. As I will later discuss, situating *Careful Coding* in relation to the university let us leverage the standing of the university as a tactic for engagement with city government. Altogether, the relational character of this project—based in commitments rather than organizational obligations—made it both distinctive and challenging.

One distinctive aspect of the *Careful Coding* project is that it had no final version of its data set, processes, and tools. Neither is there a clear sequence of iterations from one prototype to the next. In these ways, the project is in tension with familiar models of design, which usually presume an end in product or service development. However, as Paul Dourish and colleagues (2020) describe, some of these tried-and-true design processes, such as prototyping and iteration, may be at odds with the practices and needs of communities. Instead of following a formal design process (whatever that might be), this work develops along a more meandering path, led by Les and through ongoing interactions with other residents, code enforcement officers, and city council members. These interactions affect Les's aims and tactics, which in turn affect our collaborative data collection, management, and sharing; this inquiry involves a continually shifting set of orientations and alignments that continually reconfigure the civic environment. Throughout this work, the design experiment was made possible by and through—but not beholden to—the making and use of ad hoc data processes and tools, a process Helena Karasti and Karen Baker (2008) characterize as "growing one's own infrastructure."

Initially, the functionality of the tablet-based application supported residents collecting and tracking code violations over time. They needed the ability to mark a point in space, assign a series of attributes to that point, and then link a date to those attributes. In other words, what was needed was a spreadsheet, and what was useful for generating the data for that spreadsheet was a map. Technically, the app was not complicated to assemble. It was the social life of data that kept the work from being simple. First, to be useful by government, the data needed to match the city's data structures and categories they used to label infractions. Second, assigning a code violation to a geographic point was not always easy. As described at the start of this chapter, often while trying to record a violation in the neighborhood there were no addresses to be seen. It matters whether a potential violation is marked at 235 or 237 or 239 Sunset Avenue. Third, the app needed to be accessible to users with varying levels of technological skill. Finally, the app needed to be cheap. There was no dedicated budget to put toward purchasing and maintaining data collection tools for residents. For this reason, we erred toward tools and processes that would be robust even in the absence of a dedicated budget for technology. It was also crucial that our tools and processes be seen as legitimate. City employees and public officials needed to see our tools and processes as sophisticated enough to accept the data we collected, or at least not to dismiss our efforts out of hand.

Taken together, these requirements and conditions made realizing the base functionality more difficult than we expected. In our early efforts, we surveyed available off-the-shelf tools and decided on an application called SW Maps. The essential feature of this tool was its map interface. The user clicked on the map to add a point at that location, then filled in a description of the code violations in a text box and pressed Save. The record was saved to a local file on the tablet, which could be transferred off the tablet and into a spreadsheet. In general, SW Maps worked well for data collection in the field. However, it created a significant amount of data wrangling work when returning from the field. Code violations were manually input into a text entry box, and rather than listing specific violations such as "Collapsed Roof," "Burned Structure," and "Excessive Trash," it was easier to just code the structure as "Abandoned." As we later discovered, this convenience elided important distinctions between the various houses and lots.

The photos presented another problem. It was easy enough to switch from the SW Maps app to the camera app and take a photo of each site that was later reunited with the data. But the default naming convention for the photos did not reference any location. Instead, we had to retrospectively inspect the metadata for each photo, which contained the latitude and longitude of a location. Then we entered those coordinates into an online tool for reverse geo-coding (looking up a street address from latitude and longitude coordinates). This data work was tedious, so we were eager to find a way to streamline the workflow. During the summer of 2017, we had the opportunity to collaborate with our colleague, Dr. Ellen Zegura, through a National Science Foundation program for Civic Data Science that provided research experiences for undergraduates. Through this program we worked with a student named Michael Koolhang to try to solve the problem of locating the images taken during data collection. He created a script that automated the reverse-geocoding process and saved each photograph with a new name that included the street address. When attempting to match the photos with address records, however, we discovered a glitch that stemmed from the embodied experience of data collection. When taking a photograph of a house or lot, you were not actually standing at *that* location. In order to capture the full view, you would likely stand in the middle of the street or even across the street. Consequently, the address returned from the coordinates was often the address of a house across the street from the photograph. To correct this error, we looked at each photo and compared it to photos from Google Street View—an imprecise reference based on freely available tools. The process of producing a data record was inescapably messy and relied on a bricolage of tools, platforms, residents, and designers.

From Digital to Paper and Back Again

After several months of using SW Maps, a second iteration of the tools explored making the data collection nondigital. Master's students Qing Tian and Nick Tippens prototyped a paper form containing all of the information needed to document a house, building, or lot. Working in collaboration with Les, we thought a paper form would provide prompts and structures for more code violation detail. A form version would also enable volunteers to mark a violation as resolved. This feature was not present in SW Maps, and it would help Les track successful outcomes. Les also thought that he could distribute the paper forms at neighborhood events. Residents could fill out the forms, and then the sites could be checked after the fact, broadening participation in data collection. The only digital aspect the paper version retained was digitally photographing the sites. Of course, a paper form version added to the work of transcribing data into a spreadsheet.

The paper tool did not last long. More time went into its design than its use. Despite everyone's initial enthusiasm, it proved awkward when taken out into the neighborhood. This was not a case of overdesigning a tool, as so often happens. The paper tool was simple and well designed, developed with the active involvement of Les. But when taken out and used over multiple data collections, the sheets of paper became difficult to keep track of over time. And the number of volunteers working with Les remained at a handful—a number small enough to obviate the need for tools that could be widely distributed. The paper tool served a crucial role, though; it prompted a request for a form-like digital tool, rather than the map interface of SW Maps. This led to the design of another app-based data collection tool that took the structured recording of the paper form and put it onto a tablet as a sparse digital form with checkboxes.

We continued to collect and wrangle data throughout the process of designing tools. After each round of data collection, Amanda would bring the tablets back to the university and download and process the data. We used the time between data collections to reflect on how to better support the process of data collection and interpretation. One notable complication was that Les did not want to share *all* of the data with the Code Enforcement Section. Les had always protected fellow residents and did not want people to get pulled into an endless cycle of court dates and fines. Certain things in the neighborhood he just wanted to let be, while working with neighbors to address more serious problems. In other words, Les did not want to become an extension of the state. He was well aware of how people would come into the neighborhood and make judgments about its residents. He knew how Black people and poor people were judged, and how quickly a citation might saddle them with bureaucratic headaches, or worse. Yet he saw the value in documenting neighborhood violations so he and his neighbors could keep track of trends over time (Meng, DiSalvo, and Zegura 2019).

As often as possible, we would accompany Les in the field. And even when we couldn't, we were still actively involved in making the data workable, both in terms of providing the labor of data wrangling and of contributing data to the set that would, ostensibly, add to its value by associating it with city data. In this way, we were functioning as data intermediaries that were also institutional intermediaries. We were constructing connections between the data sets maintained by the city and the data collected by Block by Block. We would meet with Les to discuss the data set as it was developing, and he would share information. ("That wall that was falling onto the sidewalk has been fixed. The squatters have moved from English Avenue to North Avenue.") We would then share what we had learned from our reviews of the city's data ("It seems none of the violations on Jett Street are known to the city, but all the violations on North Avenue are included in their databases"). These regular check-ins would influence the selection of the next set of streets to walk and what data needed to be collected.

Over the next two years, we continued developing different processes and tools. Together with Les, we continued to reflect on our ongoing experiences in data collection and wrangling. A subsequent hybrid version of the tool consisted of a web-based form, two commercial Wi-Fi hotspots donated by another colleague at the university, and a paper map that was affixed to the back of the tablet. When out collecting data, a user would open the web form, then fill out information about an address, including its code violations, with a simple series of short entry fields, checkboxes, and menus. Finally, using a checkbox, they would select whether or not this particular entry should be shared with Code Enforcement or kept private to Block by Block (Meng, DiSalvo, and Zegura 2019). The paper map attached to the back of the tablet was an attempt to merge the functionality of an application with a built-in map. This map divided the neighborhood by blocks, and each sheet had map views with corresponding addresses taken from the county tax records. If an address was not readily apparent from the street, the user could consult the paper map (see figures 4.3 and 4.4).

The web-based form also addressed the ongoing challenge of associating images of locations with data. The user would shift out of the browser to the camera app and take a photo. Then they'd go back to the browser, attach the photo, and press Submit. The form uploaded the photo and automatically tagged it with the correct address and the associated code violations. As with our foraging work described in the previous chapter, connectivity was a persistent issue. The solution for *Careful Coding* was mobile hotspots.

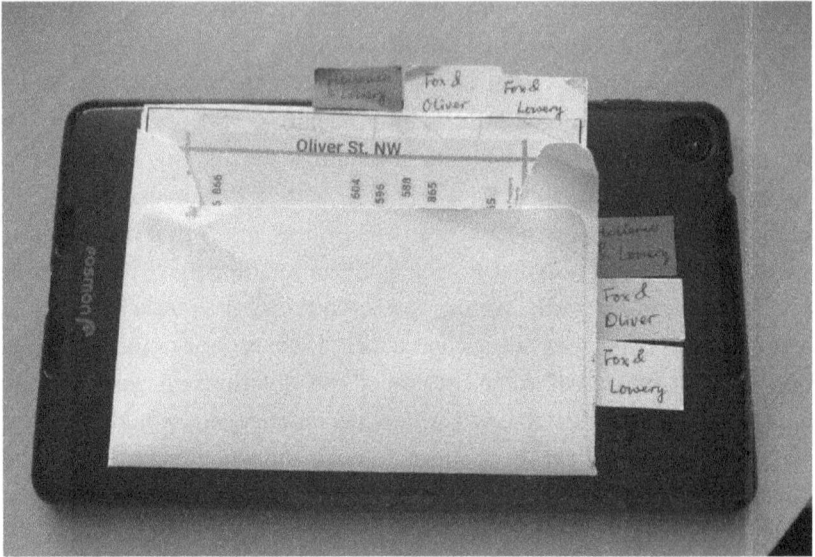

Figure 4.3
Paper maps affixed to the back of a tablet.

Figure 4.4
Using the tablet and paper maps to collect data.

The only challenge was that the user, when pressing Submit, had to be close enough to the hotspot to have network access. At times, this required a bit of back-and-forth on the street to orchestrate our positions in relation to one another. One of us would record the information, then take and attach the photo. Then we would call the volunteer carrying the hotspot closer so when we hit Submit, the data would be sent.

Our experience with *Careful Coding* demonstrated how civic data projects are often a punctuated process of trialing tools and collecting and processing data. This process is further affected by changing conditions in the civic environment. Establishing and maintaining closer relations between residents and municipal offices and their services require more than processes and tools. Establishing relationships requires generating opportunities for cooperation. These opportunities are not always given; they often must be made. And working to make them is important because it is in those moments of cooperating when we could collaboratively explore and enact configurations of action and authority within, across, and between civic institutions. Like the devices of inquiry discussed in the prior chapter, tablets and paper forms are not the subject of the design experiment. These objects—both the tools and the data—provide the conditions with and through which institutioning and democratic inquiry unfold.

From Datafication to Institutioning

Putting data to work required that we shift from designing tools to staging encounters with city government workers. Such encounters trial and establish synergies, as well as points of contestation and resistance. One way that such encounters and the corresponding activities of institutioning unfold is through dialogic modes of making, including "democratic dialogues" (Huybrechts et al. 2016). As Huybrechts and colleagues discuss, these dialogues fit within traditions of participatory design as they are intended as opportunities to broaden participation in shaping discourse, with a recognition that discourse and action are coupled.

An important aspect of the democratic dialogue is that it also affects the role of the researcher, casting them as "a creator of space for dialogue and contestation and a contributor to retooling and learning" (Miettinen 2004, 105). As I will discuss, these democratic dialogues did indeed have an effect upon our activities and subjectivities as engaged designers.

When we first began working with Les, there was a code enforcement officer assigned to the English Avenue and Vine City neighborhoods. Les developed a friendly working relationship with him. They met regularly, and Les would share a list of code violations he had collected. Together, they would walk the streets to look at the addresses on that list. The officer noted them in his official record and spoke with Les about what action might be taken. However, after that officer retired, different code enforcement officers added English Avenue to their responsibilities. Les had fewer communications with these officers because they did not seem interested in the data he collected. Perhaps they were simply busy, since they were responsible for more neighborhoods. Spread thin, they had less time for English Avenue.

In conditions of limited resources, we thought code enforcement officers would find *Careful Coding*'s data especially valuable. Our hope was that it would help direct their attention and hasten responses. However, try as we might, we could not get the attention of field officers. At Les's request, we asked for a meeting with the Code Enforcement Section to share the data we had collected. The strategy was simple; perhaps if we could convince leadership in the Code Enforcement Section of the value of our collaborative work in the neighborhood, they might encourage (or even require) field officers to meet with us. We were hopeful that tactful advocacy would help us advance our cooperative effort to address code violations. Les asked that he not be present at this meeting because he believed we might have more leverage and achieve better results if the data was presented by university researchers alone. We were not comfortable with this request, but we understood and respected his reasoning. We saw his request as recognizing the relational expertise and authority (Dindler and Iversen 2014; Huybrechts et al. 2016) we were granted as faculty, staff, and students from a technical university. And so, Amanda and I reached out to leadership in the Code Enforcement Section.

With only the modest effort of sending a few emails, we successfully arranged a meeting. To prepare, we were asked to forward the data we collected, which we did. About a week later we sat down with a senior officer and four other members of the Code Enforcement Section. We were anxious. Here we were, on our own with data we had collected with Les and his volunteers over the past year. We knew this was a chance to share that work, but we also thought it would be met with skepticism. After all, there were enough code violations from these neighborhoods in the city's databases that city employees were well aware of the extent of infractions. They were also aware of the relationship between many of these violations and absentee and delinquent landlords. We weren't presenting data that provided insights they did not already have. Our hope was more modest. By sharing this data, we wanted to assist Les in accessing city resources to support his efforts. What would count as "support" was as simple as an agreement to send a code enforcement officer out to meet with him in the neighborhood, to review the data, and discuss future engagements. In other words, our hope was that this encounter would prompt another encounter, thereby creating a pathway for future cooperation.

We arrived at the Code Enforcement Section and were ushered into a conference room. Three of us were from the university, and five from code enforcement. As we passed around printed copies of the data we had collected and brought up a map on our laptop, we were met with the reactions we anticipated. There were several sighs, a few arched eyebrows. They expressed their respect for the university and appreciation for us reaching out to them. They seemed glad we didn't think we could do this on our own, and that we had respect for the city's expertise and roles. Still, a wariness accompanied the meeting. These city employees had seen these sorts of projects before, from both residents and university faculty; they knew they would see them again. They were doubtful and cautious. Projects such as these take up their time, and moreover, they often create more work for the already stretched municipal employees.

In this tense space, we had a surprisingly fruitful conversation about the possibility of a collaboration, though it might be more apt to characterize the conversation as a negotiation. We wanted them to recognize the legitimacy of the work and commit to join us in the field. It was recognition that we earned and a commitment that we received that day—albeit with effort. I began:

"Thanks for meeting with us today. We wanted to share this data with you and talk about how we might work together, with residents, around collecting code violations."

"We have most of this data" was the quick and curt reply.

"Okay, most of it, but not all of it?" I asked, hopeful.

"Most of it."

"But is the data you don't have useful?" I probed.

"Maybe. It could be. It depends on whether it's accurate," came the hesitant, tentative answer.

I pushed: "Okay, so, honestly, is this work we are doing useful to you at all? Can you do something with it, or is this just more work for you, an annoyance? If so, we get that. That's not what we are here for. Because if this isn't useful, then we should do something else, right?"

There was a pause and a smirk from two of the officers as they looked to the most senior officer to see how she would answer. And then I prodded, "What would make it useful?"

"You should meet with the officer who works those neighborhoods. We'll put you in touch. And you should meet with Councilperson X; they are interested in doing something similar in their neighborhood."

We thanked them for their time, and they expressed appreciation for us speaking with them, which they seemed to sincerely mean. The meeting ended with us receiving our desired invitation to meet with the code enforcement officer assigned to English Avenue. The offer to make an introduction to a councilperson was a welcome surprise, and a hint that perhaps they did not think this work was entirely useless. This encounter, this democratic dialogue, thus beget another yet to come, and the experiment in different configurations of action and authority continues.

In this encounter, we moved through a series of dialogic positions and tactics, as one way of doing institutioning. Over the course of this meeting, we were simultaneously engaged in what Huybrechts and colleagues (2016) refer to as committing dialogues and questioning dialogues. As a committing dialogue, we sought to create connections in the behind-the-scenes associations between code enforcement officers and residents by appealing to the standing and relations between the institutions of code enforcement and those of the university. As a questioning dialogue, we probed and pushed against the status quo of the singular authority of code enforcement officers tracking violations. We used the data as a strategic, evidentiary asset, demonstrating that it was possible to consider differ modes and practices of tracking code violations.

Not surprisingly, arranging a meeting with the code enforcement officer assigned to those neighborhoods took some time. Officers are busy, and this type of liaison work is not a priority. In the meantime, we continued to collect and wrangle data. Two months later, we received an email from a code enforcement officer that simply stated: "I'll meet you at 8:30 a.m. at 123 English Avenue next Wednesday." And that was that. We rearranged our schedules, printed out copies of the data we had collected to date, and looked forward to this next encounter. Then it was Wednesday.

Making It All Fit

It's about 8:15 a.m. when I arrive at 123 English Avenue. There's a new house being built at that address. It's sizable. I can't tell if it's a duplex or a single-family house. There are several vans parked on the street with their doors open, piled full of building materials. About a half-dozen workers move between the house and the back of the vans, carrying what appears to be ventilation equipment. I get out of the car and look around for Qing and Les. They aren't there yet. I'm early. The workers look at me suspiciously. Then Qing drives up and parks a few car lengths in front of me. As I walk up to greet her, she gets out and says, "There's Les." I turn around and Les is walking toward us. He looks at the construction and says, "This one's going up quick." His tone reflects his concern at yet another sign of impending gentrification.

A few minutes after 8:30, a sedan pulls up with a woman driving and a man in the passenger seat. They pull over and I walk up to them. She rolls down her window and I lean toward the car. "Hello, I'm from Georgia Tech. Are you from code enforcement?" I ask.

"Yes," she replies.

"Okay, should we get in the car?" I ask.

"Absolutely not," she says, firmly. "This is a city car, you can't ride in this."

She parks and they get out. Introductions are made as she stares at the house being built. I've brought printouts of the code violations that we've collected together, organized by street, and cross-referenced with the city database. We're excited to finally share these, so I offer them to her. She holds up her hands and takes two steps back, saying, "I'm not taking those, that's not what today is about."

I mutter, "Okay," taken aback and frankly frustrated.

"Today we walk and talk—I don't need those." She looks at the house again. "I wanted you to meet me here because I wanted to talk to you about this house. Well, the house that was here—it had all sorts of problems. But they got ahead of me. In my list, that house is still here."

Clearly, she's already a bit frustrated herself. I fold up the printouts of the code violations and stuff them in my coat pocket. She starts walking and we tentatively follow. As our group walks down the street, we explain a bit of what we are doing with Les, and Les explains his motivations. She nods, seemingly listening to us while also paying attention to other things. She's got two phones that buzz insistently, and she constantly moves them in and out of her pockets to look at them. We get to a house several houses down the street, and she looks up. "Go get the stickers from the car," she says to her partner, who walks back to the car. She starts pointing out all of the things wrong with the house in front of us. "Overgrown, taller than your waist. Roof collapsing. It looks like there may have been a fire at some point, you can see the back is all wrong. It looks burned and never repaired. There's open windows along the front and sides."

Her partner comes back with a sticker the size of a magazine. She tells him to go down the side of the house to look at the back. Les takes a step to follow him and she says firmly, "No, don't you do that, you stay there." Her partner goes back and hollers that it looks like there's been a fire, and there are more open windows. We take a picture with our phone and ask if she wants it. "Why would I want it?" she asks.

"Can't you use it?" I respond.

"No, I can only use the pictures I take, with this phone—my city phone," she says, holding up one of the two phones she's carrying. She goes on to explain, "Photos are evidence. If you take a photo and send it to me, and the city takes the owner to court, the only way that photo can be used is if you show up in court too and verify it. And then you're going to get cross-examined. And likely you won't show up anyway, but if you do, you better not have anything against you, because if you do, that photo will just get thrown out."

She can't use any photos she didn't take with her city phone. That's how the evidence stays evidence. I wince at the thought of all the photos we collected, and the work we've done to associate those photos with data about infractions. She gestures to the front porch, and her partner puts the sticker on the front door. She explains that the sticker means no one is allowed on this property until they come down to city hall to sort things out. She'll file the report when she's back in the car. We keep walking. Both of her phones keep vibrating. One of the phones suddenly rings, and she walks away to take the call. A few minutes later she returns and explains that one of the phones is her city phone and the other is her own phone, but she uses her own phone for work too. If you contact her through the city phone she'll get to it, but it takes a while as she fields all the calls in order, and there are a lot of calls. But if you call or text her personal phone you will get through to her more quickly; there are fewer calls or texts to that phone. We nod and continue to walk with her.

We ask what our group can do to have these code violations addressed. She explains that she can only cite the owner, since she's not a judge. "My job is to make a decision if something crosses a line and should go to court. That's all."

"So, what about the violations we've collected?" I ask.

She replies, "If you want to be doing things, you need to look things up. A lot of what you want to tell us is in there already [referring to the city database]. And if it's in there, it's just more work for me. You also need to be sure you get it right. And it needs to matter. Safety matters. If it just doesn't look pretty, that doesn't matter. And it has to be the right time, not the wrong time. See, this house has peeling paint. I could cite that. But if I do, and the owner goes to court, he's just going to say that it's cold and he can't paint in the cold because the paint will peel. And that's true. So he won't get cited. And then nothing will happen. Because it's the wrong time."

Halfway down the next block she stops and points out another house. "Okay, a test for you—can you tell me what's wrong?" Les and Qing and I each begin listing things. She nods her head. "This is what you need to do. I saw your list before I came here. You can't just say everything's abandoned. So, it's abandoned. You've got to tell me what the violation is. And it has to be right." I ask her if using the 311 app is worthwhile, and she says yes, going on to explain how reports in 311 are routed to her. I ask her if sharing violations as we find them is worthwhile. She says maybe, if we learn to do it right. If we want to contribute and make things happen, it's our responsibility "to make it all fit and work the way it should," by which she means reporting the data. Les tells her that sometimes he just wants to look around and keep track of things before he tells anyone. She takes a pause, just looking at us. Then she responds, "That's good, because once you send it to me, I've got to do something about it. So if you don't want me to do something about it, don't tell me. If it's on my plate, I gotta serve it."

A lesson learned. Then she looks at me. "You gotta decide whose side you're on. Are you on the side of the university or him?" pointing to Les.

"I'm on his side," I stammer, taken aback by her directness.

"Uh-huh," she says, with doubt. "Well, you better be ready for the call."

"What call?" I ask.

She says, "Here's what's going to happen. You're going to report something and it's going to come to me and then it's going to turn out that the house I just put a sticker on because you helped him call it in belongs to your president's auntie, and now all of a sudden he's in a fuss. And I don't care about your president or his auntie, and so then you know what's going to happen—she's going to get a citation and then he's going to call you. That call."

"I'm okay with that, I'll take that call," I reply.

"Uh-huh," she says again. "You have to think about that and figure it out. Y'all are going to have to figure it out, how you want to make this work."

"What about this list?" I ask, referring to the code violations we've collected.

She replies tersely, "You keep making that list, and then you let me know what you want me to know about, when you want to let me know. And we'll work on this."

"Okay," says Les. There's a long pause, and I sense that we're done, for now.

"I'm going to go," she says. "I saw some things that I want to go back to and look at again." Before she goes, she pulls out her business card and writes a number on the back. "That's my number you can get through on." She hands the card to Les. We thank her, and she walks back to her car.

When she's out of earshot, Les turns to me with a grin and says, "Well, that turned out better than I thought."

"Yeah, that was rough, at the start and the end," I say, and Les laughs. We go our separate ways. Les walks back down the street in the direction of his house. Qing and I walk around the block, get into our respective cars, and drive back to campus.

The encounter had unfolded differently than I expected. It was strained, almost confrontational at the start. While the conversation warmed up as the day did, I was uncomfortable throughout. I wanted to advocate for the work Les and us had done together. I also knew that defensiveness would be counterproductive in that moment. After all, our goal was not to get praise for our data. Our goal was to bring attention to Les's concerns and direct resources to support his work. What was most disconcerting—and yet most productive—was her questioning of my commitments. In that tension the encounter expressed possibility. For that span of two hours on a December morning, Les, Qing, Officer X, and I came together to engage these conditions, to talk and act together. The awkwardness I sensed—that difficulty—was part of the work of institutioning.

Our encounters in the Code Enforcement Section offices and in the neighborhood were sites of design experiment in civics. In those encounters, the activities and outcomes of designing collapsed: we were simultaneously making and inhabiting the effects of that making. These encounters ushered us, collectively, into different modes of togetherness. These different modes of togetherness were accompanied by different, unfamiliar practices. The conversations were open and at times unsettling. Throughout, we questioned and prodded, even as we too were questioned and prodded and had our convictions and positions interrogated. In those unsure and awkward moments, through those lived experiences, we were exploring our own and each other's boundaries, our own and each other's obligations and desires, listening for opportunities to shift into new configurations; and also, in some moments, guarding existing configurations against any such shift. The work of institutioning is achieved through such encounters and conversations—"not only challenging what exists, but also constructing new articulations and new institutions" (Mouffe 2013, 11).

Navigating Institutions

A common way to define an institution is as "the rules of the game"—the conventions of doing things (North 1990). These conventions are expressed through all manner of structures and procedures, including those of the state, civil society, and culture. Scholars often differentiate institutions along disciplinary lines. For instance, one might talk of economic institutions or political institutions (see DiMaggio and Powell 2000; Powell and DiMaggio 2012). The approach to institutions within design discourse, however, tends to be conceptually and empirically messy.

Gretchen Helmke and Steven Levitsky (2004) differentiate between formal and informal institutions, and this is a helpful distinction for understanding the varied types of institutions and activities of institutioning. For Helmke and Levitsky, institutions are "rules and procedures (both formal and informal) that structure social interaction by constraining and enabling actors' behaviors." Informal institutions are "shared rules, usually unwritten, that are created, communicated, and enforced outside of officially sanctioned channels"

(2004, 727). Helmke and Levitsky go on to offer a schema for informal institutions and categorize them in relation to the effectiveness of the formal institutions they interact with. Using this schema, we can more thoroughly describe and interpret the work of the *Careful Coding* project.

Our activities with Les were attempts to stitch together informal and formal institutions. But it can be difficult to categorize whether a given institution is effective, because what it means to be effective may vary by constituent. The effectiveness of an institution may also vary considerably in relation to external factors. From the perspective of the local government of the city of Atlanta, the Code Enforcement Section may be effective: infractions are steadily identified and enforced across the city. Just because some cited infractions are not acted upon is not necessarily the fault of the Code Enforcement Section, as the responsibility could fall on others within the municipality, such as the courts or the Department of Public Works. However, for Les, there are dozens of infractions that seem to go unnoticed and persist for months, even years on end. And for Les, the rate at which citations are issued and acted upon is inadequate.

One way to describe what Les was trying to achieve—and what we were attempting to facilitate—is the making of complementary informal institutions that "'fill in the gaps' either by addressing contingencies not dealt with in the formal rules or by facilitating the pursuit of individual goals within the formal institutional framework" (Helmke and Levitsky 2004, 728). Our collection of data was intended to provide a resource on violations that may have gone unnoticed and where the Code Enforcement Section was lacking. Les's practice of regularly canvassing the neighborhood produces data with distinctive timeliness and insights grounded in local knowledge. This data and insights would otherwise not be accounted for. This pursuit, in turn, also serves Les's broader purpose to use Block by Block to sustain the neighborhood for its current residents. By working in relation to the Code Enforcement Section—as a counterpart to and supplementing their efforts—we are able to leverage their capacities to effect the desired material change in the neighborhood, while also affecting Les's desires for care.

At the same tine, there are some rules and procedures Les does *not* want to participate in. Another aspect of this work involves designing ways to change the terms of participation—or ways to not participate at all. Refusal is also a legitimate form of action, an increasingly important act with regard to data and civics (Costanza-Chock 2020). Rejecting participation is most apparent when Les chooses not to document (and thereby not to report) certain squatters, junk vehicles, and overgrown yards out of compassion for his neighbors. In these cases, we are crafting an accommodating institution by behaving "in ways that alter the substantive effort of formal rules, but without directly violating them, that contradict the spirit, but not the letter of the formal rules" (Helmke and Levitsky 2004, 729). It is not that we are violating the law by not reporting such occurrences. Rather, we are choosing not to report these occurrences—and designing features into the tools that enable us to intentionally make that choice—because we want to avoid the prescribed institutional response if we do report them. These choices and actions rework the relations between Les, the officers, and the Code Enforcement Section. Refusal becomes a means to dispute and dissent from official policy and procedure, but without direct confrontation. This eluding of direct confrontation is strategically important because it is not that Les wants to do away with these institutions; rather, he wants to engage them differently.

If institutioning involves moving between and interweaving the insides and outsides of organizations, regulations, and routines, then we can interpret the choice not to report certain violations as moments when Les moves outside of the formal institution. He is leveraging the informal agreement that if you don't want something acted upon, then you don't report it. We can take the metaphor of weaving further; the idiosyncrasies of Les's data collection and reporting might create a different pattern or welt in the fabric, but they do not unravel it. Such alternative procedures work in part because of the unstated but understood acceptance of this practice across institutional contexts. The code enforcement officer expresses the possibility of such passive manipulation by stating the formal rules and procedures, and providing an opening for acting otherwise: "So if you don't want me to do something about it, don't tell me. If it's on my plate, I gotta serve it."

In this encounter, we also witness the code enforcement officer herself interweaving the formal and informal. She too is trialing different configurations of resources and modes of engagement to achieve her ends. Her institutioning is just as significant, just as constitutive as ours. The informal use of her personal phone as a workaround is an example. The official way of contacting her remains intact. It works because there is a number a person can call that will provide an opportunity to leave a message. But she has also chosen to establish an alternate mode of engagement that is more direct and likely to initiate a faster response. She grants greater privilege to some people by giving them a prioritized way to contact her. At that moment when she gives her personal number to Les, something very important occurs. They establish a different configuration of relations by opening a passage between the formal and the informal that makes possible another set of opportunities for action.

Oftentimes, stories of designing are written as if the designer is outside of whatever they are affecting through their practice. Throughout *Careful Coding*, we—as designers—were enrolled into these engagements. In these endeavors of democratic inquiry, the formal and informal institutions of design and academia become part and parcel of the experiment. For Les, working with the university brought access to resources. Some of those resources were knowledge resources, like the know-how of working with data. Other resources were material resources, such as access to digital tablets and Wi-Fi hotspots. Still other resources were relational, such as reputation and status. For example, when Les asked us to reach out to the Code Enforcement Section and share the data, and then meet with their leadership, he was leveraging the reputation that we carry as university designers and researchers to create an opening that he and Block by Block could potentially move into. When the Code Enforcement Section leadership arranged for Les and a code enforcement officer to meet, they were constructing alignments between the university, city government, and residents. When the code enforcement officer walked with us through the neighborhood—training us in observation—she was creating new resources for her work. Throughout all of this we were, collectively, generating diverse registers and vectors for civics.

When the code enforcement officer questioned me, she brought forth a distinctive character of these design experiments in civics: the need to declare and inhabit a position, in recognition of my own institutional and intersectional subjectivity (Fox et al. 2020). Her question, "Whose side are you on?," demanded that I take a stand. The hypothetical situation she conjures—reporting a violation that results in a citation of the university president's aunt—speaks to a bundling of power, place, and race in the city of Atlanta between government, the university, and residents. In posing that question, she is asking me to consider the potential consequences of our collective actions, and in light of those consequences to articulate my commitments to both Les and her. These commitments are informal—not written down or codified in a signed memorandum of understanding—but nonetheless they are essential to establishing a foundation for ongoing collaboration. This orchestration of expressed obligation was meaningful because it was an act of informal institutioning. In that moment I was asked to make a commitment that was more than the project.

The agonism of that moment made the design experiment a site of contest and offered the potential for a minor transformation of civics (Lenskjold, Olander, and Halse 2015). Theories of agonism argue that democratic pluralism demands contestation, and part of the democratic condition occurs through such encounters (Mouffe 2013). But it is commonly assumed that the design is the provocateur, the enabler of agonism. In some cases, that is certainly the case, since one role for designing is to create spaces and conditions for agonism to manifest (Björgvinsson, Ehn, and Hillgren 2012; Kraff 2020; Sawhney and Tran 2020). But the designer—both the subjectivities and institutions of design—can also themselves be subjected to contestation, questioning, challenging, resistance, and refusal. In the encounter with the code enforcement officer, it is she—in her institutional and intersectional roles and responsibilities—who turns the table to question my actions and commitments as a designer. In that moment, what unfolds is what Huybrechts and colleagues (2016) refer to as an agonistic dialogue. In that dialogue the designer works to "promote dialogues that give room to doubts, conflicts, and disagreements" (103). But those doubts, conflicts, and disagreements are also and importantly directed back at the designer and the institutions of design. Contestation, then, is not just expressed by design toward others—it is a mutual happening (Mollon 2019). Contestation is also directed toward the designer and the institutions of design.

Design experiments in civics thus demand that we abandon any pretense that design is neutral. We should question discourses and practices that set design outside of the context of its work. Any such positioning, at least in these experiments, is contrived. The civics we are contributing to are civics we are a part of, and that communal aspect is part of what makes this work a practice of democratic inquiry. As designers and members of the institutions of design, we are enrolled into the procedures and politics of civics. We, along with the tools, processes, and data we have made, become entangled in the experiment, and in the tentative civic conditions we have sought to manifest together (Agid and Chin 2019; Fox et al. 2020; Steen 2013; Teli et al. 2020). While such perspectives echo participatory traditions and are found in emerging practices such as design justice (Costanza-Chock 2020), they are still distinct from, even counter to, the positionalities and subjectivities espoused by frameworks such as design thinking, which hinge on problematic notions of empathy (Bennett and Rosner 2019; Irani 2018). At the same time, we must acknowledge that our participation and roles may not be the same as others, and participation is not uniform or assimilationist. To claim that the same meaning is made and experienced for all would do violence to those differences that matter. For instance, after our encounter with the code enforcement officer and Les, Qing and I drove back to the university. The university is a place with very different relations to power and is an institution that has attempted to subjugate the very neighborhood where we had just been. It is important to acknowledge that while we are contributing to and participating in diverse civic relations, we do not all inhabit or experience those places and affairs in the same way.

Design Experiments as Pathways through Institutions

As a practice, institutioning does not necessarily change the scale of the work. The *Careful Coding* project remains a project "in the small." Our work engaged with a single resident, a single department within municipal government, and a handful of civil servants. Rather, institutioning changes how we situate the work, what it is placed in relation to, the breadth and diversity of those enrolled, and the extent of the associations. *Careful Coding* involved multiple subjectivities tentatively defined by geography, interest, and practice. It employed devices, data, and different organizations that formed a collective of civic institutions, composed of myriad relations. But like the commons, a collective is not inherently something "good," "civic," or "democratic." What distinguishes a collective is the character of relations within it and the experience that unfolds as we move through it. One thing design experiments in civics do is craft alternative pathways for moving through collectives of institutions, enabling and trialing different experiences of civic action (Buchanan 2019). Of course, we cannot move through these collectives seamlessly; there are barriers and constraints to institutioning (Foth and Turner 2019; Lodato and DiSalvo 2018). Part of the work navigating institutions, of crafting alternative pathways, is working in relation to those barriers and constraints.

Design experiments are never conducted alone, they are inherently cooperative. It is not designers who lead, but rather, we work together with those who face these issues, recognizing their already existing ways of working (Costanza-Chock 2020, 92). As with so much of this inquiry, the concept of the cooperative experiment finds inspiration in the work of Jane Addams and Hull-House, over a century ago. As Matthias Gross (1999) explains in his analysis of the cooperative experiments of Jane Addams and Hull-House, such experiments sit between knowledge production and application. They also straddle site-specific conditions of fieldwork and controlled conditions of the university. As such, cooperative experiments move between and weave together those institutions. Part of those institutions involves the subjectivities of those involved. But whereas the previously described design experiments in civics sought to craft subjectivities through stories or explore those subjectivities through the making and use of devices, these subjectivities are enacted in context. They are not rehearsals. They strive to be, as Marilyn Fischer (2013, 229) describes Addams's work, "an experiment in real time of the process of democratic, pragmatist political reconstruction." Moreover, experiments are cooperative to the extent that they are undertaken by more than just the designers. Though Les, the code enforcement officer, the Code Enforcement Section, myself, Amanda, and Qing each approached the event differently, it was an experience of conjoined imagination (Binder et al. 2015; Dixon 2018, 2020; Steen 2013). It was not an experiment on others, but with others (Gross 2009, 89).

Practices of making are crucial for democratic experiments, when we consider institutioning from the perspective of design. As designers, we tend to approach situations through making, even when those situations are encounters, dialogues, or other forms of living. For instance, the encounters described in this chapter as part of the *Careful Coding* project did not occur accidentally. They were outcomes of opportunistic engagements prompted by ongoing practices of designing processes and tools for data collection. Data and tools were both conduits for and the content of these experiments in civics. They were devices of inquiry into the procedures and relations of civic institutions that enabled us to enact diverse civic subjectivities in situated practice. Through them, we could ask questions about, enter into, and move through processes of governmentality.

Data was the initial impetus for our collaboration. It provided entrée to code enforcement, which prompted the encounter with the code enforcement officer. The presentation of data was made possible through the design of processes and tools for its collection. Of course, the data was questioned.

Much of it, we were told, was duplicative, some of it incorrect. Nonetheless, it influenced the Code Enforcement Section to open a more sustained conversation. We moved next to an encounter between a code enforcement officer, Les, and ourselves in the neighborhood. Through that conversation, the data was again questioned, and we were schooled in the rules and procedures of correctly categorizing infractions. Despite the tensions, the code enforcement officer did not dismiss our collective and ongoing work. Rather, I viewed her provocations as an acknowledgment of the endeavors of participation, and an invitation to continue to move together through these institutions.

The activities and outcomes of making the tools and data enable us to enter and navigate processes of governmentality in distinctive ways. The processes and tools we designed with Les enabled him to retain control over what was shared, how, and with whom. This is a different type of control than is possible with civic tech platforms like 311 or SeeClickFix, which route information directly to the city government or a third-party intermediary. The codification of participatory refusal enabled by these tools and processes is an alternative to the procedures of code enforcement officers, which require particular formalities in categorizing and documenting conditions, and follow established response sequences. Throughout our work with Les, we have emphasized designing systems that strive to enable Les and those other residents he works with to retain their agencies in their community. Reporting code violations is usually in the hands of an officer. In the model we developed with Les, the resident has the authority to decide what warrants action by the city government and what does not. Their choices in reporting data are informed by their values that prioritize the collective well-being of their neighbors. We might label these values as autonomy and justice. Inspired by the work of Nassim JafariNaimi, Lisa Nathan, and Ian Hargraves (2015), we can see these values as propositions for how to care for their neighborhood. The tools, data, and encounters manifest these values, providing the capacity to experience these propositions. Those data and the tools, then, are a means for experimenting with different configurations of action and authority; those experiments unfold through encounters; and those encounters tread and leave traces of different pathways within, across, and between civic institutions. At the same time, these endeavors are about more than data: they comprise what Roderic Crooks and Morgan Currie (2021, 1) call agonistic data practices that "mobilize the antagonisms that motivate people to act, to imagine alternative political arrangements, and to contribute to long-term collective action."

In this democratic inquiry, the collective experiences of those involved come to the fore to give substance and form to the experiment. Each encounter becomes a propositional touchpoint—a marker for referencing how relations might be differently configured. They are moments we can recall, processes that we can revise and repeat, with data as a residue. Over time, as we move through, across, and between these institutions together, we create more touchpoints that mark out different pathways. These pathways, then, are both the site of the experiment and an outcome. Similar to the work of exploring diverse subjectivities, these experiments are about imagining shifts in identities and practices. Similar to devices of inquiry, these experiments unfold through the making and use of artifacts and systems that enable us to materially probe practice and theory. Building from this mode of democratic inquiry, the ongoing experimentation of *Careful Coding* enacts these efforts in situ; what is imagined is also experienced over time—not just momentarily, but through extended engagements. Even as these encounters are tentative, contingent, and partial, even as these pathways between and through institutions may be meandering or oblique, they are also vibrant. In these encounters, we collectively experience a mode of shared governmentality—"in the small," to be sure, but also with an awareness of the potential for a more expansive field of togetherness, toward more diverse civics.

Design Appendix

Design Concept: Amanda Meng, Les Canty, and Carl DiSalvo

Data Processing: Amanda Meng

Data Tools: Michael Koolhang, Qing Tian, and Nick Tippens

Design of digital and paper-based tools for data collecting, including scripts for processing photo (Koolhang), forms for field data collection (Tian and Tippens), and paper maps for use in field data collection (Tian).

5   Events and Quasi-Events

Practicing designers, educators, and scholars often make distinctions within design by referring to different fields of design. Within most Western histories of design, those fields are organized around the kinds of objects made and the mediums in which they are made. Graphic designers tend to make visual media, and industrial designers tend to make physical artifacts, including both professional tools and consumer goods. While these labels are useful, the borders of these fields are also dynamic, as designers strive toward the new and novel and the landscape of technologies shifts boundaries and horizons. This flux is simply the condition of design, and it may be shared among all the fields and disciplines of the artificial. So it is not surprising that categories continue to blend, such that graphic design becomes communication design and includes physical and virtual artifacts, and industrial design becomes product design and includes all manner of media. To these fields we can add other fields, such as those of interaction and service design. Whereas interaction design began with an orientation toward human-computer interfaces and service design began with an orientation toward intangible goods such as banking and healthcare, these too now blend. Service design is a framework for digitally enabled products, and interaction design is common across all fields as interfaces are integral to media, professional tools, consumer goods, and services.

I have no interest in labeling yet another field of design. In fact, to do so might limit the scope of democratic inquiry, which occurs across the many fields of design. What I am interested in is understanding design experiments as a practice of making. To do so, it helps to cast the experiment as something made. The category of "events" is a useful way to do this. Conceptualizing the design experiment as an event is inclusive of all fields and mediums of making. Conceptualizing the design experiment as an event also begins to draw out characteristics of its practice as a particular mode of democratic inquiry. In colloquial terms, an event is an incident or "happening." Within an event, something transpires. What transpires, how it happens, among whom, and with what effects are vital questions to design experiments in civics. Because while not all events are experiments, all experiments aspire to be events.

The event has received significant attention in contemporary theory; Deleuze and Whitehead are progenitors of event thinking. As Mariam Fraser (2006) notes, "thinking the event" is part of a larger project of resisting reductionism and emphasizing relations. More specifically, I employ Isabelle Stengers's (2000) framing of the experiment as an event to consider the design experiment also as an event. Similarly drawing on Stengers, other scholars of design have seized on the event to capture the work of design in prototyping (Wilkie 2014), processes of "thinging" (Binder et al. 2011), and the concept of "design events" (Jönsson 2014). To this scholarship, I add the work of Elizabeth Povinelli (2011). Her feminist anthropology of late-liberalism and idea of "quasi-events" provides another perspective to quell grand narratives of the achievements of design. My hope is to draw from these intellectual wells and help their ideas flow into design experiments in civics.

In this chapter, I develop the concept of the event to understand the design experiment as a particular mode of making and a kind of made thing. Casting the design experiment as an event draws out a set of features and themes for appreciation. As I have argued from the start, the design experiment is a particular endeavor: although much of what comprises the design experiment is familiar to design, the design experiment is still distinctive. For instance, scenarios, games, sensors, maps, and apps are all familiar things that designers make across multiple fields, but in the context of the design experiment, these familiar things do different work and should be described and judged differently.

To begin with, the design experiment-as-event is not merely functional—a quality we usually ascribe to products and services. *The experiment-as-event changes the purposes and outcomes of design.* The purpose of the experiment-as-event is to spark knowledge and imagination. Knowledge and imagination initiate interest and chart courses of action. The making of the design experiment-as-event is also different from familiar practices of conceptualization and form-giving. *The experiment-as-event changes the activities of designing.* Gathering and orchestration are the activities of making that characterize the design experiment-as-event. Finally, the design experiment-as-event evokes different feelings and reactions than we presume of design. *The experiment-as-event changes the affects and expectations of design.* The affects of the design experiment include frustration, longing, and endurance. These meaningful differences cast the experiment-as-event as a particular kind of design thing, and lead us to distinctive design principles.

The Scope of the Event

The structure and presence of events are varied and often dispersed. This poses a challenge for thinking about events in relation to design, because most design practices and discourses are disposed toward definite and delineated objects and representations. We can point to a toaster and distinguish it from other toasters or a blender. We can diagram the service experience of a visit to the dentist and compare it to a visit to an oncologist or a bank. But the boundaries of events are blurred and their composition is mutable. Confounding factors further, events extend beyond familiar activities of designing and use. As Stengers (2000, 66–67) remarks, the scope of the event includes all the futures it creates, all of those who are and may still be affected by the event. The expansive and fluctuating scope of the event changes how we understand and describe the experiment as something designed, and in turn, expands our perspective on the activities and outcomes of designing.

Returning to *Fruit Are Heavy* and the use of simple sensors to detect the relative ripeness of fruit in trees by measuring the bend in the branch as the fruit grows, we could ask: What is the scope of this event? When does it begin and end? Over the course of the experiment, there were a series of happenings, each with a before and an after. For instance, there was a happening when a forager and a designer went out to a tree, climbed it, and strapped a sensor to a branch. This is clearly an identifiable episode in time and space, involving people engaged in an activity, using made things. So, we could speak of installing the sensor as an event. We could also speak of the event of sensing itself—the moment when software on the timer signals the microcontroller, which registers the change in voltage across the circuit as a stream of numbers and writes that number to the memory card along with a date and time stamp. In these cases, the before and after is readily evident, if rudimentary. There was no sensor strapped to the tree, and then there was. There was less bend in the branch, and then there was more. The bend was not previously recorded, and then it was, marked by writing data to a new line in a file.

The before and after of such incidents are important moments for describing *Fruit Are Heavy*, but they do not express the whole of the experiment-as-event. The whole of the experiment-as-event both precedes and outlives designed things and their use. It begins in the selection and crafting of the situations through which the experiment will happen. For *Fruit Are Heavy*, the experiment began with the decision to muddle precision agriculture and foraging. Before any word was scrawled on a sticky note and stuck to a wall or any use case was drafted, the experiment began in the conceptual work of opting for and fashioning some situation. This material and conceptual situation enables subsequent making, use, and interpretation.

The experiment-as-event then continues with a familiar aspect of designing: framing a phenomenon so that it is addressable through design. Designers choose which methods, techniques, and materials to use in designing. Throughout, the activities of making mingle with activities of use. In a human-centered design process, this blending occurs through iteration and testing. Prototypes are made and evaluated, offering lessons that advance the design of the artifact. Then more prototypes are made, toward a finished thing. This span of activity is most often considered the standard work of design because it emphasizes the immediate agencies of the designer and the artifact or system, and the immediate desires of users.

But the effects and affects of the experiment-as-event extend well beyond those agencies and desires. They stretch well beyond the roles of the designer and the user, and the capacities of any artifact or system. What's more, as previously discussed, those standard processes of design often do not really describe how design unfolds through these events. Design experiments also include nonuse, resistance, appropriation, misuse, obsolescence, and forgetting, accompanied by the subjectivities that express those agencies and desires. Concepts such as "de-futuring" and "designing away" bring attention to the ways the work of design might be undone, and that also should figure into the scope of the experiment (Fry 1999; Tonkinwise 2014). Practices of undoing or unmaking prompt us to consider a reparative approach to design that seeks to address prior harms done by design and work toward a redirective practice (Fry 2007; Lindström and Ståhl 2020b). Similarly, maintenance and repair reconceptualizes our understanding of the life of designed things and the diverse subjectivities of those who encounter the objects of design (Houston and Jackson 2016; Jackson 2014; Russell and Vinsel 2018). All these variations of making and use alter who is involved with the experiment-as-event and when.

The effects of the experiment may also linger or reappear, sometimes delayed, other times punctuated in effect. The experiment-as-event may continue having effect and provoking affect well after one might consider it done. For instance, if the concept of *Fruit Are Heavy* is revived and mobilized in a discussion on the potential value of municipal wireless networks years after the sensors are removed from the trees, then the experiment continues too, or rather once again has influence.

In these ways, the experiment-as-event expands the temporal frame of designing. Casting the design experiment as an event demands that we reconsider "design time." In theorizing the span of participation, Pelle Ehn (2008) offers the conceptualizations of "design before design" and "design after design" as labels to describe how creative activities of making occur both before and after the formal production of a product or service, often by people not referred to as designers. For Ehn, expanding the "when" of design is important in expanding our appreciation of who participates in design and how. Such an expanded temporal frame prompts us to consider participation anew and to recognize the creative agencies of making that occur beyond professional practice. With regard to the design experiment, understanding the expansive scope of the experiment-as-event also prompts us to consider inquiry anew and recognize a broader array of effects and affects, of purposes and outcomes of design.

Imagining the World Differently

Stengers's notion of the experiment-as-event is useful because she identifies and describes qualities and purposes of the experiment that I take to be applicable to many modes of inquiry—not only those that are scientific. One such quality is that the event is transformative; there is a difference between before and after the event. That difference produces knowledge as both a purpose and an outcome of the experiment. In other words, we know the world differently after an experiment. This outcome of knowing the world differently spans kinds of experiments, regardless of field: controlled inquiry occurs in the arts as well as the sciences. The knowledge produced also has consequences; it affects how we perceive and understand the world, and it begets further activity. Regarded as an event, experiments are the impetus for ongoing inquiry, and they have the capacity to affect the routines and character of that inquiry. As Fraser (2006, 131) succinctly summarizes Stengers's argument, "For Stengers, a scientific experiment is an event only if it makes a difference before and after, that is, if it is able to invent new practices, and new ways of thinking and feeling about a problem." Building on this idea, I want to suggest that in addition to knowledge, imagination is *also* an outcome of the design experiment. We imagine the world differently after an experiment. And imagination too begets further inquiry.

The experiment-as-event thus changes the purposes and outcomes of design. Within dominant discourses and practices of design there is an obligation to functionality and effectiveness. In part, those obligations are bound to a perceived need to demonstrate a market value to design, such that design continues to be a service and profession of commercial merit. This is also often the case in government and civil society, where design is cast as a means to innovate and achieve instrumental ends to sustain politics and society as we know it. But when the use and value of designing are not beholden to such logics or discourses (at least not only or entirely beholden), the outcomes and purposes of a design experiment may be otherwise. In the case of these design experiments in civics, which are intended to contribute to diverse civic imaginaries and practices, one purpose and outcome is imagination. That is, not only does the experiment involve imaginative making and use, the experiment also produces imagination.

Returning to *Fruit Are Heavy*, how might the design experiment be understood and appreciated as an event that generates knowledge and sparks imagination? In the experiment of *Fruit Are Heavy*, we can ask and answer questions to understand circumstances differently after we conduct the experiment. We can ask and answer whether the sensor worked. Specifically, we can ask and answer if this configuration of parts was able to register a bend in a branch over time (it was), and we can ask and answer if the housing kept the rain from the electronics (it did). We can also ask and answer whether this configuration of parts was able to stream the data (it was not). These are the obvious results of the experiment that speak to notions of functionality and effectiveness. But the value of the experiment derives from more than determining whether any single part worked. Following from Stengers's and Fraser's interpretation, the value of the experiment lies in whether our perspectives on a set of conditions and possibilities were affected. Did the experiment invent new practices, ways of making, or ways of thinking about a problem? (Fraser 2006, 13). In this case, how did the experiment-as-event change how Concrete Jungle thought about and imagined foraging and commoning as civic practices?

As a design experiment, *Fruit Are Heavy* did affect our collective conceptualizations and practices of commoning. In the processes, we, as designers together with members of Concrete Jungle, considered how the use of sensors to monitor fruit in trees around the city would affect the practices of foraging. Through our collaborative activities we considered how we would need to—and whether we wanted to—account for the new kinds of labor needed to attend to these sensors, and the new kind of labor needed to integrate the sensor data into existing practices. We began to imagine, together, new practices of foraging that folded data into work routines. We also began to imagine, beyond that particular instantiation of foraging, possibilities for using other technologies and techniques of precision agriculture for foraging. This led to considerations of the implications of inflecting data and more-than-human agencies in commoning and inspiring new figurations of the smart city that emphasized local practices of care and community economies.

The sparks of knowledge and imagination from such experiments can ignite interest and courses of action. After we know and imagine the world through the experiment, we can consider how we might differently act in the world. This brings about conundrums through our experience of emergent and unfamiliar conditions and unsure potentials, inciting further inquiry. Fraser (2006) refers to this as "inventive problem-making." As part of inventive problem-making, the experiment expresses possibilities and problematic conditions that might be attended to. Just as often as setting horizons, experiments also identify limits and boundaries and redirect action and interest. As I will discuss in the following chapter, inventive problem-making is not only a primary characteristic of the design experiment—it is also how design experiments participate in care.

There is a tension in this description of the event because there is the presumption that designing inherently contributes to problem solving.

Yoking design to operative ends remains prominent in design practice and discourse. This is particularly true in domains of design that intersect and overlap with the contexts and practices of civics—such as social design or social innovation. In these areas, addressing "social problems" is often the focus of making, and notions of "change" bubble through the expressed intentions of practitioners. Instrumental orientations can be a challenge for appreciating the uncertainty of events. At the same time, the backlash against problem solving can itself be problematic. It is true that the rush to solutions limits the scope of design and often unduly and sometimes unjustly delimits design. But it is also true that knee-jerk accusations of pragmatic design as solutionism can express positions of privilege, suddenly putting designers and design things beyond accountability.

Daniela Rosner (2018) orients her work around a non-teleological practice and theory of design, which does not reduce design to being defined and judged by rote functionalism. Such an approach retains an ethics and politics of designing that is located and accountable (Suchman 2002), while also not reducing design to a positivist project that claims to resolve issues through making alone. From a different perspective—but sharing an interest in design—Celia Lury and Noortje Marres (2015) argue for a post-instrumental notion of designed things, also drawing from pragmatism. They assert an approach to valuation that emphasizes the multiple valences of designed things. These reorientations charge designers and those who study design to be open to the things and processes of design working in more varied ways.

Whether we believe an experiment has "worked," then, does not depend upon the resolution of some circumstance, although that is an outcome one should aspire to for outcomes of the experiment to be of value in the moment and for the future. This was certainly the hope of the experiments described in this book. It is also a responsibility that we, as designers, have to our partners. That spark of imagination, that igniting of interest, and those courses of action should affect more than the field of design and the work of the designer. As an example, consider *Careful Coding* as an experiment-as-event that attempted to address conditions in the now, while also kindling desires for what conditions might become. *Careful Coding* explored how resident-led activities of collecting and managing data might draw municipal resources to a neighborhood and help residents assert which issues were attended to and prioritized. The experiment was both an attempt to enable aid in the present and to probe possible reconfigurations of authority and responsibility in local politics that might manifest in the future. Through the design experiment, residents and code enforcement officers came together with designers. Collectively, through material and embodied endeavors, we experienced how the mandates for data collection, accountabilities for the veracity of information, standards of expertise, and charges to act might be redistributed. Our process of making and using data generated knowledge about how the current processes worked. As we expressed and trialed alternative political relations, we elicited potential reconfigurations of civic institutions. Paper forms and maps, digital applications, spreadsheets, and walks through the neighborhood—all these design things comprised events through which we, collectively, produced and explored diverse civics. The experiment-as-event affected the immediate situation, while also refracting possibilities beyond the imminent functionality of use. The significance of *Careful Coding* as an event, then, is not bound *only* by whether it produces inventive modes of data collection or draws attention and resources to the municipality. The significance of the design experiment *also* lies in how it prompts us to envision how we might differently configure authority and agency within the neighborhood.

To say that the purpose and outcome of designing are the production of knowledge and the sparking of imagination shifts our expectations of what designing does and what designing might be for. Some might argue that other modes of designing contribute to knowledge production, and even that much design sparks imagination. And perhaps that is true. But what distinguished the experimental event as a mode of democratic inquiry from other practices of designing is that the production of knowledge and the sparking of imagination are a primary purpose and outcome—not secondary or tangential to some other logic or function.

When we describe and judge design experiments, then, the emphasis should be on whether knowledge and imagination were brought forth, and what courses of action they illuminated or enabled. This is not abstract or apathetic knowledge and imagination. It is situated, directed, and committed. Moreover, that knowledge and imagination are produced together with collectives of people and institutions. It is not the knowledge and imagination of designers alone, nor does it give preference to designers (Manzini 2015; Steen 2013). To achieve this requires the work of gathering and orchestration.

Gathering and Orchestration as Activities of Designing

Another question we should ask is, "What does making events entail?" Events are collective affairs that require gathering and orchestration. Gathering assembles a plurality of peoples and institutions, values, desires, facts, beliefs, objects, and experiences. Through orchestration, this plurality is bound together to produce a meaningful happening. What makes these happenings meaningful is not a matter of the quantity of things so much as it involves composing with and among the differences between things (Stengers 2005).

The experiment-as-event thus changes the activities of designing. Appreciating the work of the design experiment-as-event requires recognizing and valuing activities of gathering and orchestration as activities of making. Attention to these relational activities of making has emerged from contemporary participatory design and its interactions with science and technology studies. For Binder and colleagues (2011), this notion of gathering is basic to practices of making public things that cohere together humans and nonhumans alike toward the articulation of issues. This echoes and amplifies earlier work by Pelle Ehn and Richard Badham (2002), which expressed the idea of the collective designer: an idea of designing as both a collective endeavor and toward the construction and renewal of collectives. Both the concepts of design things and the collective designer are themselves influenced by a collection of ideas from the contemporary theory, including Lucy Suchman's artful integrations (1993, 1996), Bruno Latour's compositionism (2010), and Isabelle Stengers's cosmopolitics (2010). While quite different, these ideas share a perspective that worlding involves endeavors of assembly and arrangement, done in part through activities of making and the use of made things. Recently, designers expanding the traditions and theories of participatory design have sought to further characterize the activities of gathering and orchestration through concepts such as patch-working (Lindström and Ståhl 2014) and design events (Jönsson 2014).

In the context of democratic inquiry, the purpose of gathering and orchestration is to construct conditions for inquiry by bringing together people, artifacts, institutions, discourses, and practices, so they might intermingle, affecting one another. That interaction and affectation then sparks people's imagination, helping them envision and act on the world differently. The selection and assembly of those dissimilar, constituent parts is crucial to the experiment. These components of the experiment include the familiar mate-rialities of design, as well as less familiar things—what is present and what is absent, the human and the more-than-human.

For instance, in *Fruit Are Heavy*, fruit, trees, sensors, microcontrollers, plas-tic boxes, vinyl backpacks, designers, researchers, and foragers are conscripted to explore different practices of foraging and forms of commoning. These are the constituent parts that were present and composed through the experi-ment. But in cataloging the constituents, we should also recognize absences, such as nonexistent municipal Wi-Fi service in *Fruit Are Heavy* or the missing data in *Careful Coding*. These absences shaped our collective experiences in these experiments and altered what was gathered together. The void they left contributed to the shape and rhythm of the event.

The more-than-human factors of an experiment also demand consider-ation when cataloging these constituents and describing the experiment. Although the *Fruit Are Heavy* project was motivated by our human desire to collect and distribute wild-growing fruit as a practice of care through commoning, the qualities of the nonhumans involved in foraging influ-enced the event. These nonhumans include fruit, trees, and environments where they grow. We might also include the capacities of batteries, energy draw of the circuit, and length of the sensor as factors that exerted influ-ence on the making and use of the device. Subsequently, they also affect the staging and consequences of the experiment. This confluence of fac-tors and agencies is common to the experiment and practices of making. Research into scientific practice and the sociology of scientific knowledge repeatedly demonstrates that tools and techniques are not separable from the experiment—they are constitutive of the experiment. Practices of craft also involve constitutive parts. The origins of the clay, the potter's wheel, and the materials burned within a kiln all contribute to the aesthetics of the vessel made. The design experiment—as an experiment of and through making—similarly happens through the collection and interaction of an assortment of more-than-human qualities and agencies, which individually and collectively should be accounted for.

Working in collaboration, Tau Lenskjold and Li Jönsson (Jönsson and Lenskjold 2014; Lenskjold and Jönsson 2017) have explored how humans and nonhumans might be brought into new relations through staged encounters. This attention to the more-than-human constitution of events is part of a broader conversation in design on more-than-human encounters

(Forlano 2017; Wakkary 2021). Through a series of self-described experiments, Lenskjold and Jönsson explored how we might create devices that bring together seagulls and humans in playful ways, to rethink and potentially refigure the relations between humans and nonhumans in the city. This leads Jönsson to the articulation of a concept of "design events," which very much influences this discussion of design experiments as events. Jönsson (2014, 217) describes the more-than-human perspective of the design event as "a means to invent polite ways of entering into new relationships with nonhuman others. . . . It is a material addition that makes possible, that gives chance to expanding the repertoire of possible choices, and to explore how design can intervene and allow for different hybrid formations to emerge by moving away from a purely humanistic focus."

For Jönsson, those formations include assemblages with cameras, elders, and seagulls. In the context of *Fruit Are Heavy*, such formations might be extended to apples, bend sensors, Wi-Fi, data, and databases. The disparate character (Stengers 2000, 97) of all involved in the experiment is important because variation brings complexity and potential to the experiment and fosters a conversation between materials and practices. For instance, part of the work in *Fruit Are Heavy* was making a sensor that operated outdoors, strapped to a tree for weeks on end. The conditions of foraging exert certain burdens on the construction and use of the sensing device. Making the system work in those conditions was a knottier task than making a prototype of the system work in an engineering lab. In tandem, another part of the experiment of *Fruit Are Heavy* involved remixing the routines, motivations, and cultures of foraging with those of precision agriculture. Here the work of design experiments involved refiguring practices by piecing together seemingly contrary concepts and activities to create a sociotechnical hybrid.

The significance of the disparate character (Stengers 2000, 97) of constituents becomes more charged and promising in some experiments than others. *Fruit Are Heavy* brought the materialities and practices of precision agriculture and smart cities together within the world of foraging, and the experiment happened mostly among foragers. As such, the practices of foraging were more influenced by the practices of precision agriculture or smart cities than vice versa. In other experiments, however, practices are brought into closer relation with another to intermingle, affecting one another in uncertain ways.

PARSE was an attempt at such an intermingling, an attempt to rouse positions and perspectives and have them move one another. The project brought together people from different backgrounds, with varied interests and commitments, to collaboratively envision how they would use smart-city technologies in their everyday routines. The project used a design game to elicit ideas and fragments of stories. These fragments were then interpreted and compiled as scenarios to be shared. In this design game and storytelling, city planning, pedestrians, bicycles and cars, sensors and data, hustles and hobbies, infrastructure and its maintenance were jumbled together with the myriad identities of residents and workers. Both the activities of the design game and the subsequent scenarios were intended to animate the relations between these varied constituents of a smart Atlanta.

Similarly, the *Careful Coding* project gathered together varied constituents through the making and using of civic data. Not only was there an intermingling of materialities in this design event, formal and informal institutions also intermingled. Residents and designers collaborated with code enforcement officers, municipal information services, community organizations, and philanthropic foundations to collect local data and create civic data tools and processes. The standard way of reporting issues is through government websites and apps. For instance, the 311 app, common to many cities, provides a mobile and digital conduit between residents and municipal services. But not all residents want to use such services. Other modes of data collection might support collective rather than individual efforts. They might not solely rely upon digital platforms or provide discretion in reporting so that residents can choose to report some things and not report others. These modes of action enable residents to assert agency in shaping formal and informal institutions.

In the *Careful Coding* project, the social and political frictions between resident activists, municipal workers, professional planners, and designers imparted a distinctive feel to the experiment. The gathering together of these constituents, and their contrary temperaments, commitments, and responsibilities, had meaningful consequences. As these constituents interacted, they transformed the civic environment and affected one another. Residents came to understand municipal regulations and the structures of governance. Code enforcement officers sympathized with the concerns of residents. Designers were enrolled into the work of residents. Together, they explored and trialed what might be possible with and through data as a conduit for other relations of authority and action in the neighborhood. In the best of such situations, a conjoined literacy develops through mutual learning. This literacy is both factual and affective; it is a literacy that informs and is moving, a literacy that inspires toward apprised action.

Orchestration

As the event spans and enfolds multiple people and institutions, designing becomes a way of orchestrating associations. Orchestration, then, is a necessary complement to gathering and gives coherence to what is assembled. The work of orchestrating design experiments involves surveying and distinguishing what material and experiential aspects of one practice might affect another practice, and then combining them in ways that prompt interaction. Such attention to materialities and experiences is a practical concern because the activity of design involves rendering and manipulating materials and experience. Of course, design is also a conceptual and intellectual affair—these material and experiential aspects are expressions of ideology and values. But even these conceptual and intellectual aspects are usually explored and manifested through material and experiential demonstrations. In no way is this meant to either denigrate or valorize one mode of making or another. Nor is it meant to compartmentalize or establish borders of what is or is not designing. It is simply and humbly (with the intention of acknowledging limitations to design) to recognize that acts of design are acts of making. In this way, we can think of orchestration as form-giving. This mode of form-giving is distinctive because what is being shaped are the potentials for engagement between diverse constituents.

For example, *Careful Coding* explores the qualities and consequences of data in contemporary civics. Of all the projects discussed, it was most obviously an experiment in democratic values and conditions. Within practices of local government in Atlanta lay sets of entwined ideals and values relating to citizenship and governance. These shaped the design and use of civic technology. As in many cities, service and efficiency figured prominently in the espoused politics of the municipality. Equity was also prominent in the political discourse of city leadership. To explore these ideals and values in relation to data, the *Careful Coding* project attended to a particular instantiation of these ideologies and values: how data about the built environment is collected, managed, and acted upon. These material and experiential means expressed collective ideas about and values of civics and governance.

Similarly, *PARSE* explored the stories we tell about what smart cities are and might be. It attempted to craft stories that express more varied subjectivities than usual. This effort was both nestled in, and in tension with, ideologies about smart cities advanced by industry and government. The narratives and subjectivities they advanced tend to cast residents as passive producers and mere consumers of civic services. They tell stories of entrepreneurship progressing within formal economies, and of technology as stable and secure. The *PARSE* project sought to surface other narratives through making. These other narratives spoke to the specifics of smart-city technologies and services and also told stories about the civic conditions residents wanted to create and inhabit.

Making is thus one way to explore the interplay of values, desires, and the made world. Through the design experiments we can ask: If other means were made and used, would other values and desires manifest? Will other politics manifest, or will other modes of political action be possible? We should not presume the answer is yes; it may be no. Or likely, the results of making and use will be varied, even vague. But through making and use, we can express these questions concretely, even if we cannot answer them definitively.

Although within design experiments diverse things are gathered together, they are not fully assimilated. They remain varied, even divergent. In these particular design experiments, terms common to civic projects such as "community" become complicated. As Iris Young (1986) argues, "community" is a term that too often elides difference. It obscures that the desire for community is also what drives racism, ethnic chauvinism, and political sectarianism. Rather, says Young, "a more acceptable politics would acknowledge that members of an organization do not understand one another as they understand themselves, and would accept this distance without closing it into exclusion" (1986, 14). Difference is meaningful and should be sustained. Gathering together does not require integration or consensus.

The character of these gatherings, then, is striated, not smooth, and comes with friction (Korn and Voida 2015; Tsing 2011). It is not as if those gathered to the experiment have been crafted to fit together. Instead, the process of joinery is often a messy, seamful affair (Vertesi 2014). In some cases, such as with *Careful Coding*, the intent might be to construct such agonistic space of encounter (Björgvinsson, Ehn, and Hillgren 2012; Mouffe 2013). In other cases, such as *PARSE* and *Fictions of a Smart Atlanta*, the friction might be subtle and subdued. And at times, the friction of these gatherings leads to moments of eventfulness that are incomplete or fall apart. In fact, incompleteness and fragility are aspects of the relational work of design experiments, which gives them a character different from the often-grandiose narratives of design. The event is not always as eventful as one might hope or as designers might claim.

Different Affects and Expectations of the Design Experiment

Much of what is marked as events are dramatic happenings with vivid affects and effects. But there is a danger to emphasizing drama because designers and those who study design can become enthralled with the spectacle of events. There is also a danger in setting expectations that every event must achieve a threshold of extraordinariness. This concern is particularly relevant within contemporary design, which tends to breathlessly pursue innovation. A drive toward the exceptional is exemplified by the fascination with "disruption" in consumer products and services, medicine, education, government, and civil society. Disruption is a rallying cry for one grand event after another. But not all events are spectacular. While the before and after of an event is marked by shifts in discourse, material environments, and practice, they need not be spectacular to be consequential. Many events are discreet and mundane. Events can be partially successful or fall apart. Understanding and appreciating design as partial, fragile, and often lacking is contrary to the heroics of much of design discourse. But the design experiment-as-event evokes different feelings and reactions than we anticipate and presume of design.

Elizabeth Povinelli's (2011) feminist anthropology of late liberalism provides a vantage point on events that recognizes the mundane and engages with "the minor" (Deleuze and Guattari 1986). Povinelli speaks of "quasi-events" that do not reach the threshold of spectacle but nonetheless are meaningful. The outcome of quasi-events may be only a modest shift. Eventfulness may deny change or mark a moment that thwarts desire. Unlike the grandiosity of so much that is claimed about design, quasi-events are often "ordinary, chronic, or cruddy," and even liminal (2011, 11). The tentative nature of the experiment-as-event appreciates uncertainty—the fractional and provisional character of so much of contemporary life.

As an example of a quasi-event, Povinelli recounts moving a washing machine from one town to another, among the aboriginal Australian communities she worked with for decades (2011, 138–139). The washing machine holds the potential for providing relief from the sores and rashes and general discomfort that comes from the inability to adequately clean clothes. In the process of moving the washing machine in the back of a pickup truck, unbeknownst to Povinelli and others, the lid flies off the machine. They return later looking for the lid, only to find it along the roadside, flattened, unable to be reattached. Due to its design, the machine will not function without the lid. This has a cascade of consequences: without a functioning washing machine, clothes will not be adequately cleaned, and the sores that accompany dirty clothes will continue. Despite a desire for things to be different, and despite acting toward making things different, change is thwarted. The loss of the lid is, in all its mundaneness, a quasi-event.

> Quasi-events are a general condition of human social life. (My shoestrings snap all the time.) They are widespread (quasi-events occur across every actual and conceivable organization of social life); they confound response (their slightness often occurs below the level of accountability); they resist cause and effect characterization (it is hard to say when they occurred let alone what caused them). (Povinelli 2011, 144)

Such quasi-events differ from events more familiar to design discourse. Quasi-events occur in the context of the everyday, drawing attention to the routines of life. The commonplace becomes a site of happenings that are ordinary rather than spectacular. In some cases, the imperfect and unfinished things of a quasi-event may be closer to the actual work of design than grander, more spectacular notions of events. But the contingent nature of quasi-events makes them difficult to connect with specific outcomes. This is a challenge with regard to design because design practice and discourse tend to exude confidence in the capacities of design to effect change. Both practice and discourse in design strive for the definite. As an example, consider that in most discourses of design the prototype is distinguished from the product. The product, as a finished thing ready for sale and use, is considered the result of design. The prototype is a waypoint en route to the product. The partial and incomplete are valued primarily as means to a more permanent final state. Such latent assumptions reinforce values and beliefs about what the work of design is, should be, or strives for. However, in developing an appreciation for the design experiment—toward thinking and doing design otherwise—the imperfect and unfinished need to be given more consideration as modes of design and designing.

While design experiments strive for a significant effect, what just as often occurs is merely partial eventfulness. With *Fruit Are Heavy*, aspects of the project functioned as expected and produced meaningful insights across sites and scales. Yet, the event was thwarted and did not come to the sought-after conclusion. Technical limitations prevented the sharing of the data beyond the device. Such quasi-events are common in design experiments in civics and can be found in all the projects discussed so far. For instance, in the *PARSE* project, workshops were held, design games played, narratives crafted, and stories shared. There was interest, excitement, and plans for what should come next. However, such plans can be stymied when the administration changes, a new mayor is voted in, the former chief information officer is recruited to another city, or a public system is privatized. In the case of *Careful Coding*, tools were made for collecting data, residents collected the data, and the data was organized and analyzed. Data sets were sent off as email attachments, then councilmembers and officers emailed back to set up meetings. But over time, some residents tire of slow-moving bureaucracy, a councilmember starts their own data collection project, and a new app for data collection is developed by the city. Like the washing machine lid in Povinelli's ethnography, the stories, devices, tools, and data sets of so many design experiments sit alongside the road, separated from the machines they were made to fit with. Designers can look for what caused these disarticulations. Perhaps it is the fault of the designer or the design process, or stems from a flaw in the things made. Regardless, there will be a cascade of effects and affects.

Though the effects of quasi-events are partial, something does happen; there is a before and an after. Beyond this phenomenological fact, the effects may be diffusely distributed. Certainly, there were happenings in the workshops in *PARSE*, the sensing in *Fruit Are Heavy*, and the encounters in *Careful Coding*. However, the accomplishments of those experiments remained indefinite. As the stories from *PARSE* sit as a file on someone's desktop, planning and procurement will go on as before. While the data from *Careful Coding* waits as an unopened attachment in someone's email, the established procedures will continue. Institutions will be unaffected, and existing relations between residents and government continue unchanged. Matters of concern and care continue to be overlooked because they are unattended to, leading to disappointment and resignation.

These blurred and fragile qualities of the quasi-event are at odds with the authoritative and bold discourses and affects of contemporary design. This difference is what makes the quasi-event so pertinent and poignant; it attunes designers and those who study design to more varied outcomes, expectations, and affects. The intentions and wants of designers and their partners are hardly destined to be realized through making; experiments often disappoint. As we tell the stories of designing and use, it is important to convey moments of incompleteness, missteps, thwarted desires, and limited effects. These are not tales of "fail early and often" or worse, "move fast and break things." Rather, I am trying to describe and theorize making and use in ways that, with humility, recognize the complexity of contemporary conditions and the limitations of design. In the context of design discourse and practice, these are "new ways of thinking and feeling" (Fraser 2006, 131). Those new ways of thinking and feeling are not always joyous. Such a realization opens designers and those who study design to other affects and aspirations. Endurance is one such affect.

The outcome of a design experiment in civics is not inevitably some preferred condition. At times, the outcome is enduring—continuing to persevere and persist. To endure is itself a significant end of contemporary civics and a meaningful mode of togetherness. How peoples endure is a central theme within Povinelli's scholarship and her idea of quasi-events. As we explore what other worlds might be possible through design experiments in civics, we repeatedly confront the structures and processes of contemporary politics and economics that often work against those other worlds. It is in such moments that endurance and enduring become necessary. With *PARSE* there was initial interest in the stories created through the design game and in using the design game to facilitate more public engagement. These goals were not achieved. This was not any one person's fault; it was simply a matter of the circumstances of bureaucracy. Despite our goals not being achieved, we continue to advocate for more public engagement, share the design game, and retell the stories of what else a smart Atlanta might be. Whenever we have the chance, we remind ourselves and others of the diverse subjectivities that work and live here. Or consider the *Careful Coding* project, in which residents collected data on the built environment to advocate for responsible neighborhood improvement. The data was collected, sorted, verified, packaged, and shared. Code violations were registered in a database—and likely still reside there, awaiting action. But the change has yet to arrive. In some cases, something happens in a piecemeal way. An abandoned lot is cleared here and a dilapidated building is razed there, but still the residents live among worn conditions in their neighborhood. Yet we still work together to collect and share the data. Against uncertain odds, still we design to support these endeavors.

From the outset of this book, I have sought to identify terms and themes to describe and judge design experiments in civics. Inspired by Povinelli's notion of the quasi-event, I suggest that those terms and themes must embrace a more diverse set of affects and actions. Endurance is just one such theme. Of course, there are more themes that craft and express other collective subjectivities of design. Taking the time to notice and develop these themes is an important trajectory for future research and practice. The conjoined identities, activities, and principles of designing to endure and "struggle along with" are distinctive. They are not necessarily opposed to more familiar subjectivities of design, but they are different from the brashness that characterizes much design discourse.

One way to think about and perform more varied subjectivities of design comes from feminist and queer theory, which abandons prescribed, singular, normative positions in favor of expansive ways of being and becoming. A source of inspiration is the work of Sara Ahmed (2014, 2017) and her embrace of figures such as the willful subject and the killjoy. For Ahmed, part of the work of being a feminist is to live subjectivities such as the killjoy. By inhabiting them, we can acknowledge and indulge in figures of feminism that have been denigrated because they are "difficult." These figures produce productive frictions, rather than simply fitting in. Nassim Parvin and Anne Pollock (2020) call attention to the importance of the killjoy in relation to the unbridled enthusiasm for technology, using, in fact, smart cities as an exemplar. Beyond the killjoy or willful subject, what other identities, activities, and principles of making might vary the subjectivities of design? Cindy Lin and Silvia Lindtner (2021) call our attention to this question and its relation to an assumed trajectory of progress that aligns to positive affect. For designers working through experiments in civics, shaping different subjectivities requires alternate habits of making and ways of inhabiting the world as a maker. These may be comprised of much more varied affects than the often naïve optimism that tends to characterize design. For critics or scholars, different subjectivities of design—the diverse affects and actions that characterize design experiments in civics—change and expand what counts as design, and how we describe and interpret design.

Contingent, Provisional, Probative, and Yet Also Concrete

As I stated at the beginning of this chapter, not all events are experiments, but all experiments aspire to be events. All experiments aspire to produce effects and affects that prompt new practices of making and doing, that usher in new ways of understanding and feeling about conditions and potentials. While designers might desire for ensuing effects to be definite and distinctive—and affects to be confident and positive—that is not always the case. In fact, we should question these desires, perhaps feeling them as the residue of notions of achievement and mastery that are counter to thinking and doing design otherwise, counter to design as democratic inquiry. Drawing from Povinelli, event making also involves engagement with the "ordinary, chronic, or cruddy," and many experiences of the event are liminal. The quasi-event, then, is an apt frame for many design experiments. The experiment might cause a spark, or it might smolder. But from the start it has been clear that the design experiment is a contingent affair, provisional and probative (Ansell 2013). As Binder and colleagues describe, "When probing into futures that are inherently unpredictable, plural and sometimes impossible, it is a matter of enabling collective action in the face of uncertainty: rehearsals, attempts and failures—all are ways to try and come to terms with prevailing ambiguity" (2015, 162). Taken together, these aspects of the experiment-as-event are important in the context of civics because they provide a basis for appreciating an expanded field of designing that strives to participate in exploring new modes of togetherness, to contribute to diverse civic imaginaries and practices, in ways that often sidestep the familiar rote instrumentalism of design.

While it is contingent, provisional, and probative, the event makes the subject of the design experiment—and democratic inquiry—concrete. Rather than referring to abstractions, activities of designing instantiate a set of conditions. Through use—as well as nonuse and failure—those instantiations are questioned, disputed, and embraced, through twisting, folding, and unfurling considerations. In Alex Wilkie's work on prototyping as event, the subject of design is a disease: obesity. Obesity is a complex and contested concept in both popular and medical discourse. While that complexity and contestation remain in the design work, Wilkie (2014, 487) argues, "There is no abstract 'obesity,' because it is constantly being actualized as an event, whether through discursive envisioning or hands-on prototyping, obesity is always being specified as *this* particular form of obesity." The same could be said of the examples discussed through-out this book. The experiment-as-event does not produce an abstraction of the smart city; it produces a particular narrative of *this* smart city. The experiment-as-event does not yield a general theory of commoning; it leads to *this* particular occasion of commoning. The experiment-as-event does not produce a universal model of democracy; it produces *this* particular and inescapably local set of encounters and infrastructures of governmentality. Through the design experiment we can work to manifest civic imaginaries, if only momentarily. As they make these diverse civic imaginaries experien-tial, the design experiment can be understood as a kind of prefiguration—the lived expression of a politics in minor form (Asad 2019; DiSalvo 2016; Lenskjold, Olander, and Halse 2015).

6   Care of the Possible

Engaging in design experiments is a way to contribute to diverse civic imaginaries and practices. As a practice of inquiry, these events help us collaboratively explore and proffer ideas about how we might live together differently. Such experimentation is part of the work of democracy; it is one way we keep democratic conditions vibrant. But engaging in these design experiments is more than some form of civic duty, like voting. Engaging in these design experiments in civics is also a practice of care: the care of the possible. The phrase "care of the possible" comes from an interview with Isabelle Stengers (2011) in which she discusses how William James influenced her work. Stengers used this phrase to describe pragmatism, and it seems fitting inspiration here; pragmatism, particularly feminist pragmatism that emphasizes imagination as foundational to an experimental approach to democracy, has influenced this book. This phrase resonates with the activities and outcomes of design experiments in civics, and the values and affects that motivate those activities and outcomes.

To me, care of the possible entails a commitment to tending to diverse potentials, to conditions and consequences that have yet to be realized. In the context of democratic inquiry, these are diverse potentials of communal life. This care is made concrete through the particularities of the event. And while care occurs "in the small," it also extends beyond the immediacy of our situations to inspire our theories and desires of what civics might be. Throughout this book, we can locate care of the possible in and across the various projects. We find care of the possible for what a smart Atlanta might be, how a foraging collective might make use of emerging technologies, and how residents might make use of data to garner resources for their neighborhood. We also find care of the possible for diverse subjectivities, for what commoning might be, and how institutions might be differently configured. Such care of the possible is a practice of cultivating inspired and resourceful aspirations for our collective conditions and experiences of democracy.

There is an expansive body of scholarship on care, springing forth from feminist theory. Care is so compelling because it attunes us to the world and to each other in ways that are in stark contrast with prevailing discourses that laud domineering forms of action. Carol Gilligan's (1993) work on the ethics of care is foundational to contemporary theories of care. An ethics of care, according to Gilligan, stands apart from other forms of ethics that prize logic and reason above all else, and tend toward generalizable principles. Instead, a feminist ethics of care is relational. Because it is relational, a feminist ethics of care is not detached or impartial. Joan Tronto's work on care is particularly important for this inquiry, as Tronto articulates care and democracy. Fisher and Tronto (1991, 40) define care as "a species activity that includes everything that we do to maintain, continue, and repair our 'world,' so that we can live in it as well as possible. That world includes our bodies, ourselves, and our environment, all of which we seek to interweave in a complex, life-sustaining web." This concept of care, for Tronto, should be foundational to democracy and to our democratic institutions. Her concept of "caring with" is a call to take up the collective responsibility of care in society, and this responsibility and response becomes defining of democracy (2013).

Within the social study of science and technology there has also been an invigoration of the concept of care. This work is relevant as it tends to examine care in relation to the ways that science and technology shape and are shaped by care and develop in sociotechnical practices. Annemarie Mol's (2008) examination of how a logic of care contrasts with the prevailing logic of choice that characterizes contemporary medicine offers a corollary to issues and practices of care in civics. For María Puig de la Bellacasa (2017), care becomes a way to move beyond matters of concern, to highlight the affective attachments that underpin our relations to issues.

Much of the work on care and design is grounded in familiar caring environments, such as health and medicine. Ian Hargraves (2018, 88) poses the question: Why is design relevant for care? He offers the response that fundamentally design is a practice that works to make people matter: "Because people matter, we design." For Hargraves this concept of people mattering connects design to medicine through care. I would argue, the same articulation is possible with regard to civics. Recently the discussion of design in relation to care has expanded beyond standard caring environments. For instance, Austin Toomb's research examines how care provides an orientation to understanding practices and sites of making, such as so-called hackerspaces. What characterizes these spaces, and the activities that take place there, is not so much some virtuosity of innovation but the labor of maintenance and of tending to relations (Toombs, Bardzell, and Bardzell 2015). Eric Gordon and Gabriel Mugar's work on civic media and what they term "meaningful inefficiencies" also centers care to the work of design in the context of civics, arguing that "care is always the outcome of civic design—it is what publics, when given the chance to create together, seek to achieve" (2020, 18). More expansive still, in 2019 a group of thirty-two scholars published the Lancaster Care Charter, a declaration for aligning design with care (Rodgers et al. 2019). Significant to this inquiry, the Lancaster Care Charter is oriented toward the design of possible futures, and it looks to care as a way to approach that work, through attentiveness to "Care of Complexity," "Care of the Project," and "Care of Relations." Notably, the Lancaster Care Charter is also reflexive and circumspect—it acknowledges the limitations of design as well as offering an aspiration for design as "a means of developing better ways of caring for our world, our cities, our livelihoods, our relationships, and for each other" (77).

Given its enduring commitments to democracy and feminism, it is not surprising that care has also taken on prominence in the ever-expanding praxis of participatory design. Similar to the concept of the commons, care offers a character and purpose to designing that engages issues of equity and strives to support collective action. Kristina Lindström and Åsa Ståhl (2020a, 1) propose a practice of caring design experiments, which "aim to foster maintenance and repair for livable worlds." Their work, like this inquiry, draws from the idea of democratic design experiments (Binder et al. 2015) and then directs those experiments toward the issues of the Anthropocene. Ann Light and Yoko Akama (2014) offer an interpretation of design as an endeavor of codesigning future relations. Their interpretation is in many ways akin to much of the work described herein and is another source of inspiration for this inquiry. For Light and Akama, such an endeavor of codesigning future relations is one of care. As they state, "But we see a role for participatory practitioners as custodians of care, creating spaces for others to reflect, make mistakes, learn and debate" (160). We might think of the design experiments I have described as one example of such spaces. And the framing of the work of design as custodians of care is both reflexive and humble. Light and Akama then go on to state, "The making of futures needs care" (160). The care of the possible is this close tending to the making of futures.

I am not going to merely state, "this is all about care" and then be done with it. Rather, through this chapter I reflect on *how* care of the possible unfolds. In the process of doing so, I also acknowledge the complications of care and reflect on how an orientation and commitment to care might affect design as a field and practice. To begin with, there are at least two routes to care of the possible in design experiments in civics. The first route can be found in inventive problem-making; the second is through tinkering. Inventive problem-making extends the implications of the experiment beyond design, while also acknowledging its limits. Tinkering offers a way of characterizing the partial, while attempting to make civics work a bit better— recognizing "better" as an open, changing, and contested ambition. As a practice of care, inventive problem-making expresses issues and potentials to gather others to attend to them, while tinkering involves persistently tuning those things that matter. These are not the only ways that care of the possible occurs through practices of design and with designed things; I simply offer these expressions of care as germane to design experiments in civics.

Inventive Problem-Making as Care of the Possible

We tend to think of experiments as providing answers or solutions. But it is just as apt to say that experiments produce problems. As mentioned previously, Mariam Fraser's (2006) concept of inventive problem-making is useful for characterizing the purpose and outcomes of design experiments. As a mode of inventive problem-making, design experiments spark knowledge and imagination. That knowledge and imagination often challenges our experience of unfamiliar conditions and unsure potentials. Such unfamiliar conditions and unsure potentials are akin to what Jane Addams referred to as "perplexities," situations that require consideration, the resolution of which are not to be found in obvious or familiar courses of action ([1902] 2002). Such perplexities were fundamental to Addams's work, coupled with experimentation. As Erik Schneiderhan (2011, 596) notes in his study of Jane Addams and Hull-House, "In the pragmatist conceptualization of non-habitual action, then, perplexity and experimentation lead to growth, and this in turn fosters new perplexities and new experimentation." While the design experiment may produce some answers, it also elicits questions about the conditions and potentials that we have brought forth and articulated through the experiment. The design experiment thus does not so much solve problems as it expresses problems and articulates the factors of problems. If done well, design experiments also initiate interest and chart courses of action. Through sparking knowledge and imagination, the design experiment produces compelling topics and situations for ongoing civic work. These topics and situations are possibilities that require care. As such, design experiments in civics are a part of care work, a whole that extends beyond the practices and fields of design.

To say that a primary outcome of design experiments is inventive problem-making is not a dismissal of problem-solving altogether. Inventive problem-making simply reorients designers' relationships with problems and the activities of designing. Perhaps most significant, characterizing the outcome of design experiments as inventive problem-making creates space to admit that many problems might be better addressed through means *other* than design. In other words, inventive problem-making does necessarily produce a design problem. The outcome of inventive problem-making often directs us to look *someplace other than design* to address problems. This is in contrast with many approaches to design that look to turn all problems into design problems.

If one outcome of inventive problem-making is to realize that other practices might better address problems, then designers truly committed to those affected by those problems must make them tractable to others. The problems—their factors, relations, potentials, and consequences—need to be expressed to enable people other than designers to recognize and act on them. This is particularly important with experimentation in social and political domains that extend beyond standard competencies of designers. It is inappropriate to use design practices to address every problem. Such an assertion is not an abdication of the responsibility of designers. Rather, I merely wish to recognize humility, acknowledge the limits of design practices, and convey respect for other fields. There are always other ways of knowing, making, and doing. It would be sheer vanity and conceit to think that any problem expressed *through* design might be addressable *by* design.

Recalling the *PARSE* project demonstrates how care of the possible can identify problems rather than solve them. *PARSE* participants contributed to new scenarios of a smart Atlanta through design games. We believed that storytelling was an art of design, and that stories express subjectivities. In creating and sharing these scenarios, our intent was not to specify which services should be built. Rather, we wanted to articulate pluralistic subjectivities and then present scenarios that express those subjectivities in all their complexities. These scenarios demanded attention from different constituencies, other fields and practices with the capacities to address the issues they raised. For instance, the scenario "Game Day Parking" described a situation where a resident used city data services to determine the availability of street parking and then dynamically generated pricing for an informal community economy that sold parking in abandoned lots. The legality of "Game Day Parking" is questionable, and it could require different data structures and procedures. But it is not the responsibility or work of design to solve the legal and technical issues that undergirded this story. And designers who attempt to do so may fall victim to folly and hubris. It is the responsibility and work of design to express concepts in such a way that those who might attend to these issues are able to recognize them as meaningful. Every city has technical, ethical, and political issues in need of articulation and expression to make them tractable to others. These issues need to be recognizable to engineers, lawyers, policy makers, councilmembers, and activists as relevant to them. Quite literally, the work of design in this context is the invention of problems: the making of difficult situations that require the attention and effort of others, and doing so in ways that generate interest.

The work of generating interest is an essential aspect of inventive problem-making. By generating interest, I mean compellingly expressing the conditions, potentials, and consequences that motivate action. As Stengers (2000, 91) put it, "Concerning those who have accepted to gather around the experimental apparatus to recognize its possible relevance, we must first of all say that they have allowed themselves to become *interested*." Practices of design can be particularly valuable to provoke people to become interested; after all, design creates desire. Unlike fields and practices that purport and celebrate objectivity, much of the work of design is to capture our attention or to express arguments for how we should live in the world (Buchanan 2001). When designers craft products, services, and experiences, they make appeals to affect, character, and values. Generating interest is fundamental to the practice of design.

We can witness this, again, by returning to *PARSE*. It began with a set of playful activities to stimulate the imagination and the desire for invention. The game's format, structure, materials, and flow were intended to make the topic of smart cities accessible. Few people find the idea of spending hours talking about sensors and data compelling, because the connection between such technologies and everyday life is tenuous. The first step of the project was to craft a happening that would assemble those who might be affected by smart-city technologies but who are not attending to them or otherwise not welcome to participate in them, and to provide the impetus and means for creative expression from those people. The subsequent step was to take those abbreviated concepts and draw them together as stories. This too was an endeavor of generating interest. The stories were intentionally told and shared in formats intended to pique curiosity and draw readers in. We made decisions about the narrative forms and content with the recognition that designers were not the audience for the resulting stories. Rather, the audiences for these stories were government employees, residents, and even those in industry. Our hope was that these stories might pose problems that required *their* perspectives and capacities to address.

As design experiments in civics, these activities offer a set of conditions and experiences that enable us, collectively, to reflect upon whether or not such conditions and experiences are desirable and manifest the values we aspire to. These experiments were also prefigurative; they modeled a means-end relation through qualities of democratic togetherness (Asad 2019; DiSalvo 2016; Swain 2019; Yates 2015, 2020). In the process, they produced things like stories, devices, encounters, and experiences. These things became the material and affective remainders of design experiments—left behind as infrastructure for our ongoing imagination of democracy "in the small." The problems posed by design experiments became another component of infrastructure for imagination and continuing explorations of civics. When we speak of inventive problem-making as care of the possible, it draws our attention to ways to identify and express what might be needed if we chose to pursue those potentials. Care of the possible, then, is both "in the now" and oriented toward futures. Through the problems expressed, design experiments in civics nurture possibilities for ongoing action. These courses of ongoing action must extend beyond the work of designer and designing if they are to be democratic. As Binder and colleagues describe, through the experiment "'the possible' becomes tangible, formable, and within reach of engaged yet diverse citizens" (2015, 16).

Reflecting on the projects in this book, they are rife with inventive problem-making. Some of the problems they produce are due to inadequacies. However, we should not reductively cast all problems as deficiencies, because deficiency logics tend to reproduce oppressive binaries and hierarchies. Many of the problems they revealed were simply unresolved conundrums. *Fruit Are Heavy*, which used low-fidelity sensors to monitor the relative ripeness of fruit in trees for urban foraging, expressed shortcomings of already existing services available in smart cities. *Fruit Are Here* created an interactive digital map to track fruit trees over time and asked whether foraging data could be used for environmental monitoring. Taken together, *Fruit Are Heavy* and *Fruit Are Here* raised questions about how technologies of mediation might shape practices of commoning. *Careful Coding*, which explored how to support residents in collecting data to advocate for resources for their neighborhood, expressed the dilemmas and promise of navigating informal institutions and the capacities and limitations of using data for advocacy. Few of these problems were able to be addressed through design. Most are better suited to other disciplines and practices. This is why making the factors, relations, and consequences of problems tractable to others is vital.

Interest paves pathways to care. This idea is inspired and informed by the work of María Puig de la Bellacasa (2017) and her argument for a move from matters of concern to matters of care. The starting point here is Bruno Latour's (2004) argument for a move from matters of facts to matters of concern, marking a shift in the endeavor of scholarship, away from merely revealing conditions and consequences and toward more active engagements with issues and their publics. For Latour this is a shift in the role of the critic, who is or should be "not the one who debunks, but the one who assembles . . . not the one who lifts the rugs from under the feet of the naïve believers, but the one who offers the participants arenas in which to gather" (246). Going further, for Puig de la Bellacasa, once we have arrived at matters of concern, then we might again be moved "toward more affectively charged connotations"—toward matters of care. She offers a simple and powerful demonstration: to say "I am concerned about something" and "I care about something" are two different statements. The statement of care "adds a strong sense of attachment and commitment to something" (2017, 42).

That attachment and commitment to something—that care—should be basic to a practice of design experiments in civics and more generally to any practice of democratic inquiry. And yet, we also must acknowledge that such attachment and commitment is not basic to much of design. Standard problem-solving approaches in design make it possible to treat situations in a detached manner. If a designer believes they can definitively remedy a situation or reinvent it anew, there is no need for attachment and commitment. Within such a belief system, conditions will supposedly be so transformed as to conclusively resolve whatever "the problem" was, with no further need to attend to it. Similarly, approaches that center designers and designing render every situation as opportunistic to design. Conditions and consequences simply become possibilities to be cared for to the extent they further the occasions for design. This is why, in the context of design experiments in civics, it is crucial to appreciate inventive problem-making as an affair that seeks audiences and vectors of action other than design. We, as designers, should not participate in care to legitimize and perpetuate design; we should participate in care to cultivate possibilities for communal life.

Tinkering as Care of the Possible

Another way care of the possible unfolds in design experiments in civics is through tinkering. There are two paired qualities of tinkering that mark it as distinct from familiar perspectives on design. First, tinkering is an ongoing process without an end state. Second, tinkering is a practice of adjustment and tuning, rather than invention of the new. What makes tinkering a practice of care is the persistent attention to and pursuit of possibilities that might be "better." This "better," however, is not predetermined. This "better" is the subject of democratic inquiry through collective making, use, and consideration. What is being cared for are both the conditions in the moment and the potential that conditions might someday be otherwise.

Myriam Winance (2010) has described practices of tinkering as care by exploring how a range of actors participate in processes of adjusting wheelchairs. This tinkering does not only benefit whoever is sitting in the wheelchair—disability becomes a matter for friends and family who help maneuver the wheelchair, nurses responsible for lifting the person in and out of the wheelchair, and doctors who see the wheelchair as part of a patient's treatment or recovery. Winance calls this process "empirical tinkering," the "purpose of which, for the people involved, is to empirically shape an arrangement between the persons and the chair that suits them and that causes the emergence of movement sensations, possibilities, and abilities for everyone" (95). While the ends of this tinkering are improved movement, sensations, and abilities, the means of achieving those ends involve actions that are made possible by working with things. Getting a wheelchair into working order is an ongoing, distributed, and material affair.

In this example, while tinkering centers on the wheelchair, it is by no means limited to only the wheelchair. This tinkering occurs in adjustments to the chair, adjustments in the environment, and adjustments among all of those who make use of the chair. Such tinkering might involve raising or lowering the seat. It could involve putting a pillow on the backrest or swapping out the default handgrips for more comfortable grips. Such tinkering might also involve moving furniture in a room to accommodate the wheelchair's turning radius. Or it could involve purchasing a pair of gloves for the person in the wheelchair or for friends and family who push the wheelchair long distances. None of these adjustments will once and for all "fix" the wheelchair. These adjustments are persistent contributions to the ongoing use of the wheelchair. And through that persistent contribution to ongoing use, they express the shared values of all those who engage with the wheelchair. One such value might be that mobility is a human right. Tinkering, then, becomes one of many ways to pursue that right. At the same time, it is important to recognize that these values and ends are dynamic and relational. People's needs and desires change, as does the environment in which their efforts are embedded. Tinkering as care must therefore continue. Those who participate in tinkering do so collectively by sharing a commitment to the conditions and possibilities of all involved. Tinkering, thus, is very much a matter of possibilities—in the case of the wheelchair, it demands sensitivity to those possibilities of movements, affects, and capabilities.

Winance's conceptualization of empirical tinkering describes this second way that care of the possible occurs. In design experiments in civics, we—designers, residents, foragers, municipal workers, and so on—collectively tinker with the materials, processes, habits, and customs of civics. We tinker with the stories of smart cities to encourage them, and the futures those stories proffer, to be more expansive and inclusive. When we tinker with sensors and maps, they become devices that might augment informal systems of food provisioning. Involving ourselves with data collection tools and procedures through tinkering can cultivate and sustain more beneficent relations between residents and government. And when we engage in these activities, we are also tinkering with the constructs of civics. We are tinkering with subjectivities. We are tinkering with theories such as commoning that inspire and inform our aspirations. We are tinkering with the institutions that shape our democratic relations. To tinker as care demands an attentiveness to the ways design can both enable and constrain civic life.

Recall the *Careful Coding* project, which explored how residents collected and managed data that might be used to draw municipal resources to a neighborhood, while preserving residents' capacity to decide on how to prioritize and attend to issues. Through design experiments in civics we manifested informal institutions and relations between residents and city government. The things made and used probed existing configurations of power and responsibility and instantiated different configurations of local politics and direct democracy. Through the design experiment, residents, code violation officers, staff from the Code Enforcement Section, and designers experienced how mandates for data collection, accountabilities for the veracity of information, standards of expertise, and charges to act might be differently distributed. Through processes of making, political relations were expressed, trialed, and considered in action. The paper forms, maps, digital applications, walks through the neighborhood with residents, the cleaned and formatted spreadsheets of data—together, they comprised events within which we, collaboratively, produced and explored diverse civics. Furthermore, these events projected beyond the immediate situation and functionality. They showed that we might also reconfigure authority and agency within the neighborhood.

Although we were working with different materials and conditions than Winance, throughout the design experiment of *Careful Coding* we tinkered in ways that parallel her description of tinkering with the wheelchair. And likewise, we were engaging in care (Baker and Karasti 2018; Meng, DiSalvo, and Zegura 2019; Zegura, DiSalvo, and Meng 2018). One way this tinkering occurred was through ongoing making and modifying tools for data collection. We selected, made, and used tools as we sought to improve the process. Then we made something different and used it again to further learn.

This endeavor was different from the familiar progression of iteration and prototyping in design, because there was no assumption we would arrive at a final tool with precisely the right set of features. As a process of tinkering, there was an acceptance that the cycle of making and making adjustments would continue over and over again as we worked together.

These adjustments were not predetermined by a set of defined user requirements. Rather, these adjustments were ongoing responses to myriad and disparate factors: the differences in communication habits between code enforcement officers, the realization that our process for matching photos to addresses wasn't working, and the effect of the seasons on prioritizing and deprioritizing certain code infractions. Such design experiments, then, embrace a strategy of impromptu amendments and modifications. While we designers from the university did much of this tinkering, we were not alone in this work. Our neighborhood partner Les would adjust how the tools were used on the fly when collecting data with his volunteers. Our contacts in code enforcement would look over the data, providing feedback on what was accurate and not accurate. Another code enforcement officer might be assigned to the neighborhood, or a different neighborhood could decide to use the tool. The neighborhood could change too, so there may be less need to collect code violations, and in such a situation Les might come to believe another type of data would be more valuable in generating interest. Such design experiments in civics understand and accept that communities and the knowledge they hold are always changing.

Data was not the only site of tinkering in *Careful Coding*. Indeed, *Careful Coding* was fundamentally about tinkering with institutions. Throughout the experiment, we designers tweaked the shape and substance of encounters between ourselves and residents, between the residents and code enforcement officers in the streets, and between ourselves and the staff of the Code Enforcement Section. At the same time, residents, code enforcement officers in the street, and the leadership of the Code Enforcement Section made requests of us, as individuals and representatives of institutions. These requests influenced how we approached our research and design: *they* tweaked *our* practices, which affected the character of our affiliations. Together, we slowly manipulated both formal and informal institutions through care. As Winance (2010, 102) describes, "Here, care bespeaks a sensitivity shared and distributed among the actors. The object of care is not one single person but a collective. The work of caring involves attention that is built by the collective and directed towards the sensations and possibilities of action that emerge for the person concerned."

In these design experiments in civics, however, the focus is not on a single "person concerned," but rather on the conditions themselves, the civic environment, and the possibilities therein. In *Careful Coding,* *all* of us were working to imagine and instantiate what these relations might be. Of course, our values were different, and there were disagreements about the structure of those relations. There was friction and agonism. The persistent quality of tinkering provided an opportunity for the ongoing making, remaking, and contestation that are characteristic of robust civic engagement in democracy. Thus, tinkering-as-care is concerned with continually trying to make things work, knowing that even the definition of what it means for things to "work" is multifaceted and always becoming. We tinker with care because we believe things might be better in the future. We tinker not toward a singular grandiose story of achievement but with an acceptance of the challenges and hazy affects that accompany indefinite tending.

"Better" and "good" are important words to think about through tinkering. They are also words that should cause hesitation and concern. Design has long been normative and hegemonic. In design, to talk of "making things better" can be interpreted as an imperative to change, which when embraced uncritically, simply reinforces the status quo. But as Annemarie Mol, Ingunn Moser, and Jeannette Pols state in their introduction to *Care in Practice* (2010, 13), "Raising an argument about which good is best 'in general,' makes little sense. Instead, care implies a negotiation about how different goods might coexist in a given, specific, local practice." In other words, "better" and "good" are labels to conditions that are not universal or absolute but in constant and ongoing arbitration through discovery, invitation, and contestation.

To discuss the "good" in design opens a history of what counts as "good design" that is grossly limited, often pointing to an unacceptably narrow history of making and makers. In contrast, in the context of a feminist ethics of care, "better" and "good" are situated terms. It is these notions of "better" and "good" that should motivate care and tinkering—not the self-satisfied cultural norms of so-called good design. Continuing with Mol, Moser, and Pols (2010, 13), "In the ethics of care it was stressed that in practice, principles are rarely productive. Instead, local solutions to specific problems need to be worked out." In other words, when we tinker to make things better, that better-ness is constrained. It is a matter of improving a situation a bit and perhaps only for the moment. Tinkering is particular, not universal. In this sense, tinkering is closer in practice and affect to mending, repairing, and maintaining than to creation. These facets distinguish tinkering from domineering discourses of innovation. The "good" that is pursued through design tinkering is not an absolute—it is only good enough for now—and remains open to contestation, and the suggestion that the world might be otherwise.

Similar to inventive problem-making, tinkering is a practice of care that exists in the moment and extends into possible futures. This is another way we can speak of care of the possible—as a kind of infrastructuring or institutioning that tends to the now while producing resources and experiences that can be carried forward to nurture and provision conditions that have yet to become (Binder et al. 2011; Huybrechts, Benesch, and Geib 2017b; Le Dantec 2016). In *Careful Coding*, we tinkered with the tools and procedures of data collection in the now, and that data could continue to have an effect even after the project ended. Likewise, when we tinker with the informal institutions of governance in the now, those encounters can produce experiences of togetherness that linger and can be reproduced in other places and times. Because tinkering is never complete, it keeps us open to ongoing material and relational engagements. As long as we are tinkering, the collective conditions (and their meanings and consequences) are open to interpretation and different courses of action. In other words, tinkering is a means to resist closure, to refuse to capitulate. Tinkering is a subtle but persistent refusal to simply let things be.

A refusal to simply let things be through tinkering occurs through the material stuff, in the encounters, and in the practices and environments in which they are situated. With *Careful Coding* and *PARSE*, we are tinkering with configurations of authority and agency in local government. Through *Fruit Are Heavy* and *Fruit Are Here*, we tinkered with how the commons and commoning might be differently configured. It was not just that the procedures of data collection or activities of foraging might be different, or that the stories we told of smart cities could be more varied. It was also that the aspirations and values that undergirded those practices and characterized those environments might change. In those moments, we were tinkering with our imaginaries. Tinkering, more than being simply reformist, is a humble practice of exercising our collective political imagination.

Tinkering cares for the possible, then, in a way similar to inventive problem-making. Both strive to carry potential forward by providing opportunities for us to consider our civic environment as conditions that we might transform in small but meaningful ways. Each design experiment is an event where we explore conditions, modes of action, and consequences. One aspect that differentiates inventive problem-making and tinkering is the proximity of design and the designer in response to those conditions. In inventive problem-making, the intended outcome is often to articulate problems that people other than designers might act on. In tinkering, the designer or the activities of design are often involved in that response. Both endeavors can be understood as providing a shared commitment that we can use to understand why we do design experiments in civics. But we should also attend to the fact that care itself is complicated.

Complications of Care

While care is a significant way to attune design, it is not a panacea for its ills. We can use care as a commitment that anchors design experiments in civics. Care helps explain what we are doing in these experiments, and why we persist when faced with their recurring shortcomings. Care, however, is not without problems.

Within design, the future is often a gilded horizon. This is deceiving: what is possible may not be desirable. Even when the possible is desirable, the process of striving toward it may produce unanticipated outcomes (Parvin and Pollock 2020). This is the history of modernism, and one of the ways "wicked problems" are perpetuated. Even with care. The context of contemporary civics is particularly troubled. For example, data is pervasive throughout these experiments. All these design experiments differently participate in making and sharing data about people and their environments. That data is thick with significance, yet our use of that data is hardly innocent; research on the misuse of data in civic contexts is considerable and growing. To simply say that certain data was collected in a practice of care, or for the purposes of care, does not ameliorate these concerns or consequences. The actions we undertake under the umbrella of care may still cause harm. Possible futures may not align with the desires that provoked the experiment. There may be experiments in civics that we should not undertake and possibilities we should not explore, regardless of being motivated by care. Refusal should always remain an option.

The ways I have discussed care in this chapter emphasize its generally benevolent character. Yet this is not always the case. The discourses and practices of care have repeatedly been rallied to preserve worlds and ideologies replete with prejudice. The preservation of identities is a common example. Care is easily called upon in the service of nationalism, segregation, and other structures that perpetuate inequity. Claiming that one is "caring" for a nation or for a particular group of people can be a paternalist strategy for obfuscating nationalistic desires and racist beliefs. One might argue that such insidious strategies are perversions of care, but they exist nonetheless and remind us that the moral valence of care is complicated.

The affective valence of care is likewise complicated, because caring is not a feel-good moment. It requires long-term participation and labor. As previously discussed with regard to events and quasi-events, appreciating design experiments in civics requires being open to a broader range of affects. When we endure—an affective state of some experiments—this is not a feeling of fulfillment or success. When we endure, we tolerate, withstand, and sustain. There may be a feeling of tenacity that accompanies endurance, but it is not the same feeling as triumph. Likewise, tinkering is not the consummation of some exceptional process of creation. There may be a sense of satisfaction in the moment, but tinkering, like the experiment, begets further wants and desires. It is crucial to recognize that care is often exhausting labor.

The "something more" that characterizes care comes at a physical, emotional, and mental cost to caring people. Historically, care has been gendered and racialized. Caring-as-labor has been the work of women and people of color hired (usually at lowly wages) into caring roles. The work of care is demanding, messy, and at times unpleasant. Oftentimes, care work involves loss. While we engage in care to cultivate or sustain, what or who we care for may inevitably pass away. Consider practices of hospice: we care for those who are dying. In such instances, we do not harbor a false belief that we might mitigate the inevitable, but we still care with the hope that we might contribute to comfort and enable dignity in the face of loss.

When care scales to the level of institutions, it can also usher in the very affects and authorities of design that we want to undo. Joan Tronto (2010, 161) warns of two hazards of creating caring institutions: "paternalism, in which caregivers assume that they know better than care receivers what those care receivers need, and parochialism, in which caregivers develop preferences for care receivers who are closer to them." These concerns are endemic to design. Practitioners and critics alike have repeatedly challenged the ways that design reinforces and reproduces oppression, especially in contexts where the desired outcome is some sort of "good" (see Julier and Kimbell 2019; Nussbaum 2010). Strategies and tactics of decolonizing and feminist practice attempt to redirect these affects and authorities (Mazé and Wangel 2017; Schultz et al. 2018; van Amstel and Gonzatto 2020). But the dominant discourses of design continue to assert claims of expertise in creative problem-solving that are oppressive. This is true even for those who seek to care.

All these affects, authorities, and their complications are present throughout the projects in this book. I have attempted to be authentic and forthright, to include both the promising and problematic dimensions of design experiments in my descriptions and interpretations. In doing so, I have also attempted to demonstrate how we might talk about the activities and outcomes of designing differently, attending to its tenuousness as much as its potential. If we want to take care of the possible seriously, by committing to design experiments in civics as one way of exploring contemporary democracies, we must acknowledge and express the fullness of care. That fullness is not flawless. Neither is the design experiment, nor any practice of democratic inquiry. The design experiment is not clean and tidy, but splintered, compromised, frustrating, full of longing, and uncomfortable. Michelle Murphy (2015) offers an insightful analysis of the discourses of care and cautions scholars against taking an uncritical embrace of care and assuming an association of positive feelings. She calls for a different approach to care: "A politics of 'unsettling' care strives to stir up and put into motion what is sedimented, while embracing the generativity of discomfort, critique, and non-innocence" (717). I hope I have conveyed such an approach throughout this book. Like democracy, care is inherently contested as it is practiced. The complications of care, however, are not reasons to abandon the care of the possible and design experiments in civics. While recognizing these complications, there is nonetheless value in caring and experimenting.

Conclusion

In this book, I set out to tell stories and theorize how design practitioners and scholars might contribute to democracy, using design as a mode of inquiry. Such work is not without difficulty. In fact, it might be best characterized by the difficulties it encounters, and the ways it is fragile, contingent, partial, and compromised. A defining characteristic of this work is that it is situated: it is undertaken in relationship with others, with people and institutions, values and desires, in ever-changing circumstances. While I have attempted to closely describe such experiments and give contours to a practice, any articulation of these experiments will always be incomplete because they are always in the making.

As I write this conclusion, we are in the midst of a global pandemic. The concerns that shape our civic environments and experiences have changed. The work of democratic inquiry and design experiments changes to meet these conditions. For instance, as part of its Smart and Connected Communities funding program, the National Science Foundation has announced a call for grants that examine how communities might make use of smart-cities technologies to shape life in a post-COVID-19 era. Les's work has shifted as his worry now is supporting those who are unhoused during the pandemic. Concrete Jungle continues its work of foraging and has also expanded into a grocery delivery program distributing food to over nine hundred people a week. In each case, questions arise that warrant attention. Who will be invited and able to contribute to setting the agenda and participating in research toward a post-COVID-19 era? Can data be of use in serving those who are without the most basic asset of safe shelter? Or is collecting such data in fact counterproductive, perhaps even dangerous to those in need? What procedures and systems are needed to enable a bricolage of regional farmers, federal and state subsidies, and hundreds of volunteers to coordinate mutual aid? Engaging with such questions continues the work of democratic inquiry and design experiments. Engaging with such questions continues the work of caring for our collective futures. Working in ways that are humble, just, and collaborative enables us to participate in exploring varied democratic practices in the now and contributing to imaginaries of what might be next.

It is tempting to fixate on politics in the large—the imperatives of global development, of nation-states, of transnational regulations and policies. There is distinctive power and authority that politics in the large attends to. What's more, such politics in the large dovetails with the scale of much of contemporary technology—with artificial intelligence, machine learning, and big data. Without a doubt, that scale of politics and action is important. Yes, we need multinational pharmaceutical companies and governments to work together to develop and distribute vaccines. Yes, there is value in employing data and algorithms toward tracking, understanding, and mitigating the spread of a virus. At the same time, the scale of democracies in the small, the closeness of the conditions we experience in our daily lives, also need to be tended to. We need networks of informal organizations providing support to those in need of food and housing. There is also value in using simple tools and techniques to organize and sustain care, and at times there is value in *not* collecting data, in avoiding or resisting surveillance regimes that too often cause harm.

The question of scale, then, is not one of either/or but rather both/and (Hunt 2020). We are surrounded by crisis—the crisis of a global pandemic, the crisis of climate change, the crisis of democracy. Some of these are imminent, others are evolving. All are daunting. We need stories, theories, and practices that enable us to collectively act at different scales in these crises. My focus with these design experiments has been on local democracies. This is not because I believe that particular scale is more significant, but because of a desire for intimacy in engaged scholarship. In the close conditions of civics, democracy becomes intimate. Through design experiments we can act in that closeness, and through our actions we can perceive and experience the current conditions of democracy and also how our communal lives might be differently configured.

While these crises unfold, free-market ideologies continue to be prioritized in many civic contexts, and this threatens democracy. The prevailing discourses of smart cities remain those of efficiency through streamlining government as a service, made possible by private infrastructure and the monetization of public life. Consider the Quayside project in Toronto: a proposed smart neighborhood built from the ground up in collaboration with Sidewalk Labs. The project was critiqued from the start, and rightly so. While collaborations between industry, government, civil society, and communities are common enough, the plans for the Quayside project suggested an audacious interlacing of public and private sectors, enacted through smart-cities technologies and the medium of data. These plans were contested by more than activists and advocates. Venture capitalists referred to them as "a dystopian vision that has no place in a democratic society," and industry leaders called them "a colonizing experiment in surveillance capitalism attempting to bulldoze important urban, civic and political issues" (Cecco 2020). The advent of COVID-19 brought an end to the affair (or at least to that chapter). Due to "unprecedented economic uncertainty," Sidewalk Labs declared that the project was no longer "financially viable" and walked away (Cecco 2020). This is unsurprising. It is, however, telling. In the midst of a civic crisis, this vision of a smart city abandons the city. Perhaps COVID-19 provided an opportune set of circumstances to exit the project. But one could imagine a number of other responses to both the critiques and the crisis.

Such visions are not going away. They will reappear again and elsewhere. In many cases, such visions are much less grand and therefore much less apparent, but nonetheless pernicious. In San Diego, activists and academics are coming together to work against smart streetlights. These streetlights seem innocuous, but they are in fact data-capturing devices strewn across the city, creating a network of surveillance (Whitney et al. 2021). Even when activists succeed in convincing the city to stop the surveillance, contracts with vendors may allow the data to continue to be captured, stored, and presumably used. Similar stories exist in other cities. Technological governance and citizenship are becoming the norm in ways both spectacular and mundane. There is not yet enough public discourse or agency in decision-making concerning these technologies and procedures, which are changing the conditions and experiences of politics. Working to intercede and counter such initiatives is crucial. Design experiments can support such direct action and contestation, and that is a line of inquiry I hope others will take up.

I believe it is also important to support, sustain, and amplify efforts that offer alternative modes of communal life. That has been the focus of the design experiments in civics that comprise this book. It is fair to ask whether or not such efforts will bring about change. A common critique of such efforts is that they do not bring about change. Another is that the change they bring about is limited or exclusionary. Yet another is that such efforts are simply folded back into hegemony. All of these critiques are fair. And yet I still maintain that such work is valuable. Take foraging as an example. Foraging will not solve food insecurity. There is simply not enough produce growing wild to feed all of those in need, and most people want more than fruit to subsist on. It is easy to dismiss foraging. But for the person at the shelter who is receiving that foraged apple or pear, it matters. It matters that they have fresh fruit and healthy food that they might not otherwise have. It also matters that someone cared enough to do the work to share that fruit. To dismiss foraging or other circumscribed efforts expresses a privileged position about what kind of action is meaningful. Resident-led data collection and counter-data action are other examples. Such practices will not undo decades of systemic racism or classism. But even though the effects of systemic racism and classism persist, it matters to residents that they can collect data about their communities that enables them to tell different stories about who they are and who they want to be, to advocate and care for themselves on their terms (Meng and DiSalvo 2018; Meng, DiSalvo, and Zegura 2019; Zegura, DiSalvo, and Meng 2018). Gibson-Graham (1996, 2006) makes the argument that rejecting community economies because they are not viable against capitalism is, ironically, a fundamentally capitalocentric perspective, granting authority and destiny to a singular vision of economic life. The same can be said for civics and democracy broadly construed. Even though practices of communal life will not upend systemic racism and classism, solve food insecurity, or dismantle the regimes of big data, they offer the possibility for environments and moments that allow us to experience democratic conditions and care, if only in the small. Such experiences matter for those who participate in them.

Design Otherwise

Projects such as those described in this book are comparatively uncommon in design. Much more familiar are projects like the Quayside in Toronto—projects with designers contributing to visions of the seamless integration of public and private life through all manner of technologies. This is to be expected, given the relationship of design to industry. As Clive Dilnot (2015) argues, modern Western design was called into being by industry. Of course, then, the primary orientations of the field are going to be in relation to industry. This in and of itself is not a problem. Industry is an important component in society, and there is much that design can contribute to and through industry. But we are also in a moment in which free-market ideologies have become dangerous, oppressive, and pervasive. Practices and discourses of design that ground their purpose and meaning in producing value in free-market ideologies are misaligned to democracy. And such practices and discourses dominate design as we know it. Other approaches to design are needed. If we want to develop practices and discourses of design that find their purpose and meaning in participating in making other worlds possible, we need other theories, pedagogies, and cultures of design. As design practitioners and scholars, we need to contribute to expanding concepts of thinking and doing design otherwise—ways of designing that are not beholden to the standard histories and commitments of design and seek to proffer different subjectivities, endeavors, and purposes of making.

Beyond the democratic design experiments (Binder et al. 2015) that spurred this inquiry, ever more diverse modes of design are emerging that offer these needed theories, pedagogies, and cultures of design otherwise. These include critical fabulations (Rosner 2018), ecosocial design (Franz and Elzembaumer 2016), design activism (Fuad-Luke 2013), design justice (Costanza-Chock 2020), data feminism (D'Ignazio and Klein 2020), transition design (Irwin, Kossoff, and Tonkinwise, 2015), and pluriversal design (Escobar 2018), among others. It is easy to get caught up in these labels and their differences, but what is vital and moving is what is common among them. What is common to many of these cultures of design is a commitment to engaged practice. Such practices locate their purpose and meaning in acts of collaboration, in the work of imagining, enabling, sustaining, and in some cases bringing into being ways of living together: born of the values and desires of those undertaking that collective work. Perhaps these acts and their outcomes have market value, but it is just as likely that they not. And whether or not they have market value does not define their significance.

Rather than trying to fit such work into our standard conceptions of design, perhaps it's best just to acknowledge that such work doesn't quite fit. It seems that when we try to meld such practices and commitments together with free-market ideologies that characterize the contemporary institutions of design, what often emerges is lacking, at times pernicious (Irani 2019). I am also unconvinced that labeling such work as "public sector" is meaningful when the public sector is increasingly privatized. Moreover, as discussed in the introduction, all too often the work of government, and even civil society, is simply to reproduce governmentality as we know it (Julier and Kimbell 2019).

Just as it's fair to say that design has become an institution in contemporary society, it's also fair to say other designs are possible. And one of the tasks of research, theory, and criticism is to describe and articulate those other practices and discourses of design.

Several years ago I gave a talk on diverse civics and different models of design practice. One model cast the relationship between designers and communities in client terms. This was the most familiar model as it replicated design consultancies: the designer is outside of the community and is contracted to serve the community. Another model cast the designer as working from within a civil society organization. This model was also familiar as it replicated that of an in-house designer, a long-standing model in industry. The third model cast the relationship between the designer and communities in terms of the designer as an accomplice, drawing from activist practice (Indigenous Action Media 2014). This model generated excitement and confusion. It was unfamiliar. What seemed most difficult for the audience were the economics of this work and how it would fit with the familiar and formal institutions of design. Questions such as "Who will pay for this work?" and, perhaps more directly, "How will I get paid for this work?" jammed the conversation.

How to pay for such work and how to do such work in a way that is sustainable for all those involved *are* crucial questions. But herein is an irony. Designers take great pride in their capacity to reframe situations and practices. For the most part, however, throughout all that reframing, all that disruption and innovation of everything else, design itself is overlooked and accepted as what it has been and is. There are some, but comparatively few, attempts to differently consider the economic and social structures of design (Boehnert 2018; Elzenbaumer 2013; Julier 2017; Vlachokyriakos et al. 2018). So, while design may be an institution in contemporary society, what's needed are other institutions of design, both formal and informal.

Some of these institutions may need to be invented and made. At the same time, there are also many institutional forms that are *already* happening that we might learn from. To be clear, I am *not* suggesting that we need to disrupt or innovate design. Rather, we need to look to and humbly learn from other sites and practices of making and doing, in order to broaden our appreciation for who, what, and where design is and might be.

Here, once again, we can find inspiration and guidance in the work of Gibson-Graham. Just as Gibson-Graham argues that there are multiple economies, and that we need to acknowledge and appreciate diverse economies, and just as I have made a similar argument about civics, we might also make the same argument about design more broadly. There are multiplicities of design occurring, across varied sites. We know the dominant practices, discourses, and sites of design. These are the professions of design; they are formalized, expert, and market-driven. But by working outside the de facto institutions of design, in collaboration with others, we can broaden our understanding and appreciation of design and other modes of creative practice. This might, for instance, happen through working in collaboration with social movements (Costanza-Chock 2020; Ghoshal, Mendhekar, and Bruckman 2020), within solidarity economies (Vlachokyriakos et al. 2018), in artistic practices of noticing and unmaking (Jönsson et al. 2021), with collectives and cooperatives (Fox 2015; Jenkins 2017; Seravalli 2014), in the work of counterfeiters or forgers (Keshavarz 2018), in collaboration with Indigenous peoples and practices (Liboiron 2021), or from the critical pedagogies of the Global South (van Amstel and Gonzatto 2020). Such sites of design and their institutions are not necessarily antithetical to the dominant practices and discourses of design. Some exist in opposition, others are entangled, and most are compromised (Liboiron 2017; Shotwell 2016). What is meaningful and significant is to recognize that the sites and practices of design are numerous and varied, far beyond what is usually talked about when we talk about design, far beyond its professionalized practice as a service to industry, government, or civil society.

Design experiments in civics, then, are not a radical political practice, nor is care of the possible. As I have tried to address throughout this inquiry, design experiments in civics are modest. Their modest scale does not diminish their significance or value. Building from a pragmatist tradition, such work is essential to democracy: to explore conditions and experiences of conjoined action in an ongoing fashion. But design experiments are not grand programs of massive political or social change. They do not claim to be, nor do they aspire to be. Where we might think of designed experiments in civics and care of the possible as radical is with regard to design itself. I'm leery of the implications of the term "radical," but I am drawn to the idea of the radical as that which gets to the root of things. I am not suggesting that design experiments in civics and care of the possible upheave design as we know it. Rather, I am suggesting that design experiments in civics and care of the possible contribute to thinking about how the roots of design might find different areas for growth. And one such area would be to consider democracy itself as the grounds for practice and discourse.

A Commitment to Democracy

In the end, the reason to do these design experiments in civics comes down to a belief that they are an inherently worthy endeavor. Will our democratic institutions crumble without these experiments? No. But our experiences of democracy might be lacking. And I believe experiences that spark our interest and imagination, that provide us with capacities and desires for diverse communal life, contribute to the constant renewal of our democracies, making them more vibrant.

Through design experiments we come to know and inhabit civics differently. We also come to appreciate and practice design differently. We identify and express problems so that others might eventually address them more fully. We tinker to improve conditions, if only for the moment. Following in a pragmatist tradition, while also echoing the contestation characteristic of agonism, "there is no end-state at which we must work to arrive, but a multiple of possible future states which we seek and try out" (McKenna 2001, 83). Both design and democracy, in this sense, are process-oriented. They are undertakings that are ongoing, that find value in the action of that undertaking, in the *doing* of design and democracy. Care is similarly process-oriented. We continue to practice care, even as our actions fall short, even as our conditions are compromised, even as the goals we work toward fail to be realized. Care is not characterized by its "success." Yes, there are heroic stories of care. But there are many more stories of care that end in loss. Care brings varied and often uncomfortable affects into the practices and discourses of design. Care is stubborn—and even desperate.

In this way, we can also characterize these design experiments as hopeful. They are difficult; they are fragile, contingent, partial, and compromised. And they are hopeful. In each of the projects described in this book, those I collaborated with did their work and participated in these activities because, in varied ways, they found them worthwhile, both in the moment and toward something else beyond that moment. Much of this work is anticipatory: it looks to shape the conditions that it might grow into, with conviction but without assurances. As Rebecca Solnit (2016, xiv) puts it:

> Hope is an embrace of the unknown and unknowable, an alternative to the certainty of both optimists and pessimists. Optimists think it will all be fine without our involvement; pessimists take the opposite position; both excuse themselves from acting. It's the belief that what we do matters even though how and when it may matter, who and what it may impact, are not things we can know beforehand.

To do design as democratic inquiry, to participate in design experiments, is to choose to pursue the work of democracy with fervor and hope. We choose to participate in design experiments in civics because we care about what the conditions and experiences of democracy might be for those with whom we act together. According to Jane Addams ([1902] 2002), for democracy to be meaningful and vibrant, we must choose to seek out diverse experiences with others. Democracy must be the product of social pursuits rather than isolated, individual decisions. And we must consciously choose to embrace conditions of difference and perplexity, to care for others even though doing so may not always be comfortable. We do design experiments in civics, then, because of a basic belief: contributing to imaginaries of communal life, and exploring practices that differently configure communal life, is necessary for democratic pluralism. Such work finds its roots not in markets or government but in an attachment and a commitment to democracy itself.

References

Addams, Jane. (1899) 1982. "A Function of the Social Settlement." In *The Social Thought of Jane Addams*, edited by Christopher Lasch, 183–199. Irvington.

Addams, Jane. (1902) 2002. *Democracy and Social Ethics*. University of Illinois Press.

Addams, Jane. (1910) 1990. *Twenty Years at Hull-House*. University of Illinois Press.

Agid, Shana, and Elizabeth Chin. 2019. "Making and Negotiating Value: Design and Collaboration with Community Led Groups." In "Understanding, Capturing and Assessing Value in Collaborative Design Research," special issue, *CoDesign* 15, no. 1: 75–89.

Ahmed, Sara. 2014. *Willful Subjects*. Duke University Press.

Ahmed, Sara. 2017. *Living a Feminist Life*. Duke University Press.

Ames, Morgan G. 2019. *The Charisma Machine: The Life and Legacy of One Laptop per Child*. MIT Press.

Ansell, Chris. 2013. "What Is a 'Democratic Experiment'?" *Contemporary Pragmatism* 9, no. 2: 159–180.

Appadurai, Arjun. 1996. *Modernity at Large: Cultural Dimensions of Globalization*. Vol. 1. University of Minnesota Press.

Arendt, Hannah. 2013. *The Human Condition*. University of Chicago Press.

Asad, Mariam. 2019. "Prefigurative Design as a Method for Research Justice." In *Proceedings of the ACM on Human-Computer Interaction* 3, no. CSCW, article 200, 1–18. Association for Computing Machinery. https://dl.acm.org/doi/10.1145/3359302.

Baker, Karen S., and Helena Karasti. 2018. "Data Care and Its Politics: Designing for Local Collective Data Management as a Neglected Thing." In *Proceedings of the 15th Participatory Design Conference: Full Papers*, vol. 1, Article 10, 1–12. Association for Computing Machinery. https://doi.org/10.1145/3210586.3210587.

Bannon, Liam, Jeffrey Bardzell, and Susanne Bødker. 2018. "Reimagining Participatory Design." *Interactions* 26, no. 1: 26–32.

Barbrook, Richard, and Andy Cameron. 1996. "The Californian Ideology." *Science as Culture* 6, no. 1: 44–72.

Bardzell, Jeffrey, and Shaowen Bardzell. 2015. "The User Reconfigured: On Subjectivities of Information." In *Proceedings of the Fifth Decennial Aarhus Conference on Critical Alternatives*, 133–144. https://doi.org/10.7146/aahcc.v1i1.21298.

Bardzell, Shaowen. 2018. "Utopias of Participation: Feminism, Design, and the Futures." *ACM Transactions on Computer-Human Interaction* 25, no. 1: 1–24.

Beck, Eevi. 2002. "P for Political: Participation Is Not Enough." *Scandinavian Journal of Information Systems* 14, no. 1: 1.

Benjamin, Ruha. 2019. *Race after Technology: Abolitionist Tools for a New Jim Crow.* Polity Press.

Bennett, Cynthia L., and Daniela K. Rosner. 2019. "The Promise of Empathy: Design, Disability, and Knowing the 'Other.'" In *Proceedings of the 2019 CHI Conference on Human Factors in Computing Systems*, 1–13. https://doi.org/10.1145/3290605.3300528.

Berkowitz, Ben, and Jean-Paul Gagnon. 2017. "SeeClickFix Empowers Citizens by Connecting Them to Their Local Governments." *Democratic Theory* 4, no. 1: 121–124.

Binder, Thomas, Eva Brandt, Pelle Ehn, and Joachim Halse. 2015. "Democratic Design Experiments: between Parliament and Laboratory." *CoDesign* 11, no. 3–4: 152–165.

Binder, Thomas, Giorgio De Michelis, Pelle Ehn, Per Linde, Giulio Jacucci, and Ina Wagner. 2011. *Design Things.* MIT Press.

Björgvinsson, Erling, Pelle Ehn, and Per-Anders Hillgren. 2010. "Participatory Design and 'Democratizing Innovation.'" In *Proceedings of the 11th Biennial Participatory Design Conference*, 41–50. https://doi.org/10.1145/1900441.1900448.

Björgvinsson, Erling, Pelle Ehn, and Per-Anders Hillgren. 2012. "Agonistic Participatory Design: Working with Marginalised Social Movements." *CoDesign* 8, no. 2–3: 127–144.

Blauvelt, Andrew. 2008. "Towards Relational Design." *Design Observer*, November 3. https://designobserver.com/feature/towards-relational-design/7557/.

Bleeker, Julian. 2009. "Design Fiction: A Short Essay on Design, Science, Fact and Fiction." *Near Future Laboratory* (blog), March. https://blog.nearfuturelaboratory.com/2009/03/17/design-fiction-a-short-essay-on-design-science-fact-and-fiction.

Boehnert, Joanna. 2018. "Anthropocene Economics and Design: Heterodox Economics for Design Transitions." *She Ji: The Journal of Design, Economics, and Innovation* 4, no. 4: 355–374.

Brandt, Eva. 2006. "Designing Exploratory Design Games: A Framework for Participation in Participatory Design?" In *Proceedings of the Ninth Conference on Participatory Design: Expanding Boundaries in Design*, vol. 1, 57–66. https://doi.org/10.1145/1147261.1147271.

Brandt, Eva, Thomas Binder, and Elizabeth B.-N. Sanders. 2012. "Tools and Techniques: Ways to Engage Telling, Making, and Enacting." In *Routledge International Handbook of Participatory Design*, edited by Jesper Simonsen and Toni Robertson, 21–36. Routledge.

Browne, Simone. 2015. *Dark Matters: On the Surveillance of Blackness*. Duke University Press.

Buchanan, Richard. 2001. "Design and the New Rhetoric: Productive Arts in the Philosophy of Culture." *Philosophy & Rhetoric* 34, no. 3: 183–206.

Buchanan, Richard. 2019. "Systems Thinking and Design Thinking: The Search for Principles in the World We Are Making." *She Ji: The Journal of Design, Economics, and Innovation* 5, no. 2: 85–104.

Butoliya, Deepa. 2020. "Deepa Butoliya: There Is No Prescriptive Way to Do Speculative and Critical Design." Interview with James Auger. *SpeculativeEdu*, July 20. https://speculativeedu.eu/interview-deepa-butoliya.

Caffentzis, George, and Silvia Federici. 2014. "Commons against and beyond Capitalism." *Community Development Journal* 49, no. suppl_1: i92–i105.

Castoriadis, Cornelius. 1997. *The Imaginary Institution of Society*. MIT Press.

Castoriadis, Cornelius. 2007. *Figures of the Thinkable*. Stanford University Press.

Cecco, Leland. 2020. "Google Affiliate Sidewalk Labs Abruptly Abandons, Toronto Smart City Project." *Guardian*, May 7. https://www.theguardian.com/technology/2020/may/07/google-sidewalk-labs-toronto-smart-city-abandoned.

Chetty, Raj, Nathaniel Hendren, Patrick Kline, and Emmanuel Saez. 2014. "Where Is the Land of Opportunity? The Geography of Intergenerational mobility in the United States." *Quarterly Journal of Economics* 129, no. 4: 1553–1623.

Choi, Jaz Hee-jeong, Laura Forlano, and Denisa Kera. 2020. "Situated Automation: Algorithmic Creatures in Participatory Design." In *Proceedings of the 16th Participatory Design Conference 2020—Participation(s) Otherwise*, vol. 2, 5–9. Association for Computing Machinery. https://doi.org/10.1145/3384772.3385153.

Clarke, Allison. 2021. *Victor Papanek: Designer for the Real World*. MIT Press.

Coles, Alex, and Catharine Rossi. 2013. *EP 1: The Radical Italian Avant-Garde 1968–1976*. Vol. 1. Sternberg Press.

Connolly, William E. 2002. *Identity/Difference: Democratic Negotiations of Political Paradox*. University of Minnesota Press.

Costanza-Chock, Sasha. 2020. *Design Justice: Community-Led Practices to Build the Worlds We Need*. MIT Press.

Cowan, Ruth Schwartz. 1983. *More Work for Mother*. Basic Books.

Crampton, J. W. 2009. "Cartography: Performative, Participatory, Political." *Progress in Human Geography* 33, no. 6: 840–848.

Crivellaro, Clara, Rob Anderson, Daniel Lambton-Howard, Tom Nappey, Patrick Olivier, Vasilis Vlachokyriakos, Alexander Wilson, and Pete Wright. 2019. "Infrastructuring Public Service Transformation: Creating Collaborative Spaces between Communities and Institutions through HCI Research." *ACM Transactions on Computer-Human Interaction* 26, no. 3, Article 15, 1–29. https://doi.org/10.1145/3310284.

Crooks, Roderic, and Morgan Currie. 2021. "Numbers Will Not Save Us: Agonistic Data Practices." *The Information Society*: 1–19.

De Angelis, Massimo. 2010a. "On the Commons: A Public Interview with Massimo De Angelis and Stavros Stavrides." *E-Flux Journal* 17 (June–August): 1–17. https://www.e-flux.com/journal/17/67351/on-the-commons-a-public-interview-with-massimo-de-angelis-and-stavros-stavrides/.

De Angelis, Massimo. 2010b. "The Production of Commons and the 'Explosion' of the Middle Class." *Antipode* 42, no. 4: 954–977.

Deleuze, Gilles, and Felix Guattari. 1986. *Kafka: Toward a Minor Literature*. University of Minnesota Press.

Del Gaudio, Chiara, Carlo Franzato, and Alfredo Jefferson de Oliveira. 2016. "Sharing Design Agency with Local Partners in Participatory Design." *International Journal of Design* 10, no. 1. http://www.ijdesign.org/index.php/IJDesign/article/view/2403.

de Oliveira, Pedro J. S. Vieira. 2016. "Design at the *Earview*: Decolonizing Speculative Design through Sonic Fiction." *Design Issues* 32, no. 2: 43–52.

de Oliveira, Pedro J. S. Vieira, and Luiza Prado de O. Martins. 2014. "Cheat Sheet for a Non- (or Less-) Colonialist Speculative Design." *Medium*, September 10. https://medium.com/a-parede/cheat-sheet-for-a-non-or-less-colonialist-speculative-design-9a6b4ae3c465.

de Oliveira, Pedro J. S. Vieira, and Luiza Prado de O. Martins. 2019. "Designer/Shapeshifter: A Decolonizing Redirection for Speculative and Critical Design." In *Tricky Design: The Ethics of Things*, edited by Tom Fisher and Lorraine Gamman, 103–114. Bloomsbury.

de O. Martins, Luiza Prado. 2014. "Privilege and Oppression: Towards a Feminist Speculative Design." In *Design's Big Debates—DRS International Conference 2014*, edited by Y. Lim, K. Niedderer, J. Redström, E. Stolterman, and A. Valtonen, June 16–19, Umeå, Sweden. https://dl.designresearchsociety.org/drs-conference-papers/drs2014/researchpapers/75.

de O. Martins, Luiza Prado, and Pedro J. S. Vieira de Oliveira. 2016. "Breaking the Cycle of Macondo: Design and Decolonial Futures." *XRDS: Crossroads, The ACM Magazine for Students* 22, no. 4: 28–32.

Dewey, John. (1916) 1997. *Democracy and Education*. Free Press.

Dewey, John. 1927. *The Public and Its Problems*. Swallow Press Books, Henry Holt and Company.

Dewey, John. 1988a. "Challenge to Liberal Thought." In *John Dewey: The Later Works, 1925–1953*, vol. 15, *1942–1948*, edited by Jo Ann Boydston, 261–275. Southern Illinois University Press.

Dewey, John. 1988b. "Creative Democracy—The Task before Us." In *John Dewey: The Later Works, 1925–1953*, vol. 14, *1939–1941*, edited by Jo Ann Boydston, 224–230. Southern Illinois University Press.

D'Ignazio, Catherine, Eric Gordon, and Elizabeth Christoforetti. 2019. "Sensors and Civics: Toward a Community-Centered Smart City." In *The Right to the Smart City*, edited by Paolo Cardullo, Cesare di Feliciantonio, and Rob Kitchin, 113–124. Emerald Publishing.

D'Ignazio, Catherine, and Lauren F. Klein. 2020. *Data Feminism*. MIT Press.

Dilnot, Clive. 2015. "History, Design, Futures: Contending with What We Have Made." In Tony Fry, Clive Dilnot, and Susan Stewart, *Design and the Question of History*, 131–272. Bloomsbury.

DiMaggio, Paul J., and Walter W. Powell. 2000. "The Iron Cage Revisited: Institutional Isomorphism and Collective Rationality in Organizational Fields." *Economics Meets Sociology in Strategic Management* 17: 143–166.

Dindler, Christian, and Ole Sejer Iversen. 2014. "Relational Expertise in Participatory Design." In *Proceedings of the 13th Participatory Design Conference: Research Papers*, vol. 1, 41–50. Association for Computing Machinery. https://doi.org/10.1145/2661435.2661452.

DiSalvo, Carl. 2009. "Design and the Construction of Publics." *Design Issues* 25, no. 1: 48–63.

DiSalvo, Carl. 2012. *Adversarial Design*. MIT Press.

DiSalvo, Carl. 2016. "Design and Prefigurative Politics." *Journal of Design Strategies* 8, no. 1: 29–35.

DiSalvo, Carl, Andrew Clement, and Volkmar Pipek. 2012. "Participatory Design for, with, and by Communities." In *Routledge International Handbook of Participatory Design*, edited by Jesper Simonsen and Toni Robertson, 182–209. Routledge.

DiSalvo, Carl, Tom Jenkins, and Thomas Lodato. 2016. "Designing Speculative Civics." In *Proceedings of the 2019 CHI Conference on Human Factors in Computing*

Systems, 4979–4990. Association for Computing Machinery. https://doi.org/10.1145/2858036.2858505.

Dixon, Brian. 2018. "From Making Things Public to the Design of Creative Democracy: Dewey's Democratic Vision and Participatory Design." *CoDesign* 16, no. 2: 97–110.

Dixon, Brian S. 2020. *Dewey and Design: A Pragmatist Perspective for Design Research.* Springer Nature.

Dourish, Paul, Christopher Lawrence, Tuck Wah Leong, and Greg Wadley. 2020. "On Being Iterated: The Affective Demands of Design Participation." In *Proceedings of the 2020 CHI Conference on Human Factors in Computing Systems*, 1–11. Association for Computing Machinery. https://doi.org/10.1145/3313831.3376545.

Dourish, Paul, and Scott D. Mainwaring. 2012. "Ubicomp's Colonial Impulse." In *Proceedings of the 2012 ACM Conference on Ubiquitous Computing*, 133–142. Association for Computing Machinery. https://doi.org/10.1145/2370216.2370238.

Du Bois, W. E. B. 1975. *Darkwater: Voices from within the Veil.* Kraus-Thomson.

Dunne, Anthony. 2008. *Hertzian Tales: Electronic Products, Aesthetic Experience, and Critical Design.* MIT Press.

Dunne, Anthony, and Fiona Raby. 2001. *Design Noir: The Secret Life of Electronic Objects.* Springer Science & Business Media.

Dunne, Anthony, and Fiona Raby. 2013. *Speculative Everything: Design, Fiction, and Social Dreaming.* MIT Press.

Ehn, Pelle. 1988. "Work-Oriented Design of Computer Artifacts." PhD diss., Arbetslivscentrum.

Ehn, Pelle. 2008. "Participation in Design Things." In *Proceedings of the Tenth Anniversary Conference on Participatory Design 2008*, 92–101. Association for Computing Machinery. https://dl.acm.org/doi/10.5555/1795234.1795248.

Ehn, Pelle. 2017. "Learning in Participatory Design as I Found It (1970–2015)." In *Participatory Design for Learning*, 7–21. Routledge.

Ehn, Pelle, and Richard Badham. 2002. "Participatory Design and the Collective Designer." In *Proceedings of the 2002 Participatory Design Conference*, Malmö, Sweden, 1–10. http://cpsr.org/issues/pd/pdc2002/propdf/download.

Elfline, Ross K. 2016. "Superstudio and the "Refusal to Work."" *Design and Culture* 8, no. 1: 55–57.

Elzenbaumer, Bianca. 2013. "Designing Economic Cultures." Doctoral diss., University of London.

Erickson, Thomas. 1996. "Design as Storytelling." *Interactions* 3, no. 4: 30–35.

Escobar, Arturo. 2018. *Designs for the Pluriverse: Radical Interdependence, Autonomy, and the Making of Worlds*. Duke University Press.

Fischer, Marilyn. 2013. "Reading Dewey's Political Philosophy through Addams's Political Compromises." *American Catholic Philosophical Quarterly* 87, no. 2: 227–243.

Fisher, Berenice, and Joan Tronto. 1991. "Toward a Feminist Theory of Caring." In *Circles of Care: Work and Identity in Women's Lives*, edited by Emily K. Abel and Margaret K. Nelson, 36–54. State University of New York Press.

Forlano, Laura. 2016. "Decentering the Human in the Design of Collaborative Cities." *Design Issues* 32, no. 3: 42–54.

Forlano, Laura. 2017. "Posthumanism and Design." *She Ji: The Journal of Design, Economics, and Innovation* 3, no. 1: 16–29.

Foth, Marcus, and Troy John Turner. 2019. "The Premise of Institutioning for the Proliferation of Communities and Technologies Research." In *Proceedings of the 9th International Conference on Communities & Technologies—Transforming Communities*, 24–28. Association for Computing Machinery. https://doi.org/10.1145/3328320.3328398.

Fox, Sarah. 2015. "Feminist Hackerspaces as Sites for Feminist Design." In *Proceedings of the 2015 ACM SIGCHI Conference on Creativity and Cognition*, 341–342. Association for Computing Machinery. https://dl.acm.org/doi/10.1145/2757226.2764771.

Fox, Sarah, Catherine Lim, Tad Hirsch, and Daniela K. Rosner. 2020. "Accounting for Design Activism: On the Positionality and Politics of Designerly Intervention." *Design Issues* 36, no. 1: 5–18.

Franz, Fabio, and Bianca Elzenbaumer. 2016. "Commons & Community Economies: Entry Points to Design for Eco-social Justice?" In *Proceedings of DRS 2016, Design Research Society 50th Anniversary Conference*, Brighton, UK, June 27–30. https://lau .repository.guildhe.ac.uk/id/eprint/17555/1/Commons_and_community_econo mies_entry_po[1].pdf.

Fraser, Mariam. 2006. "Event." *Theory, Culture & Society* 23, no. 2–3: 129–132.

Freeman, Guo, Jeffrey Bardzell, and Shaowen Bardzell. 2017. "Aspirational Design and Messy Democracy: Partisanship, Policy, and Hope in an Asian City." In *Proceedings of the 2017 ACM Conference on Computer Supported Cooperative Work and Social Computing*, February, 404–416. Association for Computing Machinery. https://doi .org/10.1145/2998181.2998291.

Freeman, Guo, Jeffrey Bardzell, and Shaowen Bardzell. 2019. "Open Source, Open Vision: The MakerPro Network and the Broadening of Participation in Setting Taiwan's IT Vision Agenda." *Human-Computer Interaction* 34, nos. 5–6: 506–540.

Fry, Tony. 1999. *A New Design Philosophy: An Introduction to Defuturing*. UNSW Press.

Fry, Tony. 2007. "Redirective Practice: An Elaboration." *Design Philosophy Papers* 5, no. 1: 5–20.

Fuad-Luke, Alastair. 2013. *Design Activism: Beautiful Strangeness for a Sustainable World*. Routledge.

Ghoshal, Sucheta, Rishma Mendhekar, and Amy Bruckman. 2020. "Toward a Grassroots Culture of Technology Practice." In *Proceedings of the ACM on Human-Computer Interaction* 4, no. CSCW 1, article 054, 1–28. Association for Computing Machinery. https://doi.org/10.1145/3392862.

Gibson-Graham, J. K. 1995. "Beyond Patriarchy and Capitalism: Reflections on Political Subjectivity." In *Transitions: New Australian Feminisms*, edited by Barbara Caine and Rosemary Pringle, 172–183. Routledge.

Gibson-Graham, J. K. 1996. *The End of Capitalism (As We Knew It)*. University of Minnesota Press.

Gibson-Graham, J. K. 2006. *Postcapitalist Politics*. University of Minnesota Press.

Gibson-Graham, J. K. 2008. "Diverse Economies: Performative Practices for Other Worlds." *Progress in Human Geography* 32, no. 5: 613–632.

Gibson-Graham, J. K., Jenny Cameron, and Stephen Healy. 2016. "Commoning as a Postcapitalist Politics." In *Releasing the Commons: Rethinking the Futures of the Commons*, edited by Ash Amin and Philip Howell, 192–212. Springer.

Gilligan, Carol. 1993. *In a Different Voice: Psychological Theory and Women's Development*. Harvard University Press.

Gordon, Eric, and Paul Mihailidis, eds. 2016. *Civic Media: Technology, Design, Practice*. MIT Press.

Gordon, Eric, and Gabriel Mugar. 2020. *Meaningful Inefficiencies: Civic Design in an Age of Digital Expediency*. Oxford University Press.

Green, Ben. 2019. *The Smart Enough City: Putting Technology in Its Place to Reclaim Our Urban Future*. MIT Press.

Greenfield, Adam. 2013. *Against the Smart City: A Pamphlet*. Do Projects.

Gross, Matthias. 2009. "Collaborative Experiments: Jane Addams, Hull-House and Experimental Social Work." *Social Science Information* 48, no. 1: 81–95.

Gunn, Wendy, Ton Otto, and Rachel Charlotte Smith, eds. 2013. *Design Anthropology: Theory and Practice*. A&C Black.

Halse, Joachim, Eva Brandt, Brendon Clark, and Thomas Binder. 2010. *Rehearsing the Future*. Danish Design School Press.

Haraway, Donna J. 2016. *Staying with the Trouble: Making Kin in the Chthulucene*. Duke University Press.

Harcourt, Bernard E. 2009. *Illusion of Order: The False Promise of Broken Windows Policing.* Harvard University Press.

Hardin, Garrett. 1968. "The Tragedy of the Commons." *Science* 162, no. 3858: 1243–1249.

Hardt, Michael, and Antonio Negri. 2009. *Commonwealth.* Harvard University Press.

Hargraves, Ian. 2018. "Care and Capacities of Human-Centered Design." *Design Issues* 34, no. 3: 76–88.

Harrington, Christina, and Tawanna R. Dillahunt. 2021. "Eliciting Tech Futures among Black Young Adults: A Case Study of Remote Speculative Co-Design." In *Proceedings of the 2021 CHI Conference on Human Factors in Computing Systems*, 1–15. Association for Computing Machinery. https://dl.acm.org/doi/10.1145/3411764.3445723.

Harrington, Christina, Sheena Erete, and Anne Marie Piper. 2019. "Deconstructing Community-Based Collaborative Design: Towards More Equitable Participatory Design Engagements." In *Proceedings of the ACM on Human-Computer Interaction* 3, no. CSCW, 1–25. Association for Computing Machinery. https://dl.acm.org/doi/10.1145/3359318.

Harvey, David. 2012. *Rebel Cities: From the Right to the City to the Urban Revolution.* Verso.

Helmke, Gretchen, and Steven Levitsky. 2004. "Informal Institutions and Comparative Politics: A Research Agenda." *Perspectives on Politics* 2, no. 4: 725–740.

Hernberg, Hella, and Ramia Mazé. 2018. "Agonistic Temporary Space: Reflections on 'Agonistic Space' across Participatory Design and Urban Temporary Use." In *Proceedings of the 15th Participatory Design Conference: Short Papers, Situated Actions, Workshops and Tutorial*, vol. 2, 1–5. Association for Computing Machinery. https://doi.org/10.1145/3210604.3210639.

Hillgren, Per-Anders, Anna Seravalli, and Mette Agger Eriksen. 2016. "Counter-Hegemonic Practices: Dynamic Interplay between Agonism, Commoning and Strategic Design." *Strategic Design Research Journal* 9, no. 2: 89–99.

Honig, Bonnie. 1993. *Political Theory and the Displacement of Politics.* Cornell University Press.

Houston, Lara, and Steven J. Jackson. 2016. "Caring for the 'Next Billion' Mobile Handsets: Opening Proprietary Closures through the Work of Repair." In *Proceedings of the Eighth International Conference on Information and Communication Technologies and Development*, 1–11. Association for Computing Machinery. https://doi.org/10.1145/2909609.2909658.

Hunt, Jamer. 2020. *Not to Scale: How the Small Becomes Large, the Large Becomes Unthinkable, and the Unthinkable Becomes Possible.* Grand Central Publishing.

Huybrechts, Liesbeth, Henric Benesch, and Jon Geib. 2017a. "Co-Design and the Public Realm." *CoDesign* 13, no. 3: 145–147.

Huybrechts, Liesbeth, Henric Benesch, and Jon Geib. 2017b. "Institutioning: Participatory Design, Co-Design and the Public Realm." *CoDesign* 13, no. 3: 148–159.

Huybrechts, Liesbeth, Katrien Dreessen, Selina Schepers, and Pablo Calderon Salazar. 2016. "Democratic Dialogues That Make Cities 'Work.'" *Strategic Design Research Journal* 9, no. 2: 100–111.

Indigenous Action Media. 2014. "Accomplices Not Allies: Abolishing the Ally Industrial Complex." *Indigenous Action*, May 4. https://www.indigenousaction.org/accomplices -not-allies-abolishing-the-ally-industrial-complex/.

Irani, Lilly, 2018. "'Design Thinking': Defending Silicon Valley at the Apex of Global Labor Hierarchies." Catalyst: Feminism, Theory, *Technoscience* 4, no. 1. https://cata lystjournal.org/index.php/catalyst/article/view/29638.

Irani, Lilly. 2019. *Chasing Innovation: Making Entrepreneurial Citizens in Modern India*. Princeton University Press.

Irwin, Terry, Gideon Kossoff, and Cameron Tonkinwise. 2015. "Transition Design Provocation." *Design Philosophy Papers* 13, no. 1: 3–11.

Jackson, Steve. 2014. "Rethinking Repair." In *Media Technologies: Essays on Communication, Materiality, and Society*, edited by Tarleton Gillespie, Pablo Boczkowski, and Kirsten Foot, 221–238. MIT Press.

JafariNaimi, Nassim, Lisa Nathan, and Ian Hargraves. 2015. "Values as Hypotheses: Design, Inquiry, and the Service of Values." *Design Issues* 31, no. 4: 91–104.

Jasanoff, Sheila, and Sang-Hyun Kim. 2009. "Containing the Atom: Sociotechnical Imaginaries and Nuclear Power in the United States and South Korea." *Minerva* 47, no. 2: 119.

Jasanoff, Sheila, and Sang-Hyun Kim, eds. 2015. *Dreamscapes of Modernity: Sociotechnical Imaginaries and the Fabrication of Power*. University of Chicago Press.

Jenkins, Tom. 2014. "Prototyping Speculative Objects for the Internet of Things." In *Proceedings of the 2014 Companion Publication on Designing Interactive Systems*, 163–166. Association for Computing Machinery. https://doi.org/10.1145/2598784.2598789.

Jenkins, Tom. 2015. "Designing the 'Things' of the IoT." In *Proceedings of the Ninth International Conference on Tangible, Embedded, and Embodied Interaction*, 449–452. Association for Computing Machinery. https://doi.org/10.1145/2677199.2691608.

Jenkins, Tom. 2017. "Living Apart, Together: Cohousing as a Site for ICT Design." In *Proceedings of the 2017 Conference on Designing Interactive Systems*, 1039–1051. Association for Computing Machinery. https://doi.org/10.1145/3064663.3064751.

Jönsson, Li. 2014. "Design Events: On Explorations of a Non-anthropocentric Framework in Design." PhD diss., Royal Danish Academy of Fine Art.

Jönsson, Li, and Tau Ulv Lenskjold. 2014. "A Foray into Not-Quite Companion Species: Design Experiments with Urban Animals as Significant Others." *Artifact: Journal of Design Practice* 3, no. 2: 7–1.

Jönsson, Li, Åsa Ståhl, Kristina Lindström, and Saskia Gullstrand. 2021. "Big Enough Stories of Un/Making Pollination." Workshop at NORDES 2021. https://conference2021nordes.org/wp-content/uploads/2021/04/3_WS_Big_Enough_Stories_of_Un-Making_Polination_NORDES_2021_preliminary_description.pdf.

Julier, Guy. 2017. *Economies of Design*. Sage.

Julier, Guy, and Lucy Kimbell. 2019. "Keeping the System Going: Social Design and the Reproduction of Inequalities in Neoliberal Times." *Design Issues* 35, no. 4: 12–22.

Karasti, Helena, and Karen S. Baker. 2008. "Community Design: Growing One's Own Information Infrastructure." In *Proceedings of the Tenth Anniversary Conference on Participatory Design 2008*, 217–220. Association for Computing Machinery. https://dl.acm.org/doi/10.5555/1795234.1795280.

Kensing, Finn, and Joan Greenbaum. 2012. "Having a Say." In *Routledge International Handbook of Participatory Design*, edited by Jesper Simonsen and Toni Robertson, 21–36. Routledge.

Keshavarz, Mahmoud. 2018. *The Design Politics of the Passport: Materiality, Immobility, and Dissent*. Bloomsbury.

Keshavarz, Mahmoud. 2020. "Violent Compassions: Humanitarian Design and the Politics of Borders." *Design Issues* 36, no. 4: 20–32.

Kiem, Matt. 2013. "If Political Design Changed Anything They'd Make It Illegal: Review Essay on Carl DiSalvo's *Adversarial Design*." *Design Philosophy Papers* 11, no. 1: 31–38.

Korn, Matthias, and Amy Voida. 2015. "Creating Friction: Infrastructuring Civic Engagement in Everyday Life." In *Proceedings of the Fifth Decennial Aarhus Conference on Critical Alternatives*, 145–156. https://doi.org/10.7146/aahcc.v1i1.21198.

Kraff, Helena. 2020. "A Critical Exploration of Agonistic Participatory Design." *The Design Journal* 23, no. 1: 31–48.

Latour, Bruno. 2004. "Why Has Critique Run Out of Steam? From Matters of Fact to Matters of Concern." *Critical Inquiry* 30, no. 2: 225–248.

Latour, Bruno. 2010. "An Attempt at a 'Compositionist Manifesto.'" *New Literary History* 41, no. 3: 471–490.

Le Dantec, Christopher A. 2016. *Designing Publics*. MIT Press.

Le Dantec, Christopher A., and Carl DiSalvo. 2013. "Infrastructuring and the Formation of Publics in Participatory Design." *Social Studies of Science* 43, no. 2: 241–264.

Lee, Kipum. 2020. "From Margin to Institution: Design as a Marketplace for Action in Organizations." *Design Issues* 36, no. 4: 5–19.

Lenskjold, Tau Ulv, and Li Jönsson. 2017. "Speculative Prototypes and Alien Ethnographies: Experimenting with Relations beyond the Human." *Diseña* 11: 134–147.

Lenskjold, Tau Ulv, Sissel Olander, and Joachim Halse. 2015. "Minor Design Activism: Prompting Change from Within." *Design Issues* 31, no. 4: 67–78.

Lezaun, Javier, Noortje Marres, and Manuel Tironi. 2017. "Experiments in Participation." In *The Handbook of Science and Technology Studies*, edited by Ulrike Felt, Rayvon Fouché, Clark A. Miller, and Laurel Smith-Doerr, 195–221. MIT Press.

Liboiron, Max. 2017. "Compromised Agency: The Case of BabyLegs." *Engaging Science, Technology, and Society* 3: 499–527.

Liboiron, Max. 2021. *Pollution Is Colonialism*. Duke University Press.

Light, Ann, and Yoko Akama. 2014. "Structuring Future Social Relations: The Politics of Care in Participatory Practice." In *Proceedings of the 13th Participatory Design Conference: Research Papers*, vol. 1, 151–160. Association for Computing Machinery. https://doi.org/10.1145/2661435.2661438.

Lin, Cindy, and Silvia Margot Lindtner. 2021. "Techniques of Use: Confronting Value Systems of Productivity, Progress, and Usefulness in Computing and Design." In *Proceedings of the 2021 CHI Conference on Human Factors in Computing Systems*, 1–16. Association for Computing Machinery. https://dl.acm.org/doi/fullHtml/10.1145/3411764.3445237.

Lindström, Kristina, and Åsa Ståhl. 2014. *Patchworking Publics-in-the-Making: Design, Media and Public Engagement*. Malmö University.

Lindström, Kristina, and Åsa Ståhl. 2020a. "Caring Design Experiments in the Aftermath." In *8th Bi-Annual Nordic Design Research Society Conference: Who Cares?*, 1–9. Malmö University. http://mau.diva-portal.org/smash/record.jsf?pid=diva2%3A1513888&dswid=-6240.

Lindström, Kristina, and Åsa Ståhl. 2020b. "Un/Making in the Aftermath of Design." In *Proceedings of the 16th Participatory Design Conference 2020: Participation(s) Otherwise*, vol. 1, 12–21. Association for Computing Machinery. https://doi.org/10.1145/3385010.3385012.

Lindtner, Silvia. 2020. *Prototype Nation: China and the Contested Promise of Innovation*. Princeton University Press.

Linebaugh, Peter. 2014. *Stop, Thief! The Commons, Enclosures, and Resistance*. PM Press.

Lockton, Dan, and Stuart Candy. 2019. "A Vocabulary for Visions in Designing for Transitions." *Cuadernos del Centro de Estudios en Diseño y Comunicación*, year 19, no. 73: 27–49.

Lockton, Dan, Michelle Chou, Aadya Krishnaprasad, Deepika Dixit, Stefania La Vattiata, Jisoo Shon, Matt Geiger, and Tammar Zea-Wolfson. 2019. "Metaphors and Imaginaries in Design Research for Change." Paper presented at the Design Research for Change Symposium, London, December. https://www.researchgate.net/profile /Dan-Lockton/publication/337439129_Metaphors_and_imaginaries_in_design _research_for_change/links/5dd75c0ba6fdcc474feb7df3/Metaphors-and-imaginaries -in-design-research-for-change.pdf.

Lodato, Thomas, and Carl DiSalvo. 2018. "Institutional Constraints: The Forms and Limits of Participatory Design in the Public Realm." In *Proceedings of the 15th Participatory Design Conference: Full Papers*, vol. 1, 1–12. Association for Computing Machinery. https://dl.acm.org/doi/10.1145/3210586.3210595.

Loukissas, Yanni. 2019. *All Data Are Local*. MIT Press.

Lupton, Ellen. 2017. *Design Is Storytelling*. Cooper Hewitt, Smithsonian Design Museum.

Lury, Celia, and Noortje Marres. 2015. "Notes on Objectual Valuation." In *Making Things Valuable*, edited by Martin Kornberger, Lise Justesen, Anders Koed Madsen, and Jan Mouritsen, 232–256. Oxford University Press.

Lury, Celia, and Nina Wakeford. 2012a. "Introduction: A Perpetual Inventory." In *Inventive Methods: The Happening of the Social*, edited by Celia Lury and Nina Wakeford, 15–38. Routledge.

Lury, Celia, and Nina Wakeford, eds. 2012b. *Inventive Methods: The Happening of the Social*. Routledge, 2012.

Manzini, Ezio. 2015. *Design, When Everybody Designs: An Introduction to Design for Social Innovation*. MIT Press.

Marres, Noortje. 2012. "Experiment: The Experiment in Living." In *Inventive Methods: The Happening of the Social*, edited by Celia Lury and Nina Wakeford, 90–109. Routledge.

Marres, Noortje. 2016. *Material Participation: Technology, the Environment and Everyday Publics*. Springer.

Marres, Noortje, and Javier Lezaun. 2011. "Materials and Devices of the Public: An Introduction." *Economy and Society* 40, no. 4: 489–509.

Marttila, Sanna, Andrea Botero, and Joanna Saad-Sulonen. 2014. "Towards Commons Design in Participatory Design." In *Proceedings of the 13th Participatory Design Conference: Short Papers, Industry Cases, Workshop Descriptions, Doctoral Consortium Papers, and Keynote Abstracts*, vol. 2, 9–12. Association for Computing Machinery. https://doi.org/10.1145/2662155.2662187.

Mazé, R., and J. Wangel. 2017. "Future (Im)Perfect: Exploring Time, Becoming and Difference in Design and Futures Studies." In *Feminist Futures of Spatial Practice*, edited by M. Schalk, T. Kristiansson, and R. Mazé, 273–286. Baunach, Germany: Spurbuchverlag.

McKenna, Erin. 2001. *The Task of Utopia: A Pragmatist and Feminist Perspective*. Rowman & Littlefield.

Meng, Amanda, and Carl DiSalvo. 2018. "Grassroots Resource Mobilization through Counter-Data Action." *Big Data & Society* 5, no. 2. https://journals.sagepub.com/doi /10.1177/2053951718796862.

Meng, Amanda, Carl DiSalvo, and Ellen Zegura. 2019. "Collaborative Data Work towards a Caring Democracy." In *Proceedings of the ACM on Human-Computer Interaction* 3, no. CSCW, 1–23. Association for Computing Machinery. https://dl.acm.org /doi/10.1145/3359144.

Miettinen, Reijo. 2004. "The Roles of the Researcher in Developmentally-Oriented Research." *Development Intervention* 1: 105–121.

Miles, Christopher. 2019. "The Combine Will Tell the Truth: On Precision Agriculture and Algorithmic Rationality." *Big Data & Society* 6, no. 1. https://journals .sagepub.com/doi/10.1177/2053951719849444.

Mills, C. Wright. 1959. *The Sociological Imagination*. Oxford University Press.

Milner, Yeshimabeit. 2020. "Abolish Big Data." *Data & Society* video podcast, March 4. https://datasociety.net/library/abolish-big-data/.

Mol, Annemarie. 2008. *The Logic of Care: Health and the Problem of Patient Choice*. Routledge.

Mol, Annemarie, Ingunn Moser, and Jeannette Pols. 2010. "Care: Putting Practice into Theory." In *Care in Practice: On Tinkering in Clinics, Homes and Farms*, edited by Annemarie Mol, Ingunn Moser, and Jeannette Pols, 7–26. Transcript Verlag.

Mollon, Max. 2019. "Designing for Debate: How to Connect People to Issues through Conflictual Design Artefacts?" PhD diss., Télécom Paris.

Montuori, Bruna Ferreira, Ana Julia Melob Almeida, Viviane Mattosb Nicoletti, and Verena Lima. 2019. "Towards Relational Practices in Design." Paper presented at International Association of Societies of Design Research Conference. https:// iasdr2019.org/uploads/files/Proceedings/vo-f-1337-Fer-B.pdf.

Mouffe, Chantal. 1992. "Feminism, Citizenship, and Radical Democratic Politics." In *Feminists Theorize the Political*, edited by J. Butler and J. W. Scott, 387–402. Routledge.

Mouffe, Chantal. 2013. *Agonistics: Thinking the World Politically*. Verso.

Murphy, Michelle. 2015. "Unsettling Care: Troubling Transnational Itineraries of Care in Feminist Health Practices." *Social Studies of Science* 45, no. 5: 717–737.

North, Douglass C. 1990. *Institutions, Institutional Change and Economic Performance*. Cambridge University Press.

Nussbaum, Bruce. 2010. "Is Humanitarian Design the New Imperialism?" *Fast Company Design*, July 6. https://www.fastcompany.com/1661859/is-humanitarian-design-the-new-imperialism.

O'Brien, Daniel Tumminelli, Dietmar Offenhuber, Jessica Baldwin-Philippi, Melissa Sands, and Eric Gordon. 2017. "Uncharted Territoriality in Coproduction: The Motivations for 311 Reporting." *Journal of Public Administration Research and Theory* 27, no. 2: 320–335.

Opazo, Daniel, Matías Wolff, and María José Araya. 2017. "Imagination and the Political in Design Participation." *Design Issues* 33, no. 4: 73–82.

Opportunity Atlas. 2021. https://www.opportunityatlas.org. Accessed May 28.

Ostrom, Elinor. 2015. *Governing the Commons*. Cambridge University Press.

Papanek, Victor. 1971. *Design for the Real World: Human Ecology and Social Change*. Pantheon Books.

Parvin, Nassim. 2018. "Doing Justice to Stories: On Ethics and Politics of Digital Storytelling." *Engaging Science, Technology, and Society* 4: 515–534.

Parvin, Nassim, and Anne Pollock. 2020. "Unintended by Design: On the Political Uses of 'Unintended Consequences.'" *Engaging Science, Technology, and Society* 6: 320–327.

Pierce, James. 2015. *Working by Not Quite Working: Designing Resistant Interactive Proposals, Prototypes, and Products*. Carnegie Mellon University Press.

Pierri, Paola. 2020. "Creative Democracy: An Anthropology of and by Means of Design." PhD diss., University of the Arts London.

Povinelli, Elizabeth. 2011. *Economies of Abandonment: Social Belonging and Endurance in Late Liberalism*. Duke University Press.

Powell, Alison. 2021. *Undoing Optimization*. Yale University Press.

Powell, Walter W., and Paul J. DiMaggio, eds. 2012. *The New Institutionalism in Organizational Analysis*. University of Chicago Press.

Puig de la Bellacasa, María. 2017. *Matters of Care: Speculative Ethics in More than Human Worlds*. University of Minnesota Press.

Quesenbery, Whitney, and Kevin Brooks. 2010. *Storytelling for User Experience: Crafting Stories for Better Design*. Rosenfeld Media.

Redström, Johan. 2017. *Making Design Theory*. MIT Press.

Rodgers, Paul, Giovanni Innella, Craig Bremner, Ian Coxon, Cara Broadley, Alessia Cadamuro, Stephanie Carleklev, et al. 2019. "The Lancaster Care Charter." *Design Issues* 35, no. 1: 73–77.

Rosner, Daniela. 2018. *Critical Fabulations: Reworking the Methods and Margins of Design*. MIT Press.

Russell, Andrew L., and Lee Vinsel. 2018. "After Innovation, Turn to Maintenance." *Technology and Culture* 59, no. 1: 1–25.

Sadowski, Jathan, and Roy Bendor. 2019. "Selling Smartness: Corporate Narratives and the Smart City as a Sociotechnical Imaginary." *Science, Technology, & Human Values* 44, no. 3: 540–563.

Sanders, Elizabeth B.-N., and Pieter Jan Stappers. 2008. "Co-Creation and the New Landscapes of Design." *Co-Design* 4, no. 1: 5–18.

Sanders, Liz, and Pieter Jan Stappers. 2012. *Convivial Toolbox: Generative Research for the Front End of Design*. BIS Publishers.

Sanoff, Henry. 2000. *Community Participation Methods in Design and Planning*. Wiley.

Sawhney, Nitin, and Ahn-Ton Tran. 2020. "Ecologies of Contestation in Participatory Design." In *Proceedings of the 16th Participatory Design Conference 2020: Participation(s) Otherwise*, vol. 1, 172–181. Association for Computing Machinery. https://doi.org/10.1145/3385010.3385028.

Schneiderhan, Erik. 2011. "Pragmatism and Empirical Sociology: The Case of Jane Addams and Hull-House, 1889–1895." *Theory and Society* 40, no. 6: 589.

Schrock, Andrew R. 2016. "Civic Hacking as Data Activism and Advocacy: A History from Publicity to Open Government Data." *New Media & Society* 18, no. 4: 581–599.

Schrock, Andrew. 2018. *Civic Tech: Making Technology Work for People*. Rogue Academic Press.

Schultz, Tristan, Danah Abdulla, Ahmed Ansari, Ece Canlı, Mahmoud Keshavarz, Matthew Kiem, Luiza Prado de O. Martins, and Pedro J. S. Vieira de Oliveira. 2018. "What Is at Stake with Decolonizing Design? A Roundtable." *Design and Culture* 10, no. 1: 81–101.

Sciannamblo, Mariacristina, Marisa Leavitt Cohn, Peter Lyle, and Maurizio Teli. 2021. "Caring and Commoning as Cooperative Work: A Case Study in Europe." In *Proceedings of the ACM on Human-Computer Interaction* 5, no. CSCW 1, article 126, 1–26. https://dl.acm.org/doi/10.1145/3449200.

Seigfried, Charlene Haddock. 1999. "Socializing Democracy: Jane Addams and John Dewey." *Philosophy of the Social Sciences* 29, no. 2: 207–230.

Sengers, Phoebe, and Bill Gaver. 2006. "Staying Open to Interpretation: Engaging Multiple Meanings in Design and Evaluation." In *Proceedings of the 6th Conference on Designing Interactive Systems*, 99–108. Association for Computing Machinery. https://dl.acm.org/doi/10.1145/1142405.1142422.

Sengers, Phoebe, Kaiton Williams, and Vera Khovanskaya. 2021. "Speculation and the Design of Development." In *Proceedings of the ACM on Human-Computer*

Interaction 5, no. CSCW 1, 1–27. Association for Computing Machinery. https://dl
.acm.org/doi/10.1145/3449195.

Seravalli, Anna. 2014. "Making Commons: Attempts at Composing Prospects in the
Opening of Production." PhD diss., Malmö University.

Seravalli, Anna, Per-Anders Hillgren, and Mette Agger-Eriksen. 2015. "Co-designing
Collaborative Forms for Urban Commons: Using the Notions of Commoning and
Agonism to Navigate the Practicalities and Political Aspects of Collaboration." In
1st Thematic IASC Conference on Urban Commons, Bologna, November, 7–9.
https://www.researchgate.net/publication/286452716_Co-designing_collaborative
_forms_for_urban_commons_using_the_notions_of_commoning_and_agonism_to
_navigate_the_practicalities_and_political_aspects_of_collaboration.

Shelton, Taylor, and Thomas Lodato. 2019. "Actually Existing Smart Citizens: Expertise and (Non)participation in the Making of the Smart City." *City* 23, no. 1: 35–52.

Shelton, Taylor, Matthew Zook, and Alan Wiig. 2015. "The 'Actually Existing Smart
City.'" *Cambridge Journal of Regions, Economy and Society* 8, no. 1: 13–25.

Shotwell, Alexis. 2016. *Against Purity: Living Ethically in Compromised Times*. University of Minnesota Press.

Simon, Herbert A. 1996. *The Sciences of the Artificial*. MIT Press.

Simonsen, Jesper, and Toni Robertson, eds. 2012. *Routledge International Handbook of
Participatory Design*. Routledge.

Solnit, Rebecca. 2016. *Hope in the Dark: Untold Histories, Wild Possibilities*. Haymarket
Books.

Star, Susan Leigh. 1999. "The Ethnography of Infrastructure." *American Behavioral
Scientist* 43, no. 3: 377–391.

Star, Susan Leigh, and James R. Griesemer. 1989. "Institutional Ecology, Translations, and Boundary Objects: Amateurs and Professionals in Berkeley's Museum of
Vertebrate Zoology, 1907–39." *Social Studies of Science* 19, no. 3: 387–420.

Steen, Marc. 2013. "Co-design as a Process of Joint Inquiry and Imagination." *Design
Issues* 29, no. 2: 16–28.

Stengers, Isabelle. 2000. *The Invention of Modern Science*. Translated by Daniel W.
Smith. University of Minnesota Press.

Stengers, Isabelle. 2005. "The Cosmopolitical Proposal." In *Making Things Public:
Atmospheres of Democracy*, edited by Bruno Latour and Peter Weibel, 994–1003. MIT
Press.

Stengers, Isabelle. 2010. *Cosmopolitics*. Vol. 1. Minneapolis: University of Minnesota
Press.

Stengers, Isabelle. 2011. "The Care of the Possible: Isabelle Stengers Interviewed by Erik Bordeleau." *Scapegoat: Landscape, Architecture, Political Economy* 1: 12–17.

Sterling, Bruce. 2009. "Design Fiction." *Interactions* 16, no. 3: 20–24.

Stokes, Benjamin. 2020. *Locally Played: Real-World Games for Stronger Places and Communities*. MIT Press.

Suchman, Lucy. 1993. "Working Relations of Technology Production and Use." *Computer Supported Cooperative Work* 2, no. 1–2: 21–39.

Suchman, Lucy. 1996. "Supporting Articulation Work." In *Computerization and Controversy: Value Conflicts and Social Choices*, edited by Rob Kling, 407–423. Elsevier.

Suchman, Lucy. 2002. "Located Accountabilities in Technology Production." *Scandinavian Journal of Information Systems* 14, no. 2: 7.

Suchman, Lucy. 2007. *Human-Machine Reconfigurations: Plans and Situated Actions*. Cambridge University Press.

Swain, Dan. 2019. "Not Not but Not Yet: Present and Future in Prefigurative Politics." *Political Studies* 67, no. 1: 47–62.

Teli, Maurizio. 2015. "Computing and the Common: Hints of a New Utopia in Participatory Design." In *Proceedings of the Fifth Decennial Aarhus Conference on Critical Alternatives*, 17–20. https://doi.org/10.7146/aahcc.v1i1.21318.

Teli, Maurizio, Angela Di Fiore, and Vincenzo D'Andrea. 2016. "Computing and the Common: An Empirical Case of Participatory Design Today." In *Proceedings of the 14th Participatory Design Conference: Full Papers*, vol. 1, 1–10. Association for Computing Machinery. https://doi.org/10.1145/2940299.2940312.

Teli, Maurizio, Marcus Foth, Mariacristina Sciannamblo, Irina Anastasiu Cioaca, and Peter Lyle. 2020. "Tales of Institutioning and Commoning: Participatory Design Processes with a Strategic and Tactical Perspective." In *Proceedings of the 16th Participatory Design Conference 2020: Participation(s) Otherwise*, vol. 1, 159–171. Association for Computing Machinery. https://doi.org/10.1145/3385010.3385020.

Teli, Maurizio, Peter Lyle, and Mariacristina Sciannamblo. 2018. "Institutioning the Common: The Case of Commonfare." In *Proceedings of the 15th Participatory Design Conference: Full Papers* vol. 1, 1–11. Association for Computing Machinery. https://doi.org/10.1145/3210586.3210590.

Tharp, Bruce, and Stephanie Tharp. 2019. *Discursive Design: Critical, Speculative, and Alternative Things*. MIT Press.

Tonkinwise, Cameron. 2014. "Design Away." In *Design as Future-Making*, edited by Susan Yelavich and Barbara Adams, 198–213. Bloomsbury.

Toombs, Austin L., Shaowen Bardzell, and Jeffrey Bardzell. 2015. "The Proper Care and Feeding of Hackerspaces: Care Ethics and Cultures of Making." In *Proceedings of the 33rd Annual ACM Conference on Human Factors in Computing Systems*, 629–638. Association for Computing Machinery. https://doi.org/10.1145/2702123 .2702522.

Tronto, Joan C. 2010. "Creating Caring Institutions: Politics, Plurality, and Purpose." *Ethics and Social Welfare* 4, no. 2: 158–171.

Tronto, Joan C. 2013. *Caring Democracy: Markets, Equality, and Justice*. New York University Press.

Tsing, Anna Lowenhaupt. 2011. *Friction: An Ethnography of Global Connection*. Princeton University Press.

Turner, Fred. 2010. *From Counterculture to Cyberculture: Stewart Brand, the Whole Earth Network, and the Rise of Digital Utopianism*. University of Chicago Press.

van Amstel, Frederick M. C., and Rodrigo Freese Gonzatto. 2020. "The Anthropophagic Studio: Towards a Critical Pedagogy for Interaction Design." *Digital Creativity* 31, no. 4: 259–283.

Venturini, Tommaso, Donato Ricci, Michele Mauri, Lucy Kimbell, and Axel Meunier. 2015. "Designing Controversies and Their Publics." *Design Issues* 31, no. 3: 74–87.

Vertesi, Janet. 2014. "Seamful Spaces: Heterogeneous Infrastructures in Interaction." *Science, Technology, & Human Values* 39, no. 2: 264–284.

Vlachokyriakos, Vasillis, Clara Crivellaro, Pete Wright, and Patrick Olivier. 2018. "Infrastructuring the Solidarity Economy: Unpacking Strategies and Tactics in Designing Social Innovation." In *Proceedings of the 2018 CHI Conference on Human Factors in Computing Systems*, paper no. 481, 1–12. Association for Computing Machinery. https://doi.org/10.1145/3173574.3174055.

Wakkary, Ron. 2021. *Things We Could Design: For More Than Human-Centered Worlds*. MIT Press.

Wang, James T. 2015. "To Make or to Create? What Should Students of Design Be Taught?" *Design Issues* 31, no. 3: 3–15.

Whitney, Cedric Deslandes, Teresa Naval, Elizabeth Quepons, Simrandeep Singh, Steven R. Rick, and Lilly Irani. 2021. "HCI Tactics for Politics from Below: Meeting the Challenges of Smart Cities." In *Proceedings of the 2021 CHI Conference on Human Factors in Computing Systems*, article 297, 1–15. Association for Computing Machinery. https://doi.org/10.1145/3411764.3445314.

Wilkie, Alex. 2014. "Prototyping as Event: Designing the Future of Obesity." *Journal of Cultural Economy* 7, no. 4: 476–492.

Wilkie, Alex, and Mike Michael. 2009. "Expectation and Mobilisation: Enacting Future Users." *Science, Technology, & Human Values* 34, no. 4: 502–522.

Winance, Myriam. 2010. "Care and Disability: Practices of Experimenting, Tinkering with, and Arranging People and Technical Aids." In *Care in Practice: On Tinkering in Clinics, Homes and Farms*, edited by Annemarie Mol, Ingunn Moser, and Jeannette Pols, 93–117. Transcript Verlag.

Winchester, Woodrow W., III. 2018. "Afrofuturism, Inclusion, and the Design Imagination." *Interactions* 25, no. 2: 21–45.

Wittgenstein, Ludwig. 1953. *Philosophical Investigations.* Blackwell.

Wood, Denis. 1992. *The Power of Maps.* Guilford Press.

Wright, Earl, II. 2017. *The First American School of Sociology: W. E. B. Du Bois and the Atlanta Sociological Laboratory.* Taylor & Francis.

Yates, Luke. 2015. "Rethinking Prefiguration: Alternatives, Micropolitics and Goals in Social Movements." *Social Movement Studies* 14, no. 1: 1–21.

Yates, Luke. 2020. "Prefigurative Politics and Social Movement Strategy: The Roles of Prefiguration in the Reproduction, Mobilisation and Coordination of Movements." *Political Studies*, July. https://doi.org/10.1177/0032321720936046.

Young, Iris Marion. 1986. "The Ideal of Community and the Politics of Difference." *Social Theory and Practice* 12, no. 1: 1–26.

Zegura, Ellen, Carl DiSalvo, and Amanda Meng. 2018. "Care and the Practice of Data Science for Social Good." In *Proceedings of the 1st ACM SIGCAS Conference on Computing and Sustainable Societies*, 1–9. Association for Computing Machinery. https://doi.org/10.1145/3209811.3209877.

Index

Press
t Rossi
Main Street, 9th floor
02142

edu
t@mit.edu
253-2882

authorized representative in the EU for product safety and compliance is

Access System Europe Oü, 16879218
amäe tee 50,
10621

requests@easproject.com
56 968 939

9780262543460
ase ID: 152941459

www.ingramcontent.com/pod-product-compliance
Lightning Source LLC
Chambersburg PA
CBHW030317270326
41926CB00010B/1405